CATCH THE WHITE TIGER

How I Achieved the American Dream with $28

TONY ASSALI
with Michael Ashley

Catch the White Tiger:
How I Achieved the American Dream with $28
Copyright © 2023 by Tony Assali with Michael Ashley

ISBN: 978-1959151319 (hc)
ISBN: 978-1959151463 (sc)
ISBN: 978-1959151937 (e)

All rights reserved. No part of this publication may be reproduced, distributed, or transmitted in any form or by any means, including photocopying, recording, or other electronic or mechanical methods, without the prior written permission of the publisher, except in the case brief quotations embodied in critical reviews and other noncommercial uses permitted by copyright law.

The views expressed in this book are solely those of the author and do not necessarily reflect the views of the publisher, and the publisher hereby disclaims any responsibility for them.

The Reading Glass Books
1-888-420-3050
www.readingglassbooks.com
production@readingglassbooks.com

Author's Note

THE FOLLOWING IS based on true events. As a memoir, the described events are dependent on my best recollection of the conversations and actions of the participants. The only aspects that have been consciously changed are certain individuals' names and defining physical features so as to protect their privacy. Thank you in advance to my friends, family, and loved ones.

*This book is dedicated to my grandchildren.
I hope you follow your grandfather's steps and
reach your American dreams.*

Foreword

TWO IDEOLOGICAL PILLARS support the modern capitalist economy: competition and cooperation. All too often, the media—and our culture in general—focuses on the competitive side of this dynamic. As Americans, we like to think in terms of winners and losers, of the strong vanquishing the weak, of champions rising to the top via the dog-eat-dog, kill-or-be-killed feature of natural selection.

But while competition spurs efficiency and drives innovation, ignoring the cooperative aspect of business is foolish and self-defeating. Humans are social creatures, and we tend to do best in large groups that encourage collaboration and focus on the Greater Good. When companies pit executives and divisions against each other, the result is, inevitably, chaos and failure. Leaders who see everything as a zero-sum game, who believe the only way to succeed is for others to fail, leave little room for market expansion or economies of scale. Instead of "Look Out for #1," a wiser person says, "We do better when we *all* do better."

When I started Business Network International (BNI) in 1985, I firmly believed that referrals from trusted sources were a key component to business growth. Our motto, "Givers Gain," elegantly expresses our faith in the power of cooperation and support for one's fellow entrepreneurs. This collegial outlook succeeded beyond my wildest dreams. From small, intimate meetings at my house, BNI has grown to include more than two hundred thousand members with more than 7,600 chapters in sixty-five countries across the globe.

Tony Assali, who joined BNI in 2010, epitomizes the BNI ethos. Coming to America in the early 1970s as a teenager from Beirut, Lebanon, he used his brilliant mind, big heart, inexhaustible work ethic, and unique talent for identifying opportunities he calls "white tigers" to create a string of successful businesses. He first stacked up wins in the Boston area, then in Southern California, ultimately employing hundreds of people and changing America's food culture for the better. Have you ever bought hummus at a grocery store? You can thank Tony for that. (You will understand what I mean by the time you finish this book.)

Perhaps what's even more impressive than Tony's business success is his impact on the men and women he has led over the years. Tony made it an unwritten policy to support his staff financially during difficult times, even when the necessary funds came out of his own pocket. Believing his sales force couldn't perform effectively if they were stressed over paying their bills, he personally lent them his own money to bolster their confidence (even though, most often, he was not reimbursed). However, the most dramatic example of Tony's commitment to his people occurred during the depths of the Great Recession when he depleted his substantial personal fortune to avoid laying off a single worker.

As a member of BNI, Tony's contributions have been just as exemplary. In 2017, Tony made 986 referrals, receiving nine hundred seventy-five thousand in "thank yous for closed business." To put this in context, Tony referred nearly one million to others. That's more money in referrals from one person than some twenty- to thirty-member groups do in an entire year! In true karmic fashion, Tony's generosity has come back to reward him manifold as both tremendous abundance and deep loyalty from workers, friends, and customers alike. Ultimately, Tony's story exemplifies the enduring power of the American dream, selfless charity, and good old-fashioned human decency. In these cynical times, it's refreshing to see that good guys can still finish first.

—Ivan Misner, Ph.D., founder, BNI
September 2018

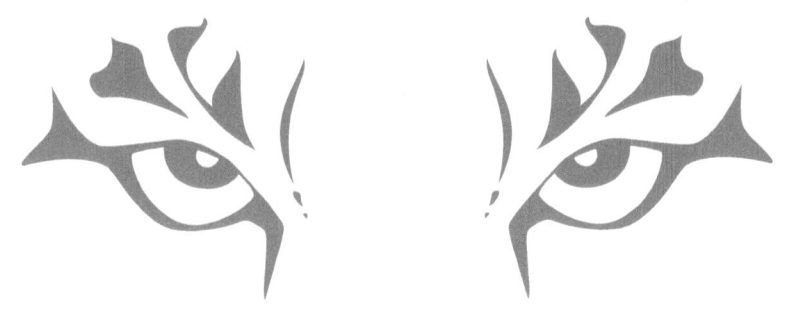

CATCH THE WHITE TIGER

Prologue

Beirut, Lebanon, 1969

I AM DREAMING of a white tiger when a car backfires. More explosions rock my neighborhood and I realize it's not a car. I know these noises. Everyone in Beirut does. It's gunfire. And it's getting closer. I turn to my bedside clock. It's only just after 6:00 a.m.

"What's going on?" my little brother, Joe, groans from his side of the room.

I throw back my covers, find my slippers, and dash downstairs. I run out into the street without my coat. The morning sun hovers above the eastern hills and the air is damp and cool. I hear shouts from the direction of St. Joseph Church, whose ancient spire rises over the rooftops. Emergency sirens echo off brick houses. A police car blasts by, nearly knocking me off my feet. I follow it.

St. Joseph is only two blocks away. It's where my family celebrates Mass every Sunday morning, where we had planned to spend the previous night, Holy Thursday. When I arrive, the place is pandemonium. People shout and scream. Several women cry hysterically. Blood stains the men's fine suits and the women's fancy dresses. I halt when I see several people splayed out on the church steps. More blood. The acrid smell of cordite assaults my nose.

"What happened?" I ask no one in particular.

"Up there," an older, gray-haired man points to the three-story building across the street. "A man with a gun started shooting. Militants."

I look up, then down the church steps, in what would have been the gunman's line of fire. Suddenly, everything spins. I feel like I'm in an elevator whose cable has just snapped, sending me plunging into a dark abyss. This is now the second time in the past two days I have experienced this sensation. The first was just twelve hours ago, when my family was preparing to leave for services. At the last second, I insisted we stay home. I had no specific reason for this demand, only the strange feeling that if we went, something awful would happen. At first, my family protested, but my pleading made them change their minds.

Now, here I am, staring at the carnage. I freeze as I recognize a victim: my best friend, Nabil Kessrousani. Sixteen years old, he was accompanying me to church when I suddenly demanded we stay home.

"You're crazy," he had told me, going off on his own.

I move to help Nabil but am pushed back by uniformed personnel carrying stretchers and medical bags. Now, police are on the scene. They herd us all to the sidelines so the first responders can do their work. I want to help, but I know there is nothing I can do.

How did I know we should've stayed away from the church? Was it gut instinct? True, I knew Beirut was becoming more dangerous, but perhaps it was divine intervention. I cannot dismiss the fact that God was looking out for me. But why? What had I done to deserve such attention? In the years to come, I will experience many eerily similar incidents. And these same profound questions will continue to vex me. Can the practical and the mysterious coexist? My incredible life story will suggest an answer to this question.

Chapter 1

"YOU HAVE TO slow down. You're killing yourself." My mother follows me around our modest house. She saw me come home from my night job just minutes ago and now stands in the hall, concern etched across her face. "I'm not going to kill myself. *I'm fine*," I insist, smiling as I comb my freshly washed hair in the bathroom mirror and change into a tailored business suit. My grin is genuine. Although I have been averaging two hours of sleep the past month, energy surges through me.

"Your father would not approve," she says.

"My father is the one who got me this job, remember? He wants me to be a success."

"We all want you to be a success," she says as I step out of the bathroom, every hair perfectly in place. "You look so handsome. You know I love you."

"I love you, too, Mom." I bend down to kiss her cheek. "Now I have to go. See you tomorrow morning."

With that, I hurry downstairs, grab the brown-bag breakfast she prepared for me, and head out the door. My bike is where I left it against the side of the house. I hop on, pedaling east.

"You're killing yourself." Those words echo through my head as I ride through Beirut's busy morning traffic. I can smell the exhaust in the air as a red Cadillac El Dorado, a light-blue Chevy Malibu and a silver Oldsmobile roar past. *Ah*, I sigh. *"La Belle*

Americaine!" This is why I'm killing myself working two jobs that keep me busy twenty hours a day, five days a week. I desire a car. No, not just a car. An *American* car. A *big* American car. A big American car that will bring me status and, more importantly, impress girls. Both of these things cost *money.* Fortunately, I seem to have a knack for making it.

You could say business is in my DNA. As my father enjoys telling my brothers, sisters, and me, Phoenician blood runs through our veins. Phoenicians were the most powerful merchants of the ancient world. One thousand years before Christ, my people dominated trade throughout the southern Mediterranean. Plato once said the Phoenicians' most distinguishing characteristic was their love of money. In that, I suppose I break with my ancestors. Oh, don't get me wrong. I love money. But even more than that, I love *making* money. It's the deal—the *sale*—that makes my blood run hot. Work is my drug of choice.

I glimpse St. Joseph Church just before I turn left onto the main boulevard that will take me toward the city center. It's been more than two months since the sniper attack and three weeks since I last talked to Nabil. Last I heard, his parents decided to take him to France for better medical care. The sniper's bullet severed his lower spine, paralyzing him from the waist down. He will never walk again. Still, his parents believe they can find a medical miracle in Paris. They probably just need to get out of Lebanon.

I understand their fear, but Beirut is my home. I adore it. Glancing around, I see nothing but beauty and the elegant hustle of urban life. They call this city The Paris of the Middle East, and it's no wonder why. Everywhere you look gorgeous architecture takes your breath away, from mighty stone buildings dating back to Ancient Rome, to modern gleaming steel-and-glass skyscrapers. Mannequins draped in the latest couture from Milan, Paris, and New York decorate the store windows I ride by. The sidewalks teem with tourists and international businessmen. In just one block, I see Arabs, Japanese, Africans, and, of course, our native Maronite Christians and Sunni Muslims. Perched at the crossroads of the Middle East, Beirut has long welcomed people of all races and faiths. How can a few militant troublemakers change centuries of tradition?

Finally, I turn onto Hamra Street, beloved by visiting Americans. Lined with hotels and shops, it caters to their taste for luxury and grandeur. Even at this early hour, the morning traffic is building strength like a gathering wave. Soon, it will crest under the mighty crush of vehicles and pedestrians. Turning off the main thoroughfare and into a rear alley, I park behind New Imperial Clothing. Quickly adjusting my suit, I smooth my hair before pulling open the door.

"I need a wool suit. Something in gray," says my first customer of the day, a fussy, blue-eyed American I judge to be in his late thirties. "Something impressive for my meeting tomorrow or I'm screwed."

"All of our suits are of the highest quality," I assure him, leading him to a rack of imports. "They come from designer boutiques in France and Italy."

His thin face darkens. "I'm not trying to pay a lot here. I'm on a budget."

"Here at our store, you'll only pay a third of what they'd charge you in Paris."

He gives me a doubtful sideways glance, but all of this is true. Europe's elite fashion designers supply us with their most sophisticated apparel—with all the labels removed, of course. That's how we can afford to sell them at such a discount.

"Here, this looks to be your size." I present a stunning charcoal gray suit.

He steps away from me. "Is there someone else here who can help me?"

I've heard this before. Customers question me all the time for being so young. No problem. I've always delighted in easing people's fears. All it takes is confidence. Without another word, I help the man into the jacket. He melts into a smile as he views himself in the mirror. I knew I would make him look good. A half-hour later, we both look good. The once-skeptical American leaves the store with his new suit, plus a complementing powder-blue Oxford shirt, wine-colored tie, and matching belt.

"Nice work." My manager claps me on the back. "I was watching. Didn't think he'd even go for the suit—then you upsold him. How'd you do it?"

I think about telling him my white tiger theory but hold my tongue. No use in sharing my little secret. But I'll tell you. In every situation, there's what I call a white tiger: something rare and precious, a treasure waiting to be seized. It's up to us to find it. My white tiger today? A package discount. By offering the picky man a more enticing deal on every item, I countered his suspicions. Instead of leaving cross with me for buying more than he bargained for, he actually shook my hand and thanked *me*, the salesperson.

Fourteen hours later, I park my bicycle in the next alley. This one is behind the Orient Prince Hotel, two miles from the New Imperial. Unlike my day job, which my father secured through his vast social network, I landed this position on my own. Upon graduating from high school, I enrolled at a private hospitality academy and became a hotel manager.

All my young life, hotels have enchanted me, especially the international ones. They represent elegance and glamour. Populated with passing travelers jet-setting the globe in style, they present life's unlimited possibilities—the chance for excitement and adventure, as well as romance. Ever since beginning as a porter at the age of twelve, I have witnessed an endless parade of beautiful women from all over the world.

"Tony, this gentleman would like to speak with you," an instructor told me one morning last fall before graduation.

"I manage the Orient Prince Hotel," the short, portly man with an impressive black mustache told me. "We're looking for a night auditor. You could be the one. I've seen your test scores. They're impressive."

"Thank you."

"Your hours will be from 11:00 p.m. to 7:00 a.m., Monday through Friday. You'll manage our books, audit the receipts. Whenever necessary, you'll man the front desk. We are a twenty-four-hour-a-day operation. You think you can handle that?"

"Of course," I said without hesitation. Out of a class of fifty students, I had been handpicked for a position in one of Beirut's finest international hotels. How could I possibly say no?

On my first day, I arrived a full hour before my shift began. Walking through the lobby, I was overwhelmed by the plush foyer, the lavish restaurant, state-of-the-art kitchen, vast function rooms, administrative offices, spa, and luxury suites. It was something out of my dreams.

"This is your uniform," the manager said. "And your name badge. You'll have your own money drawer so you can keep your funds separate from the other desk managers'."

With a firm handshake, I was on my own. The questions came fast and furious the second I took over the front desk.

"What are the best restaurants in the area?"

"Em Sherif," I replied without hesitation.

"Where is the National Museum?"

"Five blocks east. Here's a map."

"The hottest disco?"

"Pier 7."

My father, who works as an Arabic-English translator for the Union 76 oil company, taught me basic English. But I needed to pick up the latest slang to accommodate so many Americans.

"Let me call you a taxi," I tell my current customer walking down the steps with his luggage.

My offer is more than just professional courtesy. Within months of starting at the hotel, I've managed to make connections with local nightclubs and taxi drivers all over town. In exchange for my referrals, they pay me a $5 commission per taxi ride and $25 for every nightclub guest. As always, I look for the white tiger, the gem overlooked by everyone else—the special little breakthrough that will put me over the edge.

After taking care of the first gentleman, a stunning brunette in a shimmering red disco dress approaches the counter, flashing a fan of one-hundred-dollar bills. "I need Lebanese pounds. All the exchanges are closed. Can you help?"

"Of course," I say with a smile. I love the hotel business. In the morning, I will take her dollars to the exchange where I'll make 25 cents on the dollar.

Then again, I also love my retail job. But even these two salaries are not enough. It's never enough. I have dreams. Big dreams. And dreams are expensive. There's got to be a way to make more money, and I'm going to find it. Even if it kills me.

Chapter 2

TODAY, I DISCOVER my first white tiger.

I'm on a fifteen-minute break, sitting in a canvas folding chair on the sidewalk outside New Imperial Clothing, enjoying the warm summer sun, when Georges, a co-worker, hands me *Gentlemen's Quarterly.* "I know you like American magazines," he says. "A customer left this in the changing room."

I'm always eager to see the latest fashions from America. But as I thumb through *GQ*'s glossy pages, seeing predictable advertisements for Yves Saint Laurent and Pierre Cardin, I'm struck by the promotions for American blue jeans. It seems as if every third page is an ad for Levi's, Wrangler, or another American blue jean brand. I have noticed many American tourists wearing these "work pants" in lieu of traditional slacks on the streets of Beirut, but I have never seen them in local stores. *Why is no one is selling these in Beirut?*

This, I realize, is just the kind of opportunity I have been seeking to earn real money. Excited, I rush back into the store to show the magazine to my boss, Mr. Hassan. "Look." I point to a Levi's ad featuring a high fashion model clad in denim. "These are all the rage in the states. We should sell them here!"

Mr. Hassan studies the advertisement. I know he is a traditionalist when it comes to men's couture. He has often spoken disparagingly of the American and British "hippies" he sees on the news, and who occasionally wander into our store reeking of patchouli. But I also know him as a man who recognizes a business opportunity when he sees one.

"We are a fine men's fashion store," he finally says, unimpressed. "We don't sell blue jeans."

"But blue jeans *are* fashion. If they're good enough for *GQ*, they should be good enough for us. This is what our customers *want*."

Mr. Hassan's eyes return to the magazine. I can see his resistance cracking.

Sensing it's now or never, I press forward. "How about this? I'll buy the jeans myself. I'll pay for everything. All I ask is that you allow me to display them here in the store."

Now he's interested. "You'll pay me for the space?"

"We'll split the profits." I offer this without even knowing what kind of money we might be discussing. "Sixty-forty."

"Fifty-fifty," Mr. Hassan counters like the experienced negotiator he is.

"Fine. Fifty-fifty," I relent, this being the figure I'd anticipated anyway.

Mr. Hassan pushes the magazine back. "If you can get blue jeans, I'll display them."

"Good luck finding a distributor who will ship all the way to Lebanon," says Georges in a snarky tone. I turn to see him behind me and realize he must have been listening all along.

As much as I don't like it, Georges has a point. Shipping items overseas is slow and expensive. But I have an advantage neither of these men realize: my father.

"This is a great business opportunity," I tell him later that night. We have just a few minutes together before I must leave for my job at the Orient Prince, and I have rehearsed my pitch all afternoon. "You know people at the American embassy. Someone must know somebody who sells American blue jeans."

"I'll ask around," my father says. His many years working as a translator have given him connections all over the city, especially with American diplomats. "Give me a few days."

"Thank you." I give him a big hug. My affection is genuine. My father has always supported me, giving me the freedom I need to find my own path but never hesitating to help when I need it most. More than anything, I want to make him proud of me, his first-born son.

My father's "few days" seem like weeks as I run figures through my head. *What is the wholesale cost of blue jeans? How much can I sell them for here in Beirut? What about shipping costs? Customs fees? Any profit I make I will have to split fifty-fifty with Mr. Hassan. Will it be worth it?*

White tigers are rare and beautiful creatures. They're also known to eat alive the people who find them. *Will this one swallow me up?*

That Friday, my father hands me a slip of paper containing the name and number of a Wrangler wholesaler in New York City. I've seen magazine ads for this brand, and from my research, I know in America they are second only to Levi Strauss. My hands shake with nervous excitement as I dial. It's 8:30 p.m. here in Beirut, so it is early afternoon in New York. I struggle to keep my breath even as the phone rings.

"Mr. Spielman?" I ask the man at the other end of the line in my best English. "My name is Tony Assali. I'm calling from Beirut. My father is Toufic Assali—"

The man interrupts. "Yes, Tony, I've been expecting your call." His voice sounds friendly and energetic. "I understand you're looking to import Wrangler jeans. Have you done this sort of thing before?"

If I'm going to do business with him, it's important to be truthful. "This will be my first time. But if it works out, it won't be my last."

Mr. Spielman and I talk for a full half-hour. I can tell he's trying to get top dollar for his product while I insist on minimizing my expenses to make a reasonable profit. Ultimately, we make a deal. He will sell me his jeans in a variety of sizes for $3.50 each. I order fifty pairs for $175, plus shipping. *Where will I get the money?* From my own personal savings account, the money I have been saving to buy my big American car. I know it's a gamble, but if I succeed, the rewards will more than justify the risk.

The wait feels interminable. Every day, I arrive at New Imperial Clothing expecting to see a package only to be disappointed. *What if the shipment was held up in Customs? Or lost? Or stolen? What if this Mr. Spielman is just a con man, and I threw my money away for nothing?*

But then, five weeks after my phone call to New York, a large package arrives with my name on the label. Giddy, I cut the twine, tearing into the brown paper wrapping to reveal the goodies inside.

"They're here," I shout to Mr. Hassan, holding up a pair. I run my hands over the fine material. It evokes American fantasies that make my head spin: New York's urban sophistication, Los Angeles' cool celebrities strutting the Sunset Strip. "We need to get these on the floor right now."

Mr. Hassan and I clear discounted shirts off a table, stacking it with fifty pairs of jeans. I use a felt marker to make a sign on cardboard: "Wranglers. One hundred twenty Lebanese pounds." That's the equivalent of $40 U.S. As we're doing this, Georges runs his fingers over the fabric, inhaling the denim's unique aroma. There's nothing like it. Especially not in the Middle East.

But Georges is too proud of our culture to accept these imports. "These are work pants. We're selling work clothes now?"

Before either Mr. Hassan or I can respond, our first customer enters. A young Lebanese man in his early twenties, he wears a blue sports coat, tan slacks, and a white cotton shirt with an open collar.

I claim him before Georges can. "Welcome to New Imperial. How can I help you?"

"I'm looking for a suit."

"I have just what you're looking for," I assure him. But on our way toward the suit rack, I maneuver him close to my Wrangler jeans display. "These just came in this morning. We're the only store in Beirut to carry them."

I can feel Georges and Mr. Hassan watching this exchange from the other side of the store. They're both wondering the same thing: will he go for it?

"American blue jeans." His face lights up the same way mine did when I first laid eyes on this symbol of modern taste. "My friends will freak."

I throw Georges the tiniest look of triumph—and a little wink—then turn to my customer. "You can tell your buddies we gave you a great price."

He reads my handmade sign. "Just 120 pounds?"

Honestly, we could have charged double that, and I probably would have made the sale. An hour later, the customer leaves with a new Italian suit—and two pairs of Wrangler jeans. Word spreads quickly. Jeans begin flying out the door. Not only do we sell pair after pair to local customers and European tourists, we convert salespeople from the other shops on Hamra Street. They want their sweet piece of the American dream. Within two days, the display table is empty. Still, customers keep pouring through the door.

"Soon," I tell their disappointed faces. "Keep checking back." I've already called Mr. Spielman to order another hundred pairs. They can't come soon enough.

My white tiger has arrived. And to think it all began with an innocent peek at a fashion magazine. Now I'm in business. And a lucrative one at that. From every $40 sale, I first take my standard 10 percent sales commission. That's $4, covering my purchase price, plus shipping cost. The remaining $36 profit I split with

Mr. Hassan. I'm making $22 on every pair. My savings account, which I drained to make this deal happen, grows like a freshly watered flower.

Three months later, I drive out of the dealership in a new 1970-model baby- blue Ford Falcon stick shift. I am the proud owner of my *Belle Americaine*! Feeling on top of the world, I happily cruise down Beirut's bustling streets. Pretty girls stare admiringly, and I grin back. I'm delirious with happiness—and completely clueless to the dark turn my life will soon take.

Chapter 3

THE BEATLES ARE playing in all of their glorious magnificence through the factory-installed in-dash AM/FM radio of my 1970 Ford Falcon. I am cruising through the glittery streets of downtown Beirut, windows down, feeling the warm, humid, salt-tinged Mediterranean air caress my face, enjoying the prize I worked so hard to acquire.

From what I have read, the Beatles traveled a similar path to fame and fortune. John Lennon, Paul McCartney, George Harrison, and Ringo Starr began with little else besides a dream and their own hunger for more as they struggled from the back streets of Liverpool to the underground rock clubs of Hamburg—and finally—the stage of America's *The Ed Sullivan Show*.

Now, just six years after that historic appearance on February 9, 1964, the Fab Four are recognized universally as the greatest rock band of all time. I do not for a moment believe I have even a fraction of the Beatles' talent—I can't even play a musical instrument—but I believe I share the same drive that helped them achieve their success. The stunning American vehicle I now guide with near-effortless power steering attests to that.

Finally, the song finishes. It's the top of the hour and, as usual, an announcer chimes in with the news. "Gunfire rang out at a café on Mar Elias Street at approximately three-fifteen this afternoon," the gentleman intones, his practiced voice flat and emotionless. "Police found three people dead and several others wounded. A manhunt is underway for the two shooters. Authorities describe them as males in their early twenties, wearing dark jackets and wool hats. A spokesman says there is reason to suspect the shooters are refugees…"

I turn off the radio. The night is too lovely to spoil with terror. This is not a time to think about death. It is a time to celebrate life. Fifteen minutes later, I sit with my friends Michel and Yoosef at a table in La Grande, our favorite nightclub, drinking beers. Despite my best efforts to talk about anything but current events, the conversation veers to this bleak subject.

"You heard about the shooting?" Michel asks. He holds his smoldering Turkish cigarette between his second and third fingers. "It's the same thing every week."

Yoosef agrees, taking a swig of beer. "These militants. They're vermin. Cockroaches. They just keep coming."

"What do you mean?" I ask.

My friend's assured tone surprises me. "They won't stop because our government makes them feel welcome," Michel explains. "You know we provide these monsters with housing?"

"You mean camps," I correct him. I've seen newspaper pictures of refugee tents along our southern border, mile after endless mile of poverty and squalor.

"It's free housing," Michel counters. "Along with free food and medicine and schools. No wonder they keep coming. For them, every day is Christmas."

"They're Moslems." Yoosef corrects him. "They don't celebrate Christmas."

"You know what I mean," Michel snaps back. "They're parasites. And now, like cancer cells, they're attacking their host. Us. But we have an immune system to fight back."

Michel is studying to be a doctor so I'm not surprised by his medical similes, crude as they may be.

"You mean the army? The police?"

"Ha. Useless." Michel scoffs. "I'm talking about a people's army. Lebanese militias will defend our city and our country."

"Militias are against the law," I remind my friend.

"Do these jackals act like they give a damn about the law? Of course not. So why should we? The only way to beat them is to play their game."

"I've already joined a militia," Yoosef says. "So have half the guys from the neighborhood."

"There are thirty in my unit," says Michel. "We all have guns and we train every other day. The next time a terrorist tries something he'll be in his Paradise before he knows what hit him."

"What about you?" Yoosef says. "Will you join? We need you."

Michel stares at me too. We've talked about stuff like this before. He knows my stance. Still, he pushes me.

"This is your chance to make a difference. Think of your family. Your brother and sisters. Think of your friend."

I think of Nabil dying in Paris from his wounds only a few days ago, and a lump forms in my throat. I turn my head so they don't see me wipe my eyes. When I look back at my buddies' faces, I notice their mustaches, the cigarettes hanging from their lips. They want so badly to be seen as tough guys—*as men*—but all I detect is the naiveté of school children.

"You're talking about war," I tell them. "In war, everybody dies. Nobody wins."

"Are you a coward?" Michel asks accusingly. "This is our country. We must defend it."

"I have to go," I say abruptly, putting down more than enough cash to cover my share of the tab. "I have to get up early for work."

"You'll think about it?" Yoosef asks.

"Sure," I say, though I know it's a lie.

Driving home later I see my city through new eyes. For the first time, I notice the many closed and abandoned shops. The boarded windows. Graffitied walls bear pockmarked scars from gunshots and bombs. I can feel electricity in the air. A storm is coming. And neither my friends nor I, nor all the militias, can do a thing to stop it.

Chapter 4

I STUDY THE faces of the five people at the dinner table. My entire family is here: My father, mother, younger brother Joe, and sisters, Antoinette (Nunu), Josephine, and Claudia (Coco). But there is no food set before us. No drinks waiting to be enjoyed. This is not a meal nor a celebration. My father has called us together to discuss an urgent matter. My mom keeps her head lowered, her eyes refusing to meet mine. Even more than my father's grim expression, this signals something is wrong. *Is someone ill? Has a relative died? Are we in financial trouble?*

"There is going to be a war." My father gets straight to the point. His deep brown eyes are hard and unwavering. "I've been speaking to friends at the embassy. They're certain the current troubles are the beginning of civil war."

The little hairs on my arms stand up as I feel an immediate sensation of *déjà vu*. This is exactly what Michel and Yoosef were talking about. It's what *everyone* is talking about in restaurants, parks and offices throughout Beirut. The sniper attacks. The bombings. The whole city seems to be going to hell. But this is Lebanon. For decades we have been a land of peace and sanity in the Middle East. The idea that war—actual war—could erupt in our beautiful land has always seemed like a paranoid fantasy, an excuse for people like my friends to play soldier. But hearing these words from my father make it sound all too real.

"What'll we do?" Joe asks with a trembling voice. Barely a teenager, the concept of war is both confusing and terrifying to him.

"We must leave Beirut." My father's words catch in his throat. "Lebanon, too."

"And go where?" Coco blurts out. She looks as lost as Joe.

"America. My friends at the embassy can make the arrangements."

"But I don't want to go." Joe cries. "I want to stay here. I want to stay with my friends."

"We all do." My mother runs her fingers through Joe's thick black hair. "But it's no longer safe. When the war is over. If there *is* a war—"

My father interrupts. "There will be war."

My mom speaks softer. "We can come back later. I promise."

Joe starts to say something, then closes his mouth. He fidgets in his chair. I don't blame him or Coco for pacing the room. I feel nauseated. I've never known any other home but Beirut. Although I can speak enough English to get by, the idea of traveling six thousand miles to a foreign country I have seen only in the movies and on TV fills me with dread. This is not the way my life was supposed to go.

"When do we leave?" asks Josephine, always a voice of moderation. "Will we able to say goodbye to our friends?"

"Of course," my father assures her. "It may be months before we can go. There is a big demand for visas, so we can only get one to start."

Only one visa? But we can't separate!

My father turns his dark brown eyes to me, interrupting my thoughts. "Tony, you'll be the first to go."

Everyone turns to me.

"Me?" The shock sends my voice up a full octave. "Why me?"

"You speak the best English."

"But you speak better than I do. You're a translator."

"No. I have to take care of the family. You are the oldest son. You're strong and smart and can live on your own."

My mom puts her hand on mine. She's trying to calm me.

"Once you are settled," he continues. "You will send for the rest of us."

I can see my father's logic, but I'm still reluctant. I try to imagine living in a city as foreign to me as London or Beijing, unable to speak my native language and working as a… *what? What kind of jobs can a seventeen-year-old Middle Eastern immigrant get in America? Even an immigrant with a high-school education? Window washer? Bicycle messenger? Busboy?* Here in Beirut, I hold dreams of managing my own hotel. In America, I could be back to toting guests' luggage. I will be a stranger in a strange land.

"No," I say. "That's not fair. We're a family. Either we all go or we all stay. We'll find another way to get through this."

I look to my brother and sisters. They look relieved I won't abandon them.

"You must go, Tony." There's a distinct quiver in my mom's voice. Tears well up in her eyes. "It is God's will."

Joe objects. "How do you know it's God's will?"

"And who are you to question your mother?" my father snaps.

"This idea is stupid," says Coco.

The situation is spinning out of control. I must calm things down before my family faces its own civil war.

"Dad has a point," I say, pushing my chair back. "This is how it's done when families move to a new country. One person goes first."

"What are you talking about?" Joe asks.

I try to recall books from high school history classes, stories of immigrating families splitting up for the sake of the unit. "Europeans have been coming to the United States for decades. Germans, Poles, Irish, Greeks, Jews, Italians, Swedes, Russians, Armenians." I lock eyes with my dad. He nods for me to continue. "Most of them were too poor to all go at once, so they'd send the first-born son to get a foothold. Then everyone else came. Now it's our turn." I've been a salesman for years. Now I'm using my powers of persuasion to sell my family—and myself.

"Don't forget, we can still talk by telephone," my mom says.

"Right. That's something immigrants from a hundred years ago couldn't dream of. I'll be a pioneer, a cowboy, blazing a trail west so the rest of you can follow. I guess that makes me John Wayne?"

This gets a big laugh. Just what I needed to cut through the tension.

"Then he'll go." My father claps me on the shoulder hard. I know he's trying to fortify me. To remind me to be a man.

I hug him. With tears in my eyes, I tell him, "I won't let you down."

We arrive at Beirut-Rafic Hariri International Airport just after 6:00 p.m., a full two hours before my flight's scheduled departure. I have spent the last three weeks cutting all ties with the place I grew up. I submitted my resignation letter to my manager at the Orient Prince Hotel and the next day, another to Mr. Hassan at New Imperial Clothing. Both men said they were sorry to see me leave but understood. In the past few weeks, many Christians have fled. That even more have stayed gives people hope the recent wave of terrorism has run its course and civil war can be avoided. If this is true, I may be back in Beirut sooner than I expect.

My family stays close as I make my way through the quiet terminal. It's my first time in an airport, and I'm excited and nervous. Ever since the hijackings began a few years ago in Europe and North America, airports throughout the world have installed security gates with metal detectors, allowing only ticketed passengers to approach boarding gates. Beirut-Rafic Hariri is no exception. As a result, we all crowd together just outside the international security checkpoint.

"You're gonna do great," Joe tells me. "America has the best of everything. The best music. The best food. The best cars. And the best girls." He gives me a sly wink.

"I'm going to miss you so much." Coco pulls me into a big hug with wet eyes. "Write us every day."

I whisper to Josephine. "Take care of Coco. I'm counting on you."

"I'll see she stays out of trouble," Josephine promises. "You do the same."

"Here is something for when you get to Boston." My father gives me an envelope. "It's yours anyway."

"Keep it," I insist. "I have plenty of money. I'll be fine." In fact, I have only $28 in my pocket. I had saved a lot more—more than $5,000 that could have made my first weeks in America very comfortable—but I left it all with my father.

The announcer calls my flight over the loudspeaker. Suddenly, it all seems very real. Frighteningly so. I open my arms and pull everyone together for one last embrace.

My mother weeps. Her body shakes. "No! No! He can't go."

My dad tries to soothe her but she won't listen.

"What if we never see him again?"

I want to cry, too, but I push down those feelings. I clench my jaw to hold it together. "You'll see me in a few months."

I walk toward the checkpoint. Behind me, my mom wailing even harder. When I look back, I see her knees give out. Joe just barely catches her before she hits the floor.

"Go! Go!" my father insists, waving me toward the gate. "I'll take care of her. Call us when you get to America."

I give Mom one last look. "I love you."

With that, I head toward the busy checkpoint. I mustn't look back. If I do, I might fall apart too.

A uniformed agent checks my passport and ticket, then directs me to the transit tunnel. Reality hits me in the gut. No matter what I promised my family, the truth is I may never see them again. I may never see Beirut again. For the first time, I feel scared and alone.

A half-hour later, I am strapped into a narrow fabric seat gazing out the window as we rise into the night sky over Beirut. From this perspective, I see my country through new eyes. The crisscross pattern of roads, both modern and ancient, illuminated by streetlights make the city sparkle like a jewel. From this height, all is peaceful—no sign at all of the conflict or bloodshed. There is nothing here but tranquility.

Despite the beauty below, waves of sadness wash over me. I am not just leaving Lebanon. I am leaving part of myself behind. My childhood. My people. Everything I know.

Suddenly, the landscape below slides away, and we propel into the darkness, heading over the Mediterranean. The only lights come from a few distant ships in the black expanse. My heart speeds. *Is it the thrill from flying? The excitement of starting a new life in a new country? Or is it something more?* I am suddenly certain I am doing the right thing. I am a man now. A man with an unlimited future—a future I cannot wait to begin.

Chapter 5

THE SUN IS setting when my plane lands at Boston's Logan Airport, casting the complex in a golden, almost ethereal glow. Including the six hours it took me to fly to London, my half-day layover at London's Heathrow Airport, and the eight-hour flight across the Atlantic, I have been traveling for almost twenty hours. But I am not tired. The experience of flying for the first time is far too exhilarating for me to consider sleeping. This, coupled with the prospect of starting a new life, has me wound tighter than a watch spring.

After disembarking, I join my fellow passengers in the long line at U.S. Customs. It takes me nearly half an hour to get to the front. When it is my turn for processing, I step forward and present my Lebanese passport and U.S. visa to the stern-looking uniformed agent behind the glass. He studies my picture with a frown. He looks up and stares me in the eye, then studies the picture some more. At last, he gives me an expression I can only read as suspicion. If the man is trying to make me nervous, he's succeeding. Sweat forms on my forehead. I can feel my heart pounding. *What's the problem? Don't I look like myself?*

"What is the purpose of your visit?"

I clear my throat. "I'm visiting friends," I respond in English. Before leaving Beirut, my father advised me not to mention anything about the situation in Lebanon. Apparently, the U.S. government has special rules for dealing with war refugees, and the process can take years to resolve. Better to say you're a tourist.

"And how long do you intend to say?"

"A few months." I am suddenly desperate for a glass of water.

"Do you have anything to declare? Any plants, produce, liquor, or items of value?"

"Nothing," I respond honestly. I don't even bother to tell him about the $28 I have in my pocket.

He pauses with his stamp high in the air. I imagine being hauled off to prison or sent back on the next plane to Beirut. *What would my family think?* Then the stamp comes down with an echoing thud. "Welcome to the United States." He slides the documents back to me without expression.

"Thank you," I say with relief.

Grabbing my carry-on bag, I head through the gate. As I step over a broken yellow line, I realize I have officially set foot in the United States.

Everywhere I look I see bright lights and people pushing wheeled carts stacked high with suitcases. Dozens of men in chauffeur's uniforms hold signs bearing the names of the arriving passengers they are here to meet. I imagine this must be far different from what those early immigrants I told my family about experienced when they arrived half a century ago.

"Tony. Tony Assali!"

I turn to see a slender, olive-skinned man in his late twenties waving behind a rope barrier. This is Ron Elias. He's a Lebanese-American businessman I met last year while working at New Imperial Clothing. Ron was looking for bargains on Italian suits. I ended up selling him four as well as a dozen shirts and ties at a big discount, winning his trust.

"I owe you one," he had said.

He told me should I ever come to the United States, I could stay with him and his family outside Boston. After my father declared I would be moving to America, I took Ron up on his offer, writing to him. To my happy surprise, he said he would love to be my host. I later sent him my travel arrangements, and he graciously offered to pick me up at the airport. And now, here he is—wearing one of the shirts I sold him.

"Ron!" I hurry to join him. We share a quick but heartfelt embrace.

"How was the flight?"

"Great. My first time on an airplane. I've never seen the tops of clouds before. They're beautiful."

"Let's get going." Ron hustles me toward the exit. "Parking here costs a fortune."

We get my luggage from baggage claim, then hurry to the parking structure where we load my two suitcases and carry-on into the trunk of Ron's white Chevrolet Malibu. Although it's close to 10:00 p.m., the air is warm and sticky.

"That's Boston in August," Ron says and laughs.

A few minutes later, we are on the road heading north. Still wired on adrenaline, I spend the next hour with my face pressed against the window. This is my first look at America, and my impression is that America is overwhelming in size and grandeur. Leaving Logan, we pass Boston's glittering downtown towers, which I find oddly comforting. They remind me of downtown Beirut, although these buildings are massive and there are more of them. As we pass out of the city and into the suburbs, I see large areas of blackness peppered with lights from what must be small houses. I am used to Beirut's density and have never seen sprawling geography like this. *Are these shacks?*

As we continue down the highway, I find myself surrounded by American cars. *Lots of American cars.* Chevrolets. Buicks. Chryslers. Cadillacs. Plymouths. Lincoln Continentals. It feels like a dream. I glimpse only a handful of the bug-like Volkswagens and none of the smaller Citroens, Renaults, Mini

Coopers, and Fiats so common in Beirut. Virtually every car here is a *Belle Americaine*!

Ron's parents live in Manchester, New Hampshire, less than sixty miles north of Boston. As it is close to midnight and traffic is light, we make the trip in under an hour. Ron's parents are there to meet us when we arrive. Their house looks huge. Ron tells me it has four bedrooms and three bathrooms and sits on a full half- acre of land. In Beirut, this would be a mansion. But Ron assures me that, here in Manchester, a house like this is not at all unusual.

"Tony. Welcome to America!" Ron's father says in Lebanese-accented English. His hands are large, his grip strong and assured. "You had a good flight? Any problems?"

"No problems at all, Mr. Elias," I assure him, thanking him for his hospitality.

"It's our pleasure," Ron's mother says. She, too, speaks in Lebanese-accented English. According to Ron, his parents came to the U.S. more than twenty years ago. "It's our way of thanking you for taking good care of our Ronnie. Oh, my, where are my manners? You must be starving. What would you like to eat?"

In many ways, Mrs. Elias reminds me of my mother. They share the same warmth, generosity, and need to ensure everyone around them is properly fed. With a sickening feeling, I remember my own mother collapsing at the airport.

"You okay?" asks Ron.

"Fine. Fine." I pull myself together. "How about eggs?" It's late, and I want to keep things simple.

Ron laughs at my request. So do his parents.

"What's so funny? Did I just say something wrong?"

"In America, eggs are what people eat for breakfast."

"Who cares? If Tony wants eggs, I will make him eggs," Mrs. Elias says. "Ronnie, bring his suitcases."

Fifteen minutes later, I'm sitting at the Eliases' fine dining room table, looking down at a plate containing two steaming sunny side-up eggs. I take a bite. "Delicious."

"Here's some pineapple juice to wash it down."

"Pineapple juice?" I have heard of pineapples, but never pineapple juice.

"Try it," Ron says. "It's really good."

Not sure what to expect, I take a sip. I can't remember tasting anything as sweet and wonderful.

"He likes it."

"Have some milk too." Mrs. Elias sets down a small glass.

Mr. Elias notices my reticence. "What's wrong?"

"It's cold," I explain. "Is that safe?"

Ron's parents look at each other in confusion. Then Mr. Elias laughs. "It's been so long, I almost forget. Yes, the milk is safe. In America, they pasteurize milk before it goes to the market. Kills the bacteria. We drink it cold all the time."

It dawns on me that while much about this new country looks familiar, it is still a strange and foreign land. It is going to take me a long time to figure out its strange customs. After dinner, Ron's parents take me to a room they call the "den," where they have made up a couch.

"You are way too generous," I say. "Tomorrow, I'll find my own place to stay."

"Our house is yours. You can stay as long as you like."

I suspect the Eliases are just being polite. "I will find a place."

"Nonsense. We want to know all about what's happening in Beirut," says Mrs. Elias. "It's been a long time since we've been back."

Fifteen minutes later, I lie between two fresh cotton sheets, ready to enjoy the first full night's sleep I have had in days. But although my body is exhausted, my mind is still flying like the jetliner I was aboard just hours ago. Now that I am in America—*America!*—there is so much I need to do. I don't want to freeload off the Elias family, no matter how generous they may be. I need to get a job and, after that, my own place. Despite what they say.

I will be starting from nothing. The next few weeks are going to be very, very interesting.

Chapter 6

GREEN. THAT IS my first impression upon seeing America in daylight for the first time. Everything here is just so… *green*.

Beirut, like all of Lebanon, enjoys what meteorologists call a "hot-summer Mediterranean climate." While our winters can be cool and rainy, our summers are often bone dry, and many months can pass before we see even a drop of precipitation. Although we have trees—the most common of which are our celebrated cedars—forests tend to be sparse, colors muted.

By contrast, the lush, verdant landscape I see out the Eliases' living room picture window feels like the difference between an old faded sepia photograph and a vibrant new Kodachrome print. The dazzling trees and rich, verdant lawns surrounding every house on this street are so bright and vivid that the sight is, to my Middle Eastern eyes, almost painfully beautiful.

"What you are looking at?" Ronnie catches me gazing out the living room window.

"I've never seen trees so green before."

"That's nothing. If you like that you should see them in September. Everything turns red and gold. It's like they're on fire. People come from all over the country to see our fall colors. It's spectacular."

September is just a month away. I can't imagine the leaves transforming so quickly, but I look forward to seeing if Ron's right. Later, at breakfast, thoughts of trees on fire give way to more practical concerns when I tell his parents about my plans to find a job and an apartment.

"What do you know about doughnuts?" Mr. Elias asks.

Not sure what he means, I shoot Ron a glance. "Um, I know they're delicious."

"What do you know about *making* doughnuts?" Mr. Elias clarifies. "Have you ever worked in a bakery before?"

"No. I've worked mostly in hotels and retail."

Mrs. Elias jumps in. "Our daughter's husband owns a doughnut factory. They make doughnuts and sell them to stores and bakeries all over the city. They're very successful."

"We told Sylvia you were coming and might need work," said Mr. Elias. "She might be able to set you up with a job… if you want it."

I don't hesitate a second. "Of course, I want it! Thank you very much."

My excitement is genuine. Of course, working isn't my first choice of employment, but I know how important it is to secure a job and start producing income if I am going to establish myself in America. Making doughnuts is fine for now. Getting rich can come later.

"Your work visa is good, but it's not enough," Sylvia says later that week as she looks over my official documents. In her mid-thirties, she looks a lot like her younger brother—if her younger brother were a sharply dressed, good-looking woman with shoulder-length brown hair.

"What more do I need?"

"A Social Security card." She hands me back my visa. "I can't hire you without one."

For a moment, we sit in uncomfortable silence. Suddenly, I see all my dreams of making enough money to sustain myself and send home dissolve.

"But don't worry," she smiles. "I can get you what you need."

I'm grateful for Sylvia's help. At the same time, I realize how vulnerable I am in this foreign country. A few days later, Sylvia takes me to a civic building in downtown Manchester. Like most government buildings everywhere in the world, this one is cold and gray and looks like it needs a new coat of paint. Why can't a government building ever look like a nice hotel? Do all governments want their citizens to feel depressed and unwanted?

Wearing the one suit I brought from Beirut, my hair carefully combed, I stand beside Sylvia as she sits across from a dour, middle-aged woman in a tiny cubicle, her desk covered in bureaucratic forms. A small framed photo of the woman posing beside two teenage girls—her daughters, I guess—is the only sign of humanity on display.

"This is Tony's passport and H-2B work visa." Sylvia gives the woman my documents. "He's going to be working for me. Full-time. Eight hours a day, five days a week in my bakery."

I try not to look nervous but knowing my entire future hangs on this woman's impression of me causes my legs to tremble. I can only hope she does not interpret my anxiety as a sign of subterfuge.

Sylvia answers a few more questions, the specifics of which I don't hear because I'm too nervous to follow the conversation. But whatever Sylvia tells the woman does the trick because, fifteen minutes later, I walk out of the drab government building into the bright midday summer sunshine carrying my very own temporary Social Security card. A permanent version will arrive in four weeks. I can now work legally in America.

"Thank you," I tell Sylvia with genuine gratitude.

"Not a problem," Sylvia assures me. "We Lebanese stick together."

A few days later, I meet with Sylvia's husband, Mike, at their bakery. I guess Mike to be of either English or Irish descent. As I will later learn, many Americans are a mix of many, if not dozens, of nationalities, which makes the ethnic tribalism so common in the Middle East nearly impossible. It's one of the many things I will come to love about this remarkable country.

"This is our mix," Mike begins, proudly indicating bags of dust-covered baking flour lying on a heavy wooden shelf. "The manufacturer makes it especially for us."

From there, Mike walks me through the entire production process, from mixing the flour to making dough, kneading and spreading it, then using custom cutting tools to cut each doughnut from the sheet, removing the hole, and placing the raw doughnuts on a wire mesh sheet that is then lowered gently into hot canola oil.

Once the doughnuts are fried, they're finished by hand with a variety of glazes and toppings, everything from shredded coconut and chopped peanuts to multicolored candy "jimmies" and chocolate chips. Some doughnuts are injected with fillings ranging from vanilla cream to strawberry jelly. The sights and smells of the bakery are almost overpowering and it's all I can do to keep from reaching out and gobbling up as many of these tasty confections as I can lay my hands on.

As a novice, my job will be to mix the flour, knead the dough, and cut the doughnuts. Based on what Mike has shown me, it seems simple enough. Even boring. Certainly not like the responsibilities I had at either the Orient Prince or New Imperial Clothing. But being new to America, I don't have many options.

"Work starts at 4:00 a.m. so we can start delivering to our wholesale customers at 6:00 a.m.," Mike explains. "You'll go until noon, with a half-hour off for breakfast, plus two fifteen-minute coffee breaks. Think you can handle that?"

"Sure." Compared to the twenty-two-hour days I was clocking in Beirut, this will be like a vacation. Or so I think.

"Great." Mike pumps my hand. "You can start after Labor Day. Welcome aboard."

Labor Day, I learn, is a holiday honoring America's working class. By law, it always falls on a Monday, so people can have a three-day weekend. I am surprised to see so many people use this time to go shopping—many department stores proudly advertise their Labor Day sales, which means many retail workers have to work over the holiday weekend. That's funny. What kind of a holiday for working class forces them to work on a holiday?

The Tuesday after Labor Day, I wake at 2:30 a.m., eat a quick breakfast, drink a cup of coffee, then head for the bakery. I don't wish to waste money riding public transportation so I walk the five miles to work. This becomes my new routine. At first, the daily ten-mile, round-trip hike is not a problem. The air is pleasantly cool and when there is rain, the umbrella the Eliases lent me provides protection from the elements. I particularly enjoy the walk home. As Ron promised, the trees turn from green to dazzling shades of yellow, gold, and crimson. I have never seen displays like this. Set against a clear azure sky, the trees really do look like they are on fire.

But this "season" lasts only a few weeks. By late September, temperatures plunge to near-freezing. The leaves turn brown and fall to earth in piles inches thick. The trees become bare and skeletal. By month's end, it begins to snow. I am not prepared for such chilly weather. I have no boots, no gloves, not even a heavy jacket. By the time I get to the factory at 4:00 a.m., my socks are soaked and I'm half-frozen. Determined to press on, I continue to make the ten-mile, round-trip commute on foot until mid-October. But even I have a breaking point. I give in and start taking the bus.

Traveling by bus is a great relief for me physically, but it has its cost. As I am working for minimum wage, my weekly paycheck is only $45 after taxes. When I see my first pay stub, I almost have a heart attack. They not only deduct income tax, but something called "FICA," nearly 20 percent of my hourly wage.

But good things are happening, too. Shortly after beginning at the doughnut factory, the other workers invite me to join them for lunch at McDonald's. I've heard of the place, but never actually been to one. (This is 1970, long before McDonald's became an international brand.) Like my friends, I order my hamburger and French fries with a Coca-Cola. To my astonishment, my order is ready in minutes. I now know why they call this "fast food."

However, what I find even more surprising is how everyone eats their hamburgers and French fries with their hands. In Lebanon, we eat nearly everything with a knife and fork. To eat with one's hands is considered unclean.

"It's okay," one of my new friends assures me as he lifts the hamburger to his mouth. "Everybody eats like this."

"Yeah. You don't want to be weird," another co-worker warns me.

Still unconvinced, I wrap a paper napkin around each hand before carefully picking the hamburger out of its Styrofoam box. My tablemates can't help but laugh as I lean down and take a cautious bite. The hamburger is so delicious I look up and smile as I continue to chew. Gaining courage, I pick a French fry from its red cardboard container barehanded. The "fry" is hot and salty. The others applaud. Even more than getting a Social Security card, eating at McDonald's has made me a true American.

Later, as I leave, I notice the sign atop the golden arches declaring this restaurant has sold 20 billion hamburgers.

"Twenty billion?" I blink up, confused. "How can one little restaurant sell 20 billion hamburgers? That must be a mistake."

"They mean the whole company," my co-worker explains. "There are like hundreds of McDonald's all over the country."

"It started with just one drive-in in California back in the 1950s," someone else says. "It's now the biggest chain in the world."

My head is swimming. If one little drive-in could become so successful, then I have definitely come to the right country. I can be rich, too. I just need to find my white tiger. Later this month, that's exactly what I do.

Chapter 7

"**SO, HOW'S IT** going? Mike treating you okay?"

Ron and I are hanging out in the alley behind the doughnut factory. It's 8:30 a.m., and I'm on one of my two daily 15-minute coffee breaks. Ron often stops by to check on me before driving off to one of the three hair salons he owns in and around Manchester. Since I'm up and out of the house long before Ron wakes, and I am usually asleep by the time he gets in. This is one of our few opportunities to catch up on each other's lives.

"He's great," I respond between bites of a chocolate-glazed doughnut with crushed peanuts on top. I've gained 5 pounds since I began working here. Occupational hazard, I tell myself. I'll work it off once the weather warms. It's already November. Spring can't be that far off, can it? "Although I'm still stuck mixing dough. He says I can't advance to being a decorator until one of the regulars quits."

"Well, you know what they say: Good things come to those who wait."

"*Who* says that?"

I leave out the fact it's been almost six weeks and I barely have more money than I did when I started.

"We'll figure out something," Ron assures me. "Too bad you don't know how to cut hair."

Just then, I glance toward his car, a burnt-orange 1966 Pontiac GTO that I have long admired, and notice a pile of wigs covering its backseat. Blonde wigs. Brunette wigs. Red wigs. Wigs with long hair, wigs with short hair. It looks like he just came back from some crazed scalping raid.

"Why do you have so many wigs?"

"They're for my salons. A lot of my customers can only afford to come in every four or six weeks, so when their hair starts to go bad, they wear wigs. It makes for a good short-term fix."

"And you sell these?"

"It's a good side business."

"And it's profitable?"

"Very. Hell, I'd sell more if I could."

My fingers begin tingling. I am all-too familiar with this feeling. I've just glimpsed a white tiger. "What if we could sell these outside of your salons? You think you could sell more?" Even as I speak, a vision begins forming.

Ron shakes his head. "I can't afford to open a wig shop. I've checked around. The overhead's too high."

"We don't need a shop. We could go straight to the customers. At their homes."

"You mean like door-to-door? Forget it."

"You have heard of Tupperware parties?" I say. After learning about McDonald's, I've been reading about franchise business opportunities, and Tupperware parties—at which housewives gather in a neighbor's home to buy plastic food storage containers. It is one of the hottest concepts around.

"Sure. So what?" From the look on his face, I can tell he's still not making the connection.

I reach into his car and throw a platinum-colored wig on my head. "We stage wig parties."

Ron laughs. He doesn't know what to make of me.

"Choose one of your best customers. Ask her to give us her house for an evening. She invites her friends. Then we sell them, too. I'll be your salesman. I'll take a 40 percent commission on every wig I sell. You can have the rest."

Ron takes off my wig and throws it back in his car. He's not laughing anymore. "And what's in it for the woman who gives us her house?"

"What else? A free wig. But to get it, she has to bring enough friends to make it worth our while. How many wigs would that be?"

Ron knows his business and quickly runs the numbers. "At least ten."

"That could work. Everyone knows at least ten people, right? And then maybe one or two of her friends might want a free wig, too, so they let us use *their* house. And on and on and on…"

Ron's eyes now have a far-away look. This is a look I like. It means he's thinking. *Fantasizing.* But then his face changes. "I don't know. If this is such a good idea how come no one else has done it?"

"Because no one else thinks like me!"

Two weeks later, Ron and I pull up to the split-level home of one of his long-time customers, Antonia Fiorre. So much for Ron's reservations. As soon as he explained the idea to her, she sparked to it, offering to host our event. She claims to have dozens of friends who would love to buy nice wigs at the discount prices we are offering, especially with Ron himself offering to custom-style the wig for each buyer.

Ron and I have arrived a half-hour early to set up. In addition to a wide variety of wigs, which Ron was able to buy from his wholesaler for $10 apiece, we have brought several bottles of red and white wine, a package of clear plastic cups, crackers, and an assortment of meat and cheese appetizers. After all, what's a party without wine and snacks?

Our shindig is scheduled to begin at 7:00 p.m. But when the hour arrives, no guest does. Five minutes pass, and Ron looks at me nervously. "If this doesn't work, you and I are going to be eating Swiss cheese and salami for the next few weeks."

Just then, the doorbell rings. Antonia, dressed in casual slacks and a colorful printed blouse, crosses to the foyer. She cries out with delight as she greets two neighbors.

"Fashionably late," I tell Ron. He looks only slightly relieved.

By 7:30 p.m., a dozen females have crowded into Antonia's living room. All of them *oooh* and *aaah* at wigs we have displayed atop Styrofoam mannequin heads. It's showtime. I step forward and raise my hands for attention.

"Thank you all for coming," I say. "Has everyone had plenty to eat and drink?"

Smiles. Applause from the women. One of them whisper-compliments me on my accent, adding to my confidence.

"My name is Tony. This is my partner Ron. Our lovely hostess here has offered us her lovely home so we can share with you a unique opportunity to own a superior quality wig at an amazing price. Also, Ron will personally style any wig you purchase tonight to make sure it looks beautiful on you."

I approach an attractive, voluptuous brunette sipping red wine on a padded Ottoman. "What's your name?"

"Irene," she replies shyly.

"You have nice hair," I tell her. She looks away, blushing. "Is that your natural color?"

"Of course, it is." She giggles. "With a little help every few weeks." The other women laugh supportively.

"It must take hours to style like that. A lot of work."

"You have no idea." She exchanges knowing glances with the others.

"And on those days you just don't feel like spending time on your hair, I bet you could use a wig that would still make you look just as beautiful." Before Irene can reply, I pick up a nearby wig close to her chocolate hair color. "One like this. Here, try it on."

"I don't know. I've never worn one before."

"Don't worry. Here." I offer her a silk skullcap, then help her put the wig snugly over her head just as Ron showed me the day before. I straighten it, then step back like an artist revealing his masterpiece. "Well," I say to the group. "What do you think?"

As if on cue, everyone cheers. I offer Irene a hand mirror, and she gasps at her reflection. I wink at Ron. I can tell this is going to be a good night. By evening's end, we have sold twelve wigs, one to each guest. Through dealing with each woman personally, by making each one feel special, I'm able to close every sale. As promised, Ron custom styles each wig to the buyer's taste, and every woman leaves the party tipsy—and happy.

After the guests have gone, Ron and I tally our earnings. Each wig cost us $10. We sold them for $40. As agreed, I get 40 percent of the profit. For twelve wigs, that's $192. Deducting my share of the money we spent on wine and snacks, plus half the cost of the $10 wig we awarded our hostess, this still leaves me with just over $100 for one night's work. *That's more money than I make at the doughnut factory in two weeks.*

I love America.

Our idea spreads like wildfire. Customers at Ron's salons actually come up to him asking—*begging*—for the opportunity to host a wig party. By mid-November, we're doing three events a week. By early December, it's seven. The money is so good I buy Ron's 1966 Pontiac GTO from him. No more busses. I can go where I want when I want. The feeling is exhilarating.

"I'm grateful for the opportunity you gave me," I tell Mike when I return to the doughnut factory after New Year's. "But it's time to move on. I need to focus 100 percent on my wig business. This is my two-weeks' notice."

"I've been waiting for this," Mike says without any bitterness. "You're a good worker but you're just meant for bigger things."

We shake hands like gentlemen. *Like equals*. Three days later, he finds a replacement, and we agree I can leave the following day.

Throughout winter and early spring, Ron and I continue organizing wig parties all over southern New Hampshire and Northeast Massachusetts. The hours are short and the money is good. Very good. But I know women only purchase a wig once every few years at most. We're going to run out of customers soon.

I need to find a new white tiger. Something permanent. Something with a future. Luckily, my next opportunity presents itself. Her name is Stephanie. And she is beautiful.

Chapter 8

"TRY THIS COLOR. It goes with your eyes."

I hand the shimmering chestnut-colored, shoulder-length wig to the petite woman in a high-collared canary yellow dress sitting before me. She is one of more than twenty females Ron has assembled for tonight's wig party at an upscale suburban Bedford home. The young woman flashes a dazzling white smile as she slips the wig over her close-cropped auburn hair. I carefully adjust the fit, then hand her a mirror.

"You're right." She checks herself out this way and that. "You have a good eye. Is this something you learned in school? Back in…?"

"Beirut," I finish her sentence.

"That in Syria?"

"Lebanon," I say, without condescension. "Syria is to the north."

"So how long have you been in America?"

"Almost nine months," I reply, stunned to realize how much time has passed since that humid evening I landed at Logan Airport.

"Why did you move?" She inches slightly closer. She seems genuinely interested in me. Maybe even… attracted?

"Opportunity," I say. I make it a point not to discuss political problems back home. Especially not with good-looking ladies. I have learned talking politics is a great way to kill a conversation—fast. "In America, a man can be whatever he dreams. There are no limits."

"And what is it that *you* dream?"

"To be a success. To be rich. Independent. You know, the American dream."

"Looks like you're on your way." She points to the packed living room. Everyone is having a great time. Wine and laughter flow freely. Several women gather around Ron as he custom-styles a wig for a customer. "By the way, my name is Stephanie."

"Tony."

Stephanie offers her hand and I kiss it gently. It's a gesture I've picked up watching old movies. American girls always love it.

"So, what did you do back in Beirut?" Stephanie gently brushes the wig's hair from the side of her face. "Were you a student?"

"I graduated two years ago," I explain, then go on to tell her about how I worked as a night auditor at the Orient Prince Hotel and about my desire to get back into the hospitality trade. "I love hotels, especially international ones. People always coming and going. There's wealth. Glamour. A high-class international hotel is like a city. Who wouldn't want to be part of that?"

Stephanie's green-tinted hazel eyes sparkle as I express my passion. "There aren't a whole lot of international hotels around here."

"No?"

"Although the Sheraton Wayfarer is nice. They just remodeled it. Have you ever been?"

"No," I say, raising a curious eyebrow.

"You should check it out. I have a friend who works there. We could get dinner. You free Saturday?"

I am not used to women being so forward. Even American women. But who am I to judge foreign customs? As the ancient expression advises, "When in Rome, do as the Romans do." Even when they're in New Hampshire.

"It's a date."

I meet Stephanie at the bar in Bedford's Sheraton Wayfarer Hotel at 7:00 p.m. as planned. Although certainly not catering to international travelers—Bedford is not Boston—the Wayfarer is unquestionably an impressive, inviting place. Walking in, we are greeted by a towering stone fireplace rising to the top of the four-story atrium. To the right, a huge picture window overlooks a beautiful man-made waterfall lit with warm amber spotlights. Whoever designed this entrance knew what they were doing.

Stephanie and I greet each other with a hug, then proceed to a table with an impressive view of the waterfall and beyond.

"Would you like to begin with some wine?" the uniformed waiter asks, turning over my menu to reveal the limited list of red, white and blush wines printed on the back. I'm getting nervous. I want to impress Stephanie by ordering a fine bottle of wine, but even after nine months in America, my ability to read English is limited. I know better than to order by price, though. I want the wine to be excellent, not just expensive.

"May I speak with your sommelier?" I ask.

The waiter looks at me as if I have just spoken to him in Lebanese. "Excuse me?"

"Your wine steward." I glance at Stephanie. She smiles back at me.

"Um, I'm afraid we don't have one of those," the waiter says apologetically. "However, if you would like to…"

What the waiter says next becomes lost beneath the roar of a white tiger howling in my ears.

"I'd like to speak to your general manager, please. Mr. Evans?"

It's been twelve hours since my dinner date with Stephanie. Soon after receiving our wine, she introduced me to her friend, Ivy, who works as a waitress. Eagerly—perhaps too eagerly—I asked her for the name of the restaurant's general manager. When I see an opportunity, it becomes my obsession (which is probably why things with Stephanie never progressed). Now, here I am, standing in slacks and a sports jacket, my red-striped tie knotted around my neck, trying my best to project confidence and professionalism.

"I'm afraid Mr. Evans is busy right now," the stern-looking hostess says, looking me up and down. I often forget this is New England, and people who look like me aren't common. As a result, I am often viewed with curiosity, if not suspicion. To counter this, I try to act upbeat. I try to be charming.

"Not a problem. I'm happy to wait."

So, I wait. Ten minutes. Twenty minutes. Thirty minutes. Finally, a short man with a military buzz cut, wearing a tailored suit, sweeps into the room.

"You're Tony?" he asks in confusion.

"Yes, sir. Ivy suggested I speak with you."

I suddenly realize how vulnerable I am. Here I am, a seventeen-year-old kid with a foreign accent asking to speak to a manager of one of the top restaurants in the state. Planting my feet firmly, I launch into my pitch.

"I dined at your restaurant last night. The food and service were excellent," I say, hoping to break the ice with a compliment.

"Thank you," Mr. Evans replies with a cool nod.

"I can say that because I have been working in hotels since I was twelve. Before coming to America, I was night auditor at the Orient Prince, one of the finest international hotels in Beirut. I graduated from Hotel School in Lebanon when I was sixteen and speak three languages: English, French, and Arabic—"

Mr. Evans cuts me off. "That's impressive, Tony, but we're fully staffed right now—"

It's my turn to cut Mr. Evans off. "When my guest and I had dinner here last night, I was surprised to learn you have no sommelier." "Wine is very profitable. You need a sommelier to encourage wine sales, to improve your bottom line. I would like to be that sommelier."

Again, I find myself being looked up and down like I am a piece of meat undergoing inspection. I smile. I'm truly excited about this idea and want my enthusiasm to become infectious.

"Our customers aren't big wine drinkers," Mr. Evans says slowly. "Most of our liquor profits come from well drinks and cocktails."

"I understand. But a fine restaurant needs an equally fine wine selection. And like I said, wine is extremely profitable. A couple can go through one or two bottles a night."

Mr. Evans sighs. He looks like he wants to be anywhere but here. "Look, Tony, you seem like a nice kid. It's a nice idea. But I don't see you pulling it off. Maybe in a few years…"

I'm ready for this.

"I will work without an hourly wage." I remind him the minimum wage is 80 cents per hour. "We can add 15 percent to the price of each bottle. That 15 percent will be my compensation, plus any tips I earn."

I can see him shaking his head, so I plow on.

"We can have separate checks for food and wine so there's never any confusion. If I sell wine, we both do well. If I don't, you've lost nothing. Well, almost nothing."

"What does *that* mean?"

"A sommelier must look the part. I will need a red jacket, a neck chain with a medallion, a key, and a tasting cup." Mr. Evans' eyes widen the more I go on. "I would also like to print the wine list on a beautiful heavy beige paper so I can roll it up and tie it with a red ribbon. This will make the customers feel special. That way they will spend money like they believe they *are* special."

Mr. Evans rocks back on his heels, letting out a shrill whistle. "You've thought this out."

If he only knew. "Yes, sir."

He puts out his hand. We agree I will work from 5:00 p.m. until 10:00 p.m. Tuesday through Sunday on a trial basis. If I arrive by 4:00 p.m., I can get a free meal from the hotel kitchen. *Free food? Sounds good to me.*

"Just one more thing," I say as we prepare to depart company.

"What?" Mr. Evans asks, clearly wary I'm going to drop a deal-breaker.

"I would like my nametag to read '*Antoine* Assali.'"

Mr. Evans laughs. We're off to a good start. I have made big promises. The question is, can I deliver?

Chapter 9

"YOU SOUND LIKE my cat when she's looking for her litter box," a fellow Wayfarer server jokes. Ten of us sit around the hotel's noisy kitchen scarfing down free dinners while waiting for our shift to start. Pots clang. Steam rises. The enticing aromas of onion, garlic, and freshly baked bread fill the air. "She's got one of those little bells on her collar. *Jingle-jingle-jingle!*"

"That's what we should call him: Jingles!" another waiter cracks. This gets another big laugh from the group.

They're making fun of the new silver chain I wear over my velvet jacket. At the end of the chain hangs a small silver cup. This is my tastevin, literally "wine taster" in French. Invented centuries ago, it allows sommeliers to inspect the color and clarity of wines even in low illumination from candlelight. Today, the tastevin serves more as a symbol of the sommelier's profession than as an actual tool-of-the- trade. It also has an unfortunate habit of jingling against the chain whenever I walk.

Smiling pleasantly, I leave the other waiters to their gossip and garlic potatoes while I mentally prepare for the night ahead. It has been a full week since Mr. Evans hired me, and I have spent virtually every waking hour familiarizing myself with the restaurant's vast wine selection. I also visited the library to learn what varietals best match particular food groups. A week ago, I knew of only three types of wine: red, white, and blush. Now I can talk at length about cabernets, syrahs, zinfandels, and pinot noirs. I know chardonnays can be oaked or unoaked and are best served with lobster, crab, shrimp, and chicken. Let's imagine a customer orders a dinner salad. In that case, I am likely to recommend a pinot gris. I know we carry wines from Upstate New York—to satisfy the casual by-the-glass wine drinker—as well as French, Italian, and German imports for guests with more sophisticated palates.

However, no matter how confident I am with my accumulated knowledge, I recognize my paltry few weeks' worth of research makes me a brainless infant compared to a true oenophile. Any legitimate wine connoisseur could peg me as a fraud within seconds. Fortunately, this being Bedford, New Hampshire, and not Boston, my chances of being exposed are limited. Even so, I must play my best game if I want to avoid selling wigs the rest of my life.

"All right, gentlemen," Mr. Evans says with a clap of his hands. "Our customers are arriving. Let's make sure they leave happy."

I hover by the kitchen door as the first of the guests arrive. At this early hour, most appear to be older men and women traveling as couples or in groups. I have been told that in America, most older people—politely referred to as senior citizens, prefer to dine early and go to bed around 8:30 or 9:00 p.m., the same time people my age are just gearing up for the night ahead. The gray hair, bifocals, and canes I see throughout the dining area support this stereotype.

I watch carefully as a waiter takes an order from a couple in their early sixties and heads for the kitchen. I glance toward the entranceway where Mr. Evans peers at me sternly.

This is it. Showtime.

Clutching my newly printed wine list, I stride to the table and bow. "Good evening and welcome to the Sheraton Wayfarer," I say in my best English. "My name is Antoine, and I am here to ensure your evening with us is as delightful as possible. Are you celebrating any special occasion? A birthday, perhaps? An anniversary?"

"Nope," the husband grunts. Although the man is seated and wears a corduroy sports jacket, I can see he has a hefty physique. Definitely a man who likes a good steak.

"That's a lovely necklace you're wearing," I say to the wife, making sure to include her in the conversation. I know when it comes to wine purchases, it's the woman who tends to make the final decision. Even if she doesn't do so aloud.

"Why, thank you," she smiles, her cheeks showing a bit of blush. "The pendant belonged to my grandmother, who brought it over from France when she was a child."

"Ah, *France!*" I exclaim. "*Parlez-vous français, madame?*"

"Oh, my, now I feel like I'm in Europe!" She giggles.

"But why go all the way to France when we can bring a bit of France right to you?" I continue, seeing I have made a connection. I return to her husband. "You have already ordered a steak?"

"Two New York strips," the husband replies. I can tell he wishes I would vanish so he can go back to their conversation.

But his wife wants to keep chatting. "Medium-rare," she adds.

"Then may I suggest either our Napa Valley Sauvignon or Left Bank Bordeaux? Both are big and bold and will bring out the flavors in the meat," I say, making sure to maintain eye contact with the wife before turning my attention to her husband. I hand him the wine list and give him a few moments to scan the choices. This restaurant has a solid list of domestic and international selections, but it is nothing compared to the phonebook-sized volumes I remember from the Orient Prince back in Beirut.

Let's try the Bordeaux," the wife says eagerly. "It's from France, right?"

"Imported especially for us," I say with no idea if this is true or not. "You'll find it combines the flavors of cassis, blackberry, dark cherry, vanilla, coffee bean, spice and licorice. And 1969 is an excellent vintage. A perfect complement to your dinner entrée." Again, my confidence in the particulars of what I am saying is hazy at best. Do I believe I am promoting a good bottle of wine? Yes. And in the end, if the customer walks away satisfied, I have done my job.

"Pricey," the husband grumbles. Expecting this, I smile and lean down conspiratorially. "I think she's worth it, don't you?"

The couple locks eyes. The wife is sitting up straight, boring straight into him, clearly in no mood to be denigrated in front of a stranger.

"Fine," he says. "Two glasses of the Bordeaux."

"I'm sorry, but I'm afraid this wine is available only by the bottle." Before the husband can object, I am ready with the closer. "But it's a much better value. A bottle will give you five full glasses so you don't have to worry about nursing your way through the meal."

I again look to the wife and smile.

The husband sighs. "Fine. We'll take the bottle."

"Excellent choice," I say, retrieving the wine list. I hope he doesn't see my hand shaking. There are a dozen different ways I could have blown this opportunity, but my preparation paid off. I've made my first wine sale.

"Thank you," the wife says sincerely. "I wish I knew more about wine."

"That's what I'm here for. If you have any questions, just ask. I'll be back in a moment."

As promised, I return just three minutes later and, as per tradition, display the label to the husband. He nods, confirming this is the wine he ordered. I then deftly uncork the bottle and pour a thumbnail's worth into my tastevin. As the couple watches curiously, I inspect the dark red liquid, then take a quick sip.

"Perfect," I announce, then pour a small amount into the husband's glass, turning the bottle 90 degrees as I pull away. He stares at the wine for a moment as if unsure of what to do next, then lifts the glass by the stem and takes a drink. He allows the taste to linger on his tongue for a moment, then smiles, almost as if by reflex.

"That's good," he says, looking surprised. I fill his wife's glass, return to fill the husband's, then set the now nearly half-empty bottle between them.

"Your steaks should be out shortly. *Bon appétit!*"

As I return to the kitchen, I see the other waiters—many of whom are many years my senior—looking at me like I am some kind of a circus attraction. I'm only seventeen years old with a passable command of the English language, yet here I am strutting about in some comic-opera soldier's uniform, passing myself off as a wine sophisticate. Yet somehow, it works. I make it happen. And not just once, either. By the evening's end, I have sold ten bottles and four additional wines-by-the glass. After each meal, I submit my own separate invoice—and receive my own separate tip.

"Excellent job, Tony. Just excellent," Mr. Evans says after our last guests have left for the night. "Did you all see what Tony did tonight?" he asks the servers. Don't just sell the food. Sell the *experience*! Make sure they leave happy."

The skeptical looks on the other waiters' faces appear less than elated. Many of these men have been waiting tables for years. I suspect the last thing they want is to be upstaged by some punk teenager on his first day, so I try to look humble, even self-effacing.

I chuckle and say, "Beginner's luck," though I know it was anything but.

As the week goes on, my "beginner's luck" becomes a predictable routine. "You're turning my restaurant into a winery," Mr. Evans tells me. "If you keep this up, I'm going to run out of stock. What am I saying? Keep it up. I can always order more."

Surprisingly, what I thought was going to be one of my greatest handicaps—my accent—turns out to be my greatest asset. As soon as I begin speaking, customers ask me where I am from. They want to know why I came to America. In response, I am happy to tell them how much I love this country and its friendly people. Within minutes we establish a rapport. The customers like me. The customers trust me. The customers are happy to take my recommendations. And I make sure the recommendations I make are always good ones.

As weeks go by, it becomes obvious my sommelier job is a success. At a time when the federal minimum wage is just $1.60 per hour—80 cents per hour if you work for tips—I clear $600 per week. Half of each paycheck I send to my family in Lebanon. This is far more than they ever expected. Although our written communications are few and far between, I know they are proud of me.

With the other half of my check, I pay rent, buy food, clothes and, best of all, my first new American car. It is a beige and green GTO convertible with a double- carburetor and built-in 8-track music system. As I drive off the lot, top down, I breathe in the cool, humid air of late spring. I remember the feeling I had when I bought my first car back in Beirut. I have come so far in terms of both miles and life experience. But I am still lonely. I miss my family. I continue to fear for their safety. I must get them out of Lebanon and here to the United States so they can live the good life, too.

But how?

Chapter 10

LAST YEAR, BACK in Beirut, my friends insisted I join them to see the movie *Patton*, starring George C. Scott, showing in a downtown theater. From what I recall, late in the movie, Patton's army moves so fast through enemy lines their supply trucks can't keep up. When night falls, all of Patton's tanks are out of gasoline and unable to move when the Germans launch a fierce counterattack. All the Americans can do is sit there and take it.

I am reminded of this terrifying scene as Mr. Evans and I gaze upon our all-but-empty wine cabinet. The few bottles sticking out here and there from their slots only amplify how meager our supplies have become.

"What happened?" I ask, incredulous.

"You're too good," Mr. Evans replies. "You've been selling bottles faster than I can replace them."

"So why don't we order more?"

"I've been trying. But our supplier can't handle this volume. He has to adjust his shipment schedules and make new deals all the way up and down the supply line."

Anxiety grips me. "So how long until we get more wine?"

"At least two weeks."

"Two weeks!" I nearly explode.

Mr. Evans tries to calm me down. "We still have beer and cocktails."

"But the waiters sell those. If I take away their liquor sales, they'll kill me. Besides, I can't live off beer and liquor tips. I need to sell bottles—"

The hostess interrupts us. "Mr. Evans, they need you in the kitchen."

He looks relieved by the intrusion, smiling at the redhead in the black dress with the menus in her hand. "We'll figure this out later," he tells me before adding, "Maybe this would be a good time for you to take a vacation."

I stare after him. *A vacation?* That's the last thing I need. I have bills to pay and a family in Lebanon counting on me. I need to make money.

Returning to the dining room, I glimpse waiters staring at me and sharing furtive whispers. They know I'm in trouble. And they appear to be enjoying my misery. Like Patton, I've come too far, too fast. Now I'm out of fuel, out of options, and am a sitting duck for whatever these people will throw me.

Though not a drinker, I am actually thinking about having one to relieve my suddenly dry mouth, when something catches my attention across the room. I stare at it a moment, my brain considering it from various distances and angles even as my feet remain planted. To the waiters around me, I am certain this familiar object looks like nothing more than a waist-high assemblage of polished brass tubes and flat surfaces. But I see something different: a white tiger.

"Here's our answer," I announce as I wheel the gleaming European-style coffee cart into Mr. Evans' office.

"Answer to what?" he asks, seated at his cluttered desk.

"Our wine shortage."

He looks at me like I'm stupid or crazy. "You want to sell coffee? We already sell coffee."

"Have you ever heard of *Irish* coffee? Coffee with a shot of Irish whiskey, topped with whipped cream."

"I know what Irish coffee is."

"And how much of it do you sell per night?"

"Unless someone asks for it specifically, none. Tony, this is Bedford, not Boston. Not a whole lot of Irish up here."

"You don't have to be Irish to enjoy a nice cup of Irish coffee after a satisfying dinner." On cue, I pour a piping hot cup of coffee from the dispenser, add a shot of Jameson's I prepared for this moment, spoon out a dollop of freshly made whipped cream I got from the kitchen, and set it all before him with a dramatic flourish. "Try it."

Mr. Evans hesitates, sizing me up like he expects a frog to jump out of the cup, then takes a sip. The resulting smile is genuine. "All right, what's your angle?" Mr. Evans knows me too well by now.

I return my genuine smile. "Simple. At the end of every meal, I offer our diners a cup of our house specialty: Irish coffee."

"That's not our specialty."

"It could be. You normally sell Irish coffee for, what, $3 a cup?"

"Uh—"

"You do. I've checked. Now we sell it for $5 a cup. And I get to keep the extra $2."

Mr. Evans rocks back in his chair, slipping his arms behind his head. He takes in a deep breath, and his eyes roll up to the ceiling. He sits like that for a good minute, saying nothing, doing nothing. The silence goes on so long it becomes unbearable. I open my mouth to say something—

"You know what I wish, Tony?"

"No, sir."

"I wish the others here had half your initiative. All right. Let's give it a try. I just hope we don't run out of Jameson."

That night, as planned, I wheel the freshly polished brass coffee cart to a booth just as a couple finishes their meal.

"You enjoyed the monkfish?" I ask.

"Perfect," the man replies. I can see from their glasses that the man and his companion have been drinking cocktails, which means they're probably loose and suggestible.

"I have the perfect way to top off your meal. Our specialty: Irish coffee."

"A regular coffee will be fine for me," the man says.

I act like I don't hear him. "We start with our signature dark roast from Bolivia, brew it to precisely 205 degrees Fahrenheit, then add a shot of Jameson, Ireland's premium Irish whiskey. We add a dollop of freshly made whipped cream created right here in our kitchens. It goes down smooth and will keep you warm all the way home." This last part I say to his companion, the pretty woman beside him with the full red lips.

There's a moment of awkward silence, then…

"Oh, let's try one." She grabs her husband by the elbow. "It'll be fun."

"Fine," the man says, like it's his idea. "Make it two."

As hoped, my dramatic presentation has caught the ear of nearby diners. Now they want to seal their meals with our premium beverage.

In the following days, I make my presentation even more theatrical. With practice, I learn to extend my arm to its full height while pouring Jameson whiskey into the glass three feet below. I do it over and over until I can do it without spilling a drop. This little flourish always captures the room's attention, and tables clamor for me to perform the same trick again and again. Soon, I am selling, on average, seventy-five cups per night. My $150 nightly share is the equivalent of selling ten whole bottles of wine, which balances things out nicely.

At the end of the month, our wine supplies are finally restored. Antoine Assali, wine steward extraordinaire, can return. But Mr. Evans is not ready to shut down what has quickly become one of his restaurant's key profit centers.

"We're making Irish coffee part of our standard bill o' fare." He proudly shows me a newly printed menu in which "World-Famous Wayfarer Irish Coffee" is listed as a house specialty. "I want you to teach all the other waiters how to do that pouring trick. The guests freakin' love it."

"My pleasure."

"Oh, and one other thing." Mr. Evans turns to face me. "I talked to corporate. We're going to push Irish coffee in *every* Sheraton in North America it's such a hit. I've hired a local ad agency to create a brochure. Four-color. Gloss-coated. The works. And I want to put you on the cover."

"Me?"

"Pouring the Irish coffee." Mr. Evans pantomimes my routine, raising his right arm. "You're a natural."

Since coming to America nearly a year ago, I've been sleeping on the Elias family's couch. Now, from selling both wine and Irish coffee at the Sheraton Wayfarer, I'm finally making enough money to rent a place of my own. And I am more than eager to do so.

In another benevolent coincidence, a studio apartment opens up in a building owned by Ron's uncle, Ernest Elias, just a few blocks away. I check the place out. It's only about 400 square feet, but it's furnished. And compared to the couch I've been sleeping on, it's a mansion.

"You're a friend of the family, so you can have it for $40 a month, plus utilities," Ernest tells me. "And the first month is free. Give you a chance to get on your feet."

"I'll take it," I say without hesitation and move in the next day. The following week, my telephone is installed. The first thing I do is call my family in Beirut. "I have my own apartment," I announce to cheers at the other end. "I'm going to be in the phone book."

"The phone book?" my mother says, her voice sounding a million miles away. "What is a phone book?"

In Lebanon, there are no phone books. Friends and business associates either just share numbers or dial the operator for assistance.

"It's a list of everyone in town and their numbers," I explain. "But how is everything in Beirut? Have there been more attacks?"

"Not many," my father says, getting on the line. "Maybe things will be quiet again and you can come home."

"Right," I say half-heartedly. I like the life I have here in America and am not eager to give it up. Not now. I have my own car and my own bachelor pad, and my personal life is picking up. Working at the Wayfarer, I have no trouble finding beautiful girls to go out with me. They find me exotic.

And as for finding a special girl, that's something I am not yet interested in. Therefore, when Ron tells me, "Tony, there's a girl I want you to meet," I don't take him seriously.

Little do I know my life will never be the same.

Chapter 11

I AM NOT fond of blind dates. Agreeing to go out with a woman I have never met before makes about as much sense as buying a car sight-unseen. Besides, it's not like I'm desperate for companionship. I get off work at 10:00 p.m. every night, a time when there is still plenty of action happening at the Wayfarer and nearby clubs. Still, to placate Ron and his wife, Frances, I agree to attend dinner along with the mysterious Sara they have talked so much about.

It is a cold autumn night when I arrive at Ron's in the Bedford suburbs. I have promised myself that, if things go badly, I will feign sickness and leave early. If this Sara is not my type, there's no sense wasting my time… or hers.

Ron greets me at the door before I can ring the doorbell. "Right on time." Before I can say a word, Ron ushers me in, taking my heavy overcoat. "Grab yourself a drink."

He escorts me into the well-appointed living room where Frances and a pretty young woman of about twenty sit on the sofa sipping wine. Seeing me, they rise to their feet.

"Tony!" Frances cries, running over to hug me. "Thank you for coming. I've been telling Sara all about you."

I turn and smile at the young woman nervously holding her glass in both hands. Slender and wearing a miniskirt, she appears to be about five foot three with long brown hair and brown eyes. Immediately, she breaks into a smile that could light up Times Square. Any notions I may have had about pretending to be sick vanish.

"Hi," she says, offering her hand. She turns to Frances. "You never told me he was *this* handsome!" The women laugh and I relax.

"Your wine looks low. Let me get you a fresh one," I offer. I pull out the dark red bottle I brought from the hotel. "This is a 1970 Chateau Margaux, straight from our special reserves. Charles de Gaulle drinks this." I have no idea if that last statement is true, but all is fair in love and war.

"*Viva la France!*" Ron declares as he pops the cork. "Now let's get to the table before the food gets overdone." Offering Sara my hand, I escort her to the dining room. I pull out her chair as she sits.

"A real gentleman," Sara says.

"If I wasn't already married to Ronnie, you'd have to fight me for him," Frances says and giggles.

The meal is excellent, but I pay little attention to it, as all my attention is focused on Sara. She's not only extremely attractive, but bright, quick to laugh, and possesses a surprisingly rich knowledge of the hospitality industry from working as a cocktail waitress and hostess.

Finished eating, Ron and Frances kick their matchmaking efforts into higher gear. "Don't worry about clean-up," Frances says. "Ronnie and I can take care of everything."

"I'm sure you two would like to spend some time alone together without us old married folks getting in the way," Ron adds.

I glance at Sara. She seems game.

"If you're sure you don't need help—" I say, but Frances cuts me off.

"Go. Get out of here before we kick you out."

After thanking our hosts, Sara and I find ourselves standing on the sidewalk under a glowing white-orange mercury vapor streetlamp, a light snow falling from the starless sky.

"Here's my car, if you need a ride." I motion to my GTO.

"Actually, I drove myself." Sara gestures to a yellow Volkswagen Beetle parked down the block.

"Well…" I say, hoping she will offer some kind of suggestion.

"Hey, look, there's a Dunkin' Donuts at the end of the block." She points to a neon-lit store where this street meets a busy commercial avenue not too far away. "They have good coffee."

Five minutes later, we sit across from each other in the most generic Dunkin' Donuts you can imagine, sipping very good coffee. We talk about anything and everything. I learn she just moved here from Vermont and is currently staying at her cousin's. I tell her how my family sent me to America to avoid civil war. Sara gets excited when I tell her about my various business ideas. She appears to like my energy. I certainly like hers. When the manager finally closes the shop at midnight, we still haven't run out of subjects to talk about.

I don't know if you can call what I experienced *love at first sight*, but *instant infatuation* is appropriate. Over the next few weeks, Sara and I meet often. Since she lives with her cousin, any sleepovers take place at my studio apartment, as modest as it is. For convenience's sake, she brings over a spare set of toiletries. Then several changes of clothes. Then her favorite records. Before I know what's happening, she has officially moved in.

Contrary to the male stereotype, I do not at all feel trapped by this arrangement. Sara and I get along great. We share the same tastes in food and music. We both love shopping and dancing for hours. Best of all, she shows no resentment over the hours I work or how I flirt with my female customers. I could not ask for anything more.

Three months later, I find myself standing at the counter of a local jewelry store. A slim, balding man in his late forties, dressed in a finely tailored suit, approaches me. "Can I help you? Are you looking for anything special?"

"An engagement ring," I reply, unable to take my eyes off the dazzling gems displayed in the glass cabinet below me. "I want something nice—but simple. Elegant. I don't make a lot of money and…"

"I understand. And I'm sure we can find just what you're looking for." He keys open one of his cabinets and pulls out a small box he lays on the counter. Pulling back the black fabric, he reveals what must be two dozen rings, each containing a small, sparkling jewel. "When buying diamonds, the first thing to look for is quality. Even smaller stones can be impressive if the color, cut, and clarity are high. And, remember, you can put any stone into any setting. If you like one stone but a different ring, we can do that for you."

"What price range are we looking at here?" I inquire, even as I feel my heart beating rapidly in my chest.

"These run anywhere from $500 to $2,500," the clerk replies. Seeing the expression on my face, he adds, "I know a ring is a major purchase. Especially for a young man like yourself. Which is why we offer a long-term payment plan so you can buy the ring you want now and pay for it in easy, affordable monthly installments."

As a professional salesman, I know how important it is for a customer to believe he's getting a good bargain even if he ends up paying more in the long run. But, in this instance, I am also a customer, and I am not immune to the phrase "easy, affordable monthly installments."

The following Monday is my day off. That evening, I take Sara out for dinner at Cicero's, one of her favorite Italian restaurants. This being a Monday, the place is quiet and we secure a secluded booth in the corner. I'm dressed in a coat and tie. She wears a pleated red dress and a gold pendant. We begin by splitting a Caesar salad and an order of fried calamari with spicy marinara sauce. For our main course, she picks chicken piccata while I have poached salmon with penne pasta. We split a bottle of

Chianti. The conversation is light and casual. She does most of the talking.

Only when we have finished our entrées does her mood suddenly darken.

"Are you all right?" she asks. "You've been quiet tonight."

"I've been thinking."

"About work? Tony, you never stop."

"No. Thinking about us," I say. I think I can actually hear her breath catch in her throat. A statement like this can mean one of two things. I hurry to clarify my position. "These past few months have been amazing. I've never been happier. When I am with you, all the colors of the world are brighter, all the sounds more musical..." I'm stumbling for words. I feel like an actor in a bad movie but Sara appears transfixed. "You know about my white tiger theory. Something that is rare and valuable must be pursued, and pursued quickly, before it vanishes. There is no time for hesitation."

Sara's face turns bright red as I reach into my pocket.

"I want to spend my life with you. Will you...?"

"Yes!" Sara leaps to her feet before I can finish. She rushes around the table and pulls me into a big bear-hug and a kiss. I'm grateful the restaurant is only one-third full. As it is, the staff showers us with enthusiastic applause.

As Sara tries on her ring, our waiter approaches. "Congratulations. Tonight, dessert is on the house."

Neither Sara nor I are interested in a big, expensive wedding. My income is improving, but I could barely afford the ring. We agree to wed at the Hillsborough County Courthouse. Ronnie and his uncle Earnest, my landlord, serve as witnesses. Halfway through the ceremony, I say a silent prayer to my family back home, wishing they could be here to share this moment with Sara and me.

After the brief ceremony, the four of us go to dinner at an upscale seafood restaurant. I have never felt more alive in my life.

There is no time—nor are there funds—for a honeymoon, so I return to work. As Sara and I have discussed, our plan is to live frugally and save enough so we can buy a house large enough for a family. In the meantime, she will use birth control so we don't have to worry about taking on obligations we can't afford. It's the perfect arrangement. I'm no longer lonely. I have someone to love. Someone to love me. I have a great job, great friends, and a future that looks bright and…

"I'm pregnant," Sara announces one day as I'm getting ready for work.

"What?" I can't believe what I'm hearing.

"I saw the doctor yesterday," she continues, unable to make eye contact. "I'm due in early November."

"But, how?" I sputter. "You're on the pill."

"I stopped."

"When?"

"About three months ago. I see how you flirt with women at the restaurant and I thought…"

"You thought what?" My confusion turns to rage. I do not like this feeling but cannot help myself.

"We got married so quickly." Tears well up in her eyes. "What if you got tired of me and left? I thought that, if we had a child…"

"It would force us to stay together?" I finish her sentence. "That's smart thinking. My God, look at how we live. We're renting a 400-square-foot apartment. I work nights six days a week. You work temp jobs during the day. How are we supposed to raise a kid like this?"

"So, what are you saying? You want me to get an abortion?"

"No," I cry. The word itself is like a dagger through my heart.

"Then we *are* going to have the baby?"

Yes, we will have the baby. And on November 2, 1971, Scott Assali enters the world. Seeing Scotty lying in his mother's arms changes something inside me. All my life, I viewed the world from my personal perspective. I was the hero in my own movie, and everyone else was just a supporting player. But now, as I gaze down at my newborn son, I realize I am not so special, just part of a larger continuum, including all my ancestors who came before me and all my descendants to come. Scotty will live longer than I will. He will experience things I cannot even imagine. My job—my most important job—is to ensure he grows up healthy, happy, and equipped with values that will allow him to meet life's challenges in the years ahead.

"Welcome to the world, Scotty," I whisper. "Welcome to America." Great relief washes over me as I realize that Scotty, born here in Manchester, is an American citizen. He can never be threatened with deportation. He can never be denied civil rights because of his legal status. He is an *American*, and he will enjoy the benefits being an American brings.

I have never been prouder of anything before in my life. I also know I can never trust Sara ever again.

Chapter 12

NOW THAT I am a new father, making money has become more important than ever. Working as a wine steward brings in steady income, but my after-tax wages are not enough to support Sara and Scotty comfortably, let alone enough to afford the kind of larger apartment we need.

My solution comes, from all places, Jamaica. Yes, Jamaica, that island paradise in the northern Caribbean. The man's name is Bobby, and he's one of four Jamaican waiters that Mr. Evans brings home when returning from his annual two-week vacation. Of the four, Bobby is by far the cheeriest and most gregarious, and we quickly become friends. We have much in common. He is a workaholic. I am a workaholic. He has great ambitions. I have great ambitions. But while he sees waiting as the path to the American dream, he views my sommelier route as a dead end.

"You are good with the customers," Bobby tells me during a break. "You make them feel at ease. Best of all, you get them to spend their money—happily. You should be a waiter."

"Do waiters make good money?"

"In an upscale restaurant like this?" Bobby laughs. "You'll be making twice as much waiting tables as you do serving wine. Also, remember, not everyone who comes to dine here orders a bottle of wine, but they all order food."

He has a good point. That afternoon, I corner Mr. Evans in his office.

"I'm going to be waiter," I announce without any preamble. "This is not a request. This is not a negotiation. I'm going to be a waiter. Even more than that, I'm going to be the best waiter you've ever had. Your customers will be thrilled with their experience, and this restaurant will thrive as never before."

There is an awkward silence as Mr. Evans gives me that look again, like I'm some green-skinned alien who has just stepped out of a flying saucer. It takes a second or two for his mind to process this new information.

"And wine. You'll still sell wine?" he asks.

"Of course. In fact, I will train all our waiters on the fine art and science of wine selling."

Mr. Evan gives me the other look he sometimes bestows: one mixed with awe and stupefaction. "You'd do that?"

"Of course. Why wouldn't I?"

"It's just that… well, I have never really had an employee like you."

Damn right, Mr. Evans. That's what I think. But I don't say it.

"I guess you could start—"

"Tomorrow," I say. "I'd like to start training tomorrow. I've already cleared it with HR."

Mr. Evans grins like a Cheshire cat. "Of course, you did. You know the waiters work in teams here. You can work with—"

"Bobby," I interject. "We already work well together."

"Fine. Send Bobby in here and—"

"He already knows."

Mr. Evans bursts out laughing. "Is there anything else you want to tell me?"

I soften my approach. There's a fine line between being proactive and being a jerk. "We still needed your approval, sir. We just didn't want to bother you with the details. We know you're an important man."

"Thank you. I appreciate that."
"And Mr. Evans…?"
"Yes?"
"Congratulations on making an excellent decision."
He slaps me on the shoulder. "You're one in a million."

To prepare for my new responsibilities, I spend the next week in intensive training like before. I memorize our extensive menu. I learn how to take quick, precise notes others can easily interpret. I practice pairing orders with customers, even customers sitting at different tables. I learn to balance large trays of food and move through crowded aisles while avoiding physical contact. Best of all, I sample all of our restaurant's dishes, including appetizers, entrées, and desserts so I can speak with authority when asked. My months as a sommelier have already prepared me to expertly help customers pair the perfect wine with whatever entrée they select.

In short, I am ready.

But all the practice in the world can't prepare you for life's twists and turns. For my debut, Mr. Evans puts me on the 5:00 p.m. Monday shift. Our first two customers look like businessmen who have just finished a long day of traveling. I watch our hostess seat them. Then I give them a few moments to scan the menu before I glide to their table with an air of ease and purpose.

"Good evening, and welcome to the Wayfarer," I say with a big smile—but not too big. My intention is to project amity, not mania. "My name is Antoine, and I will be taking care of you this evening. Is this table to your liking?"

"It's fine," the larger businessman says. His brown hair is thinning, his complexion ruddy, and his tie askew.

"Would you like to start off with some drinks? Perhaps a cocktail? Beer? We have an excellent selection of wines, both by the bottle and by the glass."

"Just get me a Chivas, rocks," the big guy says.

"I'll have a Bud," his companion chimes in. He, too, wears business attire that appears to have endured a long plane flight, road trip, or both. "In the glass."

"Excellent." I make a note on my pad. Glancing down, I notice the larger man's suit jacket opening, exposing a not-so-subtle paunch. "By the way, our special tonight is a sixteen-ounce Porterhouse steak. Premium grade. Hand-rubbed with a select variety of spices, then *hand-grilled* over an open mesquite flame to seal in the juices."

I can practically see the drool forming at the side of the portly businessman's mouth. "Sounds good."

"I'll be right back. Take your time." After delivering the drink orders to the bar, I attend to my next set of customers, three older women here for a night on the town.

"Your accent is so unusual," one says. "Your name is Antoine, but you don't sound Italian. I have Italian in-laws, and they don't talk like you."

"I am Lebanese. From Beirut. The Paris of the Middle East. And while I may not be Italian, I know good Italian wines. How about I start you off with a bottle of pinot grigio?"

And so it goes. Over the course of the evening, I serve eight different parties and manage to screw up only one order—serving asparagus to a customer who ordered sautéed green beans. I also sell three bottles of wine.

"Nice work," Bobby says as we share cigarettes in the back alley.

"You think tonight was good? Just watch me."

In the coming weeks, I hone my performance to a fine art. I greet my customers warmly, often complimenting the ladies on some piece of jewelry or attire. I am careful to be polite and helpful but never pushy. I smile and pay attention but never hover. I make jokes but am never crude. I watch each table to determine the optimum moment to clear their dishes or offer coffee and dessert. Never too early. Never too late.

Because of my diligence, word gets around. Customers ask for me by name. If the restaurant is busy, diners will wait for an hour or more just to sit in my section. Best of all, I feel less and less like a foreigner. People like my accent. To them, I am exotic but also personable. A friend.

And Bobby is right. The money is better. Man, is it better. On a good night, I can clear twice what I did as a sommelier. The only downside of working at the Wayfarer is returning home afterwards. As soon as I walk through the door, Sara and I start to fight.

Scotty is misbehaving. He needs new clothes. I need to spend more time with him. When are we going to move out of this pit and into a real apartment? When can we go out for a nice dinner?

It goes on like this until the morning of February 5, 1972. I am preparing to leave for work when the phone rings.

"Hello?" The connection is loud and scratchy. I recognize it instantly as long distance.

"Hello? Tony? It's Joe." The voice at the other end sounds choked and panicked. I know something is wrong.

"Joe, what's the matter?"

"It's father. He's… had a stroke," Joe can barely utter the words.

I can't breathe. "How bad is it? Did he make it? Is he alive?"

"He's been in the hospital since Monday. His right side is paralyzed."

"Permanently?" I ask, already knowing the answer.

"They think so." Although Joe is thousands of miles away, I can see the tears in his eyes. "He's going to be in a wheelchair for the rest of his life."

"I'll send money."

"No," Sara cries, nearly tearing the telephone handset from me. "We need that money for Scotty. For us!"

"Thank you, Tony, but we can handle it here. I'm leaving private school. I'll use the money for Dad."

"No, no, stay in school," I insist. "If you need money for that, I can help with that, too. I'm doing well in America. And when you come here, too, you'll need your education."

I can see Sara shaking her head but I continue talking to my brother for another few minutes. Joe and I agree I will send the family $200 per month as long as necessary.

This arrangement does not sit well with Sara, and she lets me know it. "You have responsibilities here." She points to Scotty in his playpen.

"I know. But this is something I must do. It'll work out in the end. Trust me."

She doesn't say another word. She goes to our bedroom and slams the door. More and more, Sara is showing her selfish side. Yes, it's a side I understand—we are all driven by self-interest—but hers has an unpleasantness to it that makes me increasingly uncomfortable. When I vowed to stay with her for better or worse, I meant it. But more and more, I wonder if I made a mistake.

Chapter 13

LIKE MOST CULTURES of the Middle East, the Lebanese one is patriarchal. For centuries, men have been the undisputed heads of the country's institutions, from the government and church all the way down to the family. As a member of this patriarchy, a Lebanese man must have sons—ideally, several, to ensure the perpetuation of the family name and thereby his legacy. In Lebanon, failing to produce a male heir is tantamount to failing as a human. By the same token, Lebanese men are expected to revere their fathers, to honor, and, if necessary, protect them as they would their own offspring. Should a Lebanese father fall ill or become infirm, it is up to his sons to see to his care and welfare.

Although I now reside in America, my soul is still very much Lebanese, and I cannot ignore the obligations that hundreds of years of tradition have placed upon me. So far, I have done my duty by siring Scotty, extending the Assali bloodline for at least one generation. Now, news of my father's debilitating stroke has created yet another familial obligation I must assume. And this is proving to be a prickly issue with Sara.

"For God's sake, Tony, your dad has his whole family to take care of him," she says as I tell her of my plan to send a third of my pay to Beirut. "He has your mom. Your brothers. Your sisters. That should be enough."

"You don't understand." Already, the walls of our tiny studio apartment feel like they're closing in on me, causing me to sweat and my hands to shake. "I am the first-born son. When my father's ill, that makes me head of the household, even if I'm on the other side of the world. If I don't do this, I will be seen as less of a man by every member of my family… including me." *Especially me.*

"*I* am your family," she counters. "*Scotty's* your family. Your job is to take care of me and to take care of Scotty. Isn't there something in the Bible about a man leaving his parents and cleaving to his wife? Isn't that what it says?"

"The Bible also commands us to honor thy father and thy mother," I remind her.

"That doesn't mean pay their medical bills."

"You can be so selfish," I hear myself say. I regret these words as soon as they leave my mouth.

"*I'm* selfish? I'm trapped in this cell every evening taking care of *your* son so you can flirt and do God-knows-what with women at your fancy hotel, and *I'm* selfish? Tony, go to hell."

This is not one of my finer moments. At the risk of fracturing my delicate marriage further, I ignore Sara's objections and quietly arrange to send a third of my take-home pay to Joe for our father's care. However, subsequent correspondences with Joe suggest that, due to Lebanon's deteriorating political situation, good medical care is becoming harder to acquire. If our father is going to have any hope of recovery, he must come to the United States. For that to happen, I will have to sponsor the family. And to sponsor the family, I need to become an American citizen.

Days later I approach Ron's father at home with my request. I go to him first because I know he's well-connected in Manchester's business and legal community. "I want to become an American," I tell him. "How do I do that?"

Mr. Elias offers me coffee and sits me down at his kitchen table. "It's a complicated process. You'll need a lawyer who specializes in this."

My mind can't help wandering to the worst possible outcomes, my father growing sicker, my family back home overwhelmed. Worse, my father passing away. I control my trembling hands by gripping my cup harder.

Mr. Elias takes my shoulder. "Luckily, I know a good lawyer. Martin Green. He works downtown. I'll give you his number and let him know you'll be contacting him."

"Thank you," I say, my voice cracking. "You don't know how much this means to me."

"Actually, I do."

Martin Green, attorney at law, works out of a suite of law offices on the fourth floor of a modern, marble-faced office building in downtown Boston. He is one of six partners and specializes in immigration law. Slightly shorter than me, trim, and sporting a rust-red mustache, Green projects an air of calm and confidence that puts me at ease.

"So, you're here on an H-2B temporary work visa?" he says, seated behind his polished mahogany desk.

"Yes." I sit in a plush armchair that's just low enough that I have to look up to make eye contact. "I came here in August 1970."

"And you're gainfully employed?"

"I work as a waiter at the Sheraton Wayfarer hotel restaurant."

"You've been there how long?"

"Over a year. I started as a sommelier. Now I'm a waiter. It pays better."

"Any record of criminal behavior? Arrests?"

"Absolutely not."

"Don't worry. I just had to ask," Green says calmly, jotting down more notes. "Tell me, why do you want to become an American citizen?"

"The truth?" My thoughts return to my sick father in Beirut.

"Um, yes. I find that's usually the best approach."

"For my family. I have a son, an infant, born here in America, and I need to make sure he can never be taken from me. Also, the rest of my family is still in Lebanon. If you've been reading the newspapers, you know life is getting bad there."

"So I hear."

This is the first time I have ever explained my situation so plainly to anyone since arriving in America, and words come pouring out. "The plan was for me to come to the U.S. first, then for me to help bring the rest of them over later. But I can only sponsor them if I am a citizen. Also, my father is very ill. He just had a stroke."

"I'm sorry to hear that," Green says with genuine sympathy. "How bad?"

"Bad enough. He's paralyzed on one side. He can't work. Can't support his family. That's up to me now. Can you help me?"

"I can certainly help you fill out the paperwork and make sure it gets to the right people. But the system here runs slowly. Getting you full citizenship could take some time."

"What do you mean? A few weeks?"

Green shakes his head. "No, Tony. A few years."

Chapter 14

THE CAB RIDE from Manchester to Boston's Logan Airport is long and uneventful. When I last travelled this route, with Ronnie three years ago, we were leaving the city, the hour was late, and Interstate 93 was nearly empty. As a result, we made the fifty-three-mile trip in less than an hour. This time, travelling into the city center with Sara and Scotty, now two years old, it's midmorning, and commuter traffic is as thick as Boston chowder. Almost two hours have elapsed by the time we pull up to the airport's international terminal. We have only forty-five minutes until our international flight departs.

"What if they don't let you back into the country?" she asks fearfully as we stand in the long, snaking queue at the BOAC ticketing station.

"They'll let me back in. Martin Green tells me my visa is still good."

"And what about Scotty?" she asks as she balances the restless two-year-old on her hip. "We're going to be traveling for fourteen hours. He's gonna go crazy."

"Look, we've talked about this for months. It's important my family meet my wife and son. They can't come here so we must go there, which is what we're doing."

Sara has been against this trip since I proposed it. During the last week she has become increasingly quarrelsome about the subject. She wants to find any excuse to back out. In the last forty-eight hours alone, she has suggested we could become gravely ill from drinking the local water, catch a strange disease, or even fall victim to an airplane hijacker. She has told me point-blank there are many, many things she would rather spend our limited funds on than a trip to Beirut. But, as I see it, we have no choice. Family is everything, and it's high time Scotty meets his.

After checking our bags, we run madly through the terminal to the departure gate with five minutes to spare. We are soon nestled in our narrow seats watching Boston fall away as our Lockheed TriStar thunders into the sky.

Scotty is at first fascinated with the sights and sensations of flight but reverts to being a restless two-year-old who wants to run and jump and kick and make our lives as miserable as possible. Fortunately, the day's stimulation—and perhaps the cabin's low air pressure—soon takes its toll on his tiny body. He settles down and drifts off to sleep.

Grateful for the break, Sara and I settle back, trying to remain as quiet as possible. This accomplishes two things. First, it ensures Scotty remains undisturbed. Second, it keeps Sara and me from starting any conversation that might escalate into yet one more argument. The result is we spend the bulk of our transatlantic trip clenching our jaws and struggling to avoid eye contact.

Following a two-hour layover at London's Heathrow Airport, the three of us board a smaller Trans Mediterranean Airways (TMA) Boeing 707 for the trip to Beirut. When we touch down at Beirut-Rafic Hariri International Airport, it is 3:40 local time.

"Tony!" I hear a familiar voice call as we leave Customs. It's Joe, waving amidst a large crowd gathered to greet the new arrivals.

I take Sara's hand, literally dragging her the fifty or so feet to where Joe waves his arms like a castaway signaling a passing ship. As we come closer, I see he's not alone. My sisters, Coco and Nunu, are here along with my mother.

Then I look down and see my father. He's in a wheelchair and appears much smaller and frailer than I remember. He leans at an odd angle, his left side clearly unresponsive. But there is a bright gleam in his blue-gray eyes, and a broad smile blossoms on his stubbled face as we approach.

I all but throw myself at my mother, nearly crushing her in my embrace. I can feel her heaving sobs as I hold her close to my heart. Then, in turn, I hug Joe, Coco, and Nunu, finally kneeling so I can look my father in the eye.

I'm surprised his face appears blurred and unfocused. Then I realize, like everyone else, I'm crying. I awkwardly wipe the tears from my eyes and take my father's hand in mine. It seems so much smaller and more delicate than the one I shook when I left for America just three years ago.

"Father, I'm sorry I couldn't have come sooner."

"I understand. It's a long trip," my father says, his voice surprisingly strong. "And who is this great beauty?"

I turn and realize I have forgotten Sara and Scotty, both of whom are standing nearby in awkward silence. I jump to my feet.

"Father, this is my wife, Sara," I say with perhaps too much formality. "And this little guy is Scotty. Scotty, say hello to your grandfather."

My father reaches out with his good right hand as I lower Scotty onto his lap. Despite all the confusion, the boy is surprisingly calm as he settles into place and looks up at my father with his big, shiny brown eyes. My dad strokes the boy's curly brown hair. "Such a handsome young man. He clearly takes after his mother."

This brings a smile to Sara's face and helps break the ice. I quickly introduce her to the rest of my family, and there are big hugs all around.

Finally, Joe steps forward and takes my arm. "Let's get your luggage. We have another surprise."

"What surprise? You know I hate surprises."

"You'll see."

Together, we head for the baggage claim area on the terminal's lower level. When we arrive, I find it more crowded than I had expected. It takes me only a few moments to realize why. Only about half of those waiting are travelers from our London flight.

The other half are people from our neighborhood. Men. Women. Even kids. All are dressed in their best party clothes. There's a cry of delight when we're first recognized, and more than fifty people of all ages surge toward us like a human tsunami. The hugs and handshakes go on for several minutes as I'm welcomed back to Beirut, and I take the opportunity to introduce Sara and Scotty to people whose names and faces are still as familiar to me as the day I left.

We finally get our luggage and join Joe in what turns out to be the lead car of a twenty-vehicle-long motor caravan. This rag-tag convoy leaves the airport, winds its way into the central city and finally stops just short of our neighborhood, which I'm stunned to see has been roped off in preparation for what appears to be a major street festival.

Long tables have been set up throughout the street and colorful bunting hangs from the street lamps. On the tables are trays of freshly made Mediterranean foods, including kebabs, *falafel, shawarma, tabbouleh, kibbeh, dolma, hummus,* and *baba ghanoush.* As our neighbors hurriedly exit their cars, wine begins to flow freely, a local four-man street band strikes up a traditional folk song, and we all sit down to enjoy this incredible spread.

I look over at Sara and see she is thoroughly overwhelmed by our reception. I imagine that, to her, a young woman who has never ventured more than a hundred miles from home, these foreign sights, sounds, and tastes must be intense. Even frightening. Scotty, however, seems to be adapting quickly. As soon as Sara puts him down, he runs straight for the sweets table and grabs a handful of honey-glazed baklava.

Ironically, like Sara, this celebration fails to relax me. Instead, it puts me on edge. As much as I feel honored by all this attention, I feel uncomfortably unworthy of such reverence. After all, what have I done to warrant such adulation? I went to the U.S. and found gainful employment. I got married and had a child. This story is no different than thousands of other stories. After three years, I have not built a business empire, nor have I made enough to buy my own house. I still can't even manage to achieve U.S. citizenship, let alone bring the rest of the family to America. Yet, here, everyone is celebrating as if I just brought home an Olympic medal. I feel like an imposter in danger of being exposed at any moment.

Later that night, while the others are still eating, drinking and dancing, I manage to take my father aside for a quiet conversation.

"So how goes it in America? Are you keeping the wolf from the door?"

"I'm making good money," I tell him. "But not as much as I want."

"And I know you want quite a lot. Always have. Ever since you were a boy. But you were never afraid of hard work. That is what made you special."

"I'm still working hard. And I'm going to keep working hard until I can bring you, Mom, and everyone else to America." I don't mention I'm already sending part of my take-home pay to help pay for his care. My brother and I agreed this arrangement will remain our secret.

"And when might that be? As you can see, I'm not getting any younger."

"It's complicated. I'm working with a lawyer. A good one. But I have to work in the U.S. for five years before I can apply for citizenship. That's the law."

"Five years?"

"I've already been working for three, so I'm more than halfway there."

"I don't know that we can last that long," my father confesses. "I don't know what the American newspapers are saying, but the situation here is getting worse by the day. It's not safe."

I look over at my smiling sisters beside my mom and have to hold back the tears welling in my eyes. "I wish I could do more."

"And this girl you married…" he changes the subject.

"Sara."

"Not Lebanese."

"No. She's a mix of Scot, Irish and Italian. But we are good together."

"Are you?" He turns in his chair, his face hardening. "I've been watching you. You barely spent five minutes with her all evening."

"I've been a little distracted."

"She's not for you," my father says without hesitation.

For the moment, I am speechless. My first instinct is to tell my father he's wrong, that despite our differences, Sara and I make a good couple. But then I realize that, in just a few minutes, my father has seen what I have failed to recognize in more than two years: she and I are doomed to separate.

The question now is how do I leave her and still keep Scotty?

Chapter 15

MY TRIP TO Beirut is an unqualified success. Not only have I introduced Scotty to his extended family, but also, my misgivings about Sara have been confirmed by people whose opinions I trust. The woman I once viewed as my life partner is not right for me. The way I see it, divorce is only a matter of time. Sara's feelings toward me have similarly turned south. Since our return, our relationship has become increasingly frosty. We now live more like roommates than husband and wife. During the day, I watch Scotty while Sara works part-time at a nursing home. At 3:30 p.m., she returns, and I leave to wait tables.

When I return at 11:00 p.m., both Scotty and Sara are usually asleep. Sara and I occasionally see each other at breakfast, but our conversations are brief and superficial. We still share the same bed, but there is no intimacy. She knows this marriage isn't working, but like me, she doesn't know what to do about it. We are stuck at a crossroads.

According to Newton, an object at rest will remain at rest unless acted upon by an outside force. In the case of my dying marriage, that outside force is named Roberta. A waitress recently hired by Mr. Evans to replace Bobby, she is my new serving partner.

"I don't feel good about this," I tell Mr. Evans when he informs me of the new arrangement.

"Why not? Roberta is smart. Experienced. She's good with people. I think you'll work together well. And you know I'm a good judge of people, right? After all, I hired you."

I have no doubts about Roberta's bona fides. And she's clearly an attractive woman, a natural blonde standing a slim five-foot-six, with a narrow nose, high cheekbones, and piercing green eyes. Under other circumstances, she would have my undivided attention. It's just that...

"I've never worked with a woman before. I think things might be a bit... awkward."

"Don't worry, I don't bite," Roberta says, having obviously overheard our conversation. She steps forward, offering her hand. "I hear you're the best waiter here. I'm excited to learn from you."

As Roberta locks her green eyes with mine, my reservations melt away. No wonder Mr. Evans hired her. This woman is irresistible.

It takes only a few days for Roberta to learn our staff's methods and rhythms. Our customers seem as enamored with her as I am. They eagerly order any appetizer, entrée, drink, or dessert she recommends—which tends to increase the size of each dinner check significantly. As her partner, I receive 50 percent of her tips, just as she receives half of mine. Between us, we are doing great.

"I told you we'd make a good team," she says slyly as she counts our receipts at the end of the night.

There's an obvious spark between us. I feel it. Roberta appears to feel it too. Within a week, we're an item. With her, I just feel good again. Do I feel guilty about cheating on my wife? I know I should. But at this point, Sara is my wife in name only. Maybe I am subconsciously trying to give her an excuse to leave me—to put this marriage out of its misery.

The more I think about it, the more I want to divorce Sara and marry Roberta. But I must stop myself. Impulsivity is what got me into this mess. I need to slow down—to assess my options. Only then can I move forward in a considered, logical manner. I also need emotional support, the kind I can only get from my family.

This requires yet another trip to Beirut. I broach the subject of such a trip with Roberta, realizing how crazy the idea sounds as soon as it leaves my mouth. Surprisingly, she's on board.

"I'd love to meet your family. They sound like wonderful people. But will Sara let you go?"

This is the real question. Sara is not stupid. She probably already suspects I'm having an affair. If I suggest returning to Beirut, with or without Scotty, an explosive confrontation is inevitable. As bad as living with Sara-the-ice-queen has been, dealing with red-hot-angry-I'm-going-to-claw-your-eyes-out-with-my-bare- hands Sara is bound to be ten times worse.

It takes me a few days to work up the courage, but finally I propose a trip to Lebanon to Sara over breakfast. "I need some 'getaway' time," I say, trying to couch the idea in the softest terms. "I need more time with my family. Just me and Scotty, without worrying about whether or not you're bored or feeling uncomfortable. I think some days apart would be good for both of us."

I look away as I wait for the Mt. Sara volcano to explode.

Instead, she says, "If that's what you want to do." Before adding, "Are you sure you can take the time off from work?"

I'm so stunned by her reaction it takes me a full three seconds to respond. "I still have more than two weeks of vacation time I haven't used. I'm sure it won't be a problem."

She gets up from the table and loudly drops her plate into the sink. "Then have fun. Truthfully, I'd rather stay here. It's safer."

And just like that, the decision is made. I still can't believe it. Sara blessing my trip to Beirut—and even allowing me to take Scotty—is the last thing I expected. I have to believe her lack of concern is a sure sign she is as eager as I am to see this marriage end. *So why doesn't she just leave me? Would she rather it be me to sever things, allowing her to play the role of the victim*? If so, it's an arrangement I have no problem accommodating.

Three weeks later, I am again airborne, headed for London and a connecting flight to Beirut. Scotty, now on his second transatlantic flight in just one year, lounges beside me, deep into a coloring book. Roberta sits by the window. I never told Sara I was taking Roberta on this trip. I don't know what her reaction would have been if I had, but I decided not to kick that particular hornet's nest.

As for Scotty, I introduced him to Roberta just before boarding the plane. I explained she was my "friend" and would be going with us to Lebanon. Roberta then gifted Scotty with a plush teddy bear, which he, of course, loved. Ever since, they've been fast friends. When we return to Manchester, I'm sure Scotty will have plenty to say to his mom about "Daddy's friend," but by that time it probably won't matter either way.

Our arrival in Beirut is in stark contrast to our previous homecoming. This time, there are no crowds. No motorcades. No block parties. In fact, only my brother Joe is at the Customs gate to greet us. After retrieving our luggage, the four of us drive to our family house where my father, mother, and sisters are waiting. My mother has prepared a lovely dinner, and we all enjoy the food and drink in a warm, relaxed mood.

Later that night, after dessert, my father takes Roberta aside for a talk. I spend the next hour chatting with my mom and siblings about work, Scotty, and my home life, all the while keeping one eye on the conversation going on in the corner. Finally, I see Roberta lean down to give my father a hug, which he clearly enjoys. I excuse myself from the kitchen table and walk over to the fireplace where my father has parked himself.

"Well?" I ask. "You spent a long time talking to Roberta. What do you think?"

"Much better than the other one. So, when is the wedding?"

I can't keep the smile off my face. I'm thrilled my father not only likes Roberta but blesses any future union.

However, my euphoria is short-lived. The next morning, I receive a long-distance call from Sara. "Something's happened…"

My breath hitches in my throat.

"I'm pregnant, Tony."

I don't know how long the silence lasts. Probably only a few seconds, but it feels like hours.

"Are you sure?" I finally ask, already knowing the answer.

"Of course, I'm sure. I saw the doctor this morning. I'm eight weeks along."

My mind reels. This doesn't make sense. Sara and I haven't been together in months. "Who's the father?"

The volcano finally erupts. "*What do you mean,* Who's the father? You are."

I try to stay calm as I shift the receiver to my other ear. "That's impossible. You know it's impossible."

"The baby is yours. This is your responsibility."

I am tongue-tied. Another child is about to enter my life, a child who is clearly not mine, carried by a woman who is lying to me. As if my life weren't difficult enough—things just got way more complicated.

Chapter 16

BOSTON IS COOL and drizzly when Roberta, Scotty, and I return from Beirut. Together, we take a shuttle to the airport's long-term parking lot to retrieve my car. With Scotty buckled snuggly into the backseat, we head back to Manchester, the atmosphere thick with tension.

"What are you going to tell Sara?" Roberta finally asks as we turn north onto Interstate 93.

"I don't know. She's trying to trap me. I don't know why. Our marriage has been dead a long time. Now she's pregnant with someone else's child, and she thinks it's going to fix things?"

"Please keep me out of this, okay? This is between you and her. I don't know Sara. I don't want to be dragged into something I have nothing to do with."

I pat her hand, telling her I understand. And I really do understand her position. She may be *the other woman* in this real-life soap opera, but Sara and I had grown apart long before she arrived. My relationship with Roberta was the result of my estrangement from Sara, not the cause of it. She should not be punished for deeds she had no part in.

Arriving in Manchester, I drop Roberta off at her house, then drive to our apartment building. My homecoming reception is as chilly as the weather outside. No warm embrace or torrent of kisses greets my return. Instead, when I enter, Scotty on my shoulder, I find Sara sitting on the couch watching TV. Her face is blank, her gaze fixed on the flickering screen. I have to walk between her and the TV to get a reaction. When it finally comes, it is just the merest semblance of recognition.

"Hello," she says in a monotone.

"You're really pregnant…" I say, getting right to the point. When Scotty reaches for her, she puts him in her lap but keeps her eyes averted.

The lack of emotion in her voice is chilling. "Yes. I'm due in July."

I click the TV off. "The child is not mine. We haven't been together in nearly a year."

"You're my husband. The child is yours."

"This is ridiculous." My temper frays by the second. "I'm moving out. Scotty will need to stay here. This is his home. I don't want to upset him more than I have to."

"That's probably a good idea," Sara says with surprising equanimity. "We don't want to upset Scotty."

I had expected a fight. At least some resistance. Some bitter recriminations. An angry hurling of charges and countercharges. But Sara already seems to have accepted the fact that our marriage is over. Any quarrels at this point would be useless.

A half-hour later, I have packed my clothes and toiletries and am out the door. There is an apartment complex a half mile away catering to out-of-town executives and local divorcés. Here I rent a furnished studio apartment to hold me over until I can arrange for more permanent accommodations.

The next night, when I return to work, I tell Roberta what I have done.

"I'm sorry," she says uncomfortably. "I never told you this, but my parents divorced when I was eleven. I'm still not over it. I don't think they are, either. We grew up believing that love conquers all, that we each have one special soulmate we're destined to share our lives with. But the truth is, love can fade, and marriage is hard work. They say 50 percent of marriages end in divorce, and that rate is even higher for people who marry young like you did. You're older now. A different person. So is she."

"So, it's for the best?"

"It probably doesn't feel that way now, but, yes, it probably is," Roberta says. In the brief time I have known her, I have always regarded her as unusually intelligent. Now I recognize in her a wisdom far beyond her years. No wonder I've fallen for her.

"And what about us? Do we have a future?"

She hesitates. "No."

This hits me hard. I've been envisioning spending the rest of my life with this woman. Even my family back in Beirut love her.

"I don't understand," I sputter. "I thought we were a couple."

"We had a great time together, but I don't want to marry you. You already have one child and another on the way. Even if you divorce, Sara will always be a part of your life. I'm sorry. Maybe I'm selfish. But a relationship like that is just too complicated."

A week later, Roberta leaves the Sheraton Wayfarer to work at a restaurant on the other side of the city. My phone calls to her go unanswered, and we never speak again. My world has been turned upside down and I feel disconnected from reality, like I'm floating in space. At work, I go through the motions, but my enthusiasm hits an all-time low. I just don't feel the same spark to succeed.

Eight months later, Sara gives birth to another son. She names him Jimmy. As I suspected, he looks nothing like me. While Scotty has my dark Mediterranean coloring and curly black hair, Jimmy is pure white and blond.

"It's time we settle this," I tell her when visiting her apartment before taking Scotty for a trip to the park. "I want a divorce. Jimmy isn't mine, but I'll still pay child support, just to avoid a fight. I just want this over with."

"We can do that." She offers no more resistance than she did when I proposed my trip to Beirut. "Just send me the papers and I'll sign them."

Sara and I officially divorce in April 1975. A few weeks later, she remarries. Her husband is the man she was dating before she met me. He's also white and blond. But Roberta was right. Even after a divorce, a marriage is never truly over. Not when there are children involved. And Scotty is about to become a major issue in our now-separate lives.

Chapter 17

BEING SEPARATED FROM Scotty is one of the hardest things I've had to face in life. As part of our divorce settlement, Sara and I agreed I would take him on Saturdays and Sundays every other week. In the two-plus years since we finalized our divorce, I have never missed a weekend.

Even so, every time I arrive at Sara and her new husband's townhouse to pick up my son, I feel like an intruder. Scotty grows so fast I need time to adjust to whatever new words, ideas, and passions he's developed since our last get-together. One week he's crazy about his Etch A Sketch. The next he's into Mattel Hot Wheels. One day he can't stop talking about Scooby-Doo, and when I see him next, he's obsessed with *Land of the Lost*. It's like I'm meeting a new child every time I come to the door. While I'm always thrilled to see him any way I can, I miss all the mundane day-to-day interactions—the questions, the discoveries, the demands, the games, the laughs, the hugs—even the fights—that help shape the young man I now see so infrequently.

Today I arrive as scheduled at 9:00 a.m. to pick up Scotty for our weekend together. Sara answers the door. She's dressed in sweats, her hair pulled back, her face in minimal makeup. She looks pale and tired.

"Hello, Tony," she says without enthusiasm.

"Hi. How are you?"

"Fine." She turns and calls into the house, "Scotty, your father's here."

I remain on the front porch as Scotty appears next to his mother. He's already dressed in jeans, a long-sleeved shirt, a windbreaker, and he has a change of clothes in his Bugs Bunny backpack. But he wears a strangely sullen expression and refuses to make eye contact.

"What are your plans?" She asks.

"I thought we'd go to the park, then get some burgers." I turn to Scotty for some kind of reaction, but his attention remains elsewhere.

Looking through the doorway, I catch a glimpse of Frank, Sara's new husband. In his late twenties, he's slightly overweight with thinning blond hair. He sits in the living room, reading the sports section. He makes no effort to acknowledge me. Such indifference is not unusual for him, but today I find his chilly vibe especially odd. Something's off here.

"Just have him back tomorrow by 5:00."

Sara pushes Scotty onto the stoop and closes the door on us. Now I'm certain something is weird. She has never been this eager to relinquish our son, certainly not without so much as a hug or a kiss.

"You ready, buddy?" I ask him in my most upbeat voice. He nods, so I take him by the hand to my car.

"You're quiet today," I say, buckling him into place. "You feeling okay?"

"Fine," he says, again avoiding eye contact.

I drive us to a large park about a mile away. As soon as I open the door, Scotty is out of the car and heading to the playground. Strolling through the grass, I find a bench and settle down to watch him play with other children. The sky is partly cloudy, the temperature a pleasant 65 degrees with a calm, warm wind blowing from the south. It's hard to imagine a more perfect spring day. Like the trees beginning to bud, here in this open, unthreatening space, my son again shows signs of life. Climbing on the monkey bars, sliding down the slide, he looks giddy.

As promised, we later visit a diner. Scotty gets a regular burger and fries. I order the same, and we split a Coke. I watch my son carefully as he devours his meal. He seems content now, free of whatever anxieties were plaguing him earlier. A few hours in the sunshine appear to have done him good.

That night, as I prepare Scotty for bed, his demeanor darkens again. He becomes quiet and withdrawn. When I look at him, he glances away as if in fear. After he brushes his teeth, I help him change out of his clothes and into his pajamas. It's then that I see them.

Ugly purple bruises cover his back and upper arms, making me gasp. Some of these discolorations are partially faded, indicating they're at least a few days old.

"Where did you get these?"

He does not reply. I can't tell if he is scared or ashamed.

"It's okay," I assure him.

His little lip quivers. Still, he says nothing.

"I'm your father. You can tell me."

A teardrop slides down his cheek. "Frank," is all he can say.

I do my best to hide the fact that my blood is boiling.

"When was this?" I ask in as soothing a voice as possible.

"I was being bad, so he hit me."

"Has Frank hit you before?" "Y-yes."

"A lot?"

"Sometimes."

"For being bad?"

"I try to be good." Scotty wipes his nose with the back of his hand.

I think about his little brother. "What about Jimmy? Does Frank hit him, too?"

"No." His voice cracks. "Only me."

It occurs to me it's because Scotty is not his real son. Scotty is vulnerable and a constant reminder of me. Immediately, I fantasize about giving this man a taste of his own medicine. But I am in America on a guest worker visa. I can't afford to screw up. I must be cleverer than that. I have to bide my time.

The next evening, I return Scotty to Sara at the appointed hour.

"How did everything go?" she asks.

"Fine." I make no mention of my discovery. "We had a good time."

When I look Sara straight in the eye, she appears to flinch a bit. My look is intended to let her know I know what's been going on between these walls. Her pursed lips and shortness of breath suggest she gets my message.

It's not enough, though, and I can't sleep. I can't eat. I lie in bed imagining Frank raising his hand to my son. That this coward would resort to such tactics, and that Sara would allow it, fills me with white hot rage. The more I think about it, the angrier I get.

I'm so worried I might do something drastic and stupid, jeopardizing everything I have built here, that I make an appointment to meet with Martin Green, my immigration lawyer. When I tell him what I suspect, he asks if there is any evidence. I tell him about the bruises, the way Scotty acts like a different child—scared and intimidated.

"He can't be left alone in that house," I tell him.

"I'm not a family lawyer—" Martin begins.

"We have to get him out."

"Then we'll need to take both Frank and Sara to court."

"Will that work?"

"Maybe. If we get the judge to give you full custody." He looks me straight in the eye. "You ready for that? You ready to take Scotty full-time?"

I hadn't considered this. Taking care of a five-year-old child full-time is a serious responsibility. *How would this even work?* I still have my job at the Sheraton Wayfarer. I work evenings and nights. Who would look after him then? No matter. I'll figure it out.

"Let's do it," I tell Martin. "Let's take them to court."

It takes a full month, but finally we get a hearing in front of a family court judge. I enter the courtroom wearing my best navy-blue three-piece suit. Sara, Frank, and Scotty are already there along with their own attorney, a short, balding fellow in a brown tweed suit.

My palms sweat even though it's freezing in here. I fear my accent and immigrant status will hurt me. *What if I don't pull this off? Will Frank do something worse to Scotty as payback?* I force myself not to think of that.

"Don't worry, Tony, you're going to do fine," Martin squeezes my hand as we take our seats at the table.

"So, Mr. Assali, I understand you're asking for full custody of your son on the basis he currently resides in an unsafe environment," says the judge, a heavy-set man with jowls and in his late forties.

"Yes, your honor." Martin rises to his feet. "We have reason to believe this child has been subjected to a pattern of physical abuse at the hands of his stepfather—"

"That's a lie!" Frank shouts, only to be silenced by his attorney.

"And therefore, Mr. Assali, his biological father, should be granted sole responsibility for his upbringing."

"Have you brought evidence of such abuse?" The judge peers over his glasses to read his notes. "Photographs? A doctor's report?"

I have a sinking feeling.

"No, your honor. I'm afraid there hasn't been time. But we do have testimony from the child himself. As well as the marks on his body."

"Your honor, this is clearly a waste of the court's time," says Sara's lawyer, now also on his feet. "Scott is a boy, prone to exaggeration and flights of fantasy. And as a five-year-old, he's very physical. He plays. He roughhouses. He falls. Any contusions he may have are perfectly normal for a child his age and in no way a sign of abuse. As for Mr. Assali, while his intentions may be noble, the court must recognize he's an alien living in this country as a guest of the U.S. government. As such, he could be deported at any time. Above all else, Scott needs domestic stability, the kind only a home with his mother and step-father, both U.S. citizens, can provide."

I knew Sara's lawyer would play the immigrant card, but still it fills me with anger. A wave of nausea passes over me as I realize that, without hard forensic evidence of abuse, I will lose this case. Scotty and I lock eyes. I feel I have failed him.

No one says a word as the judge ponders his options. At last he looks up. "I'd like to speak to the boy myself. In chambers alone. Bailiff, could you please help our young friend find his way? This court is now in recess."

The uniformed bailiff approaches Sara's table. She whispers something in Scotty's ear, and Scotty cautiously takes the man's hand. Together, they follow the judge out of the courtroom.

"So, what happens now?" I ask Martin.

"We wait."

"What are our chances?"

"It all depends on your son. How much he's willing to talk. How comfortable is he with strangers?"

It took half a day for him to reveal Frank's abuse to me. I can't imagine any circumstances under which he'd freely divulge such embarrassing information to a total stranger.

Catch the White Tiger

    We all wait in tense silence for a good thirty minutes. Any time I look over, Frank glares at me with open hostility. I want to return the look—to do worse— but I force myself to back down. It won't don't any good. It might even make things worse.

    Finally, the judge re-enters. We all rise as the bailiff returns Scotty to Sara. As the judge takes his seat at the bench, my stomach clenches.

    It's so unfair. I know I am about to lose my son.

Chapter 18

I HAVE NEVER before been in a courtroom, neither here in the U.S. nor back in Beirut. Because I work nights, I've had little opportunity to watch legal dramas like *The Bold Ones* or *Owen Marshall: Counselor at Law* to familiarize myself with the workings of the American legal system. I therefore have little reason to expect a favorable verdict. I also have scant physical evidence to support my charges. My only witness is a clearly traumatized five-year-old boy. Add to this the uncertainty of my legal status, and my situation appears hopeless.

I prepare myself for the worst as the judge again peers over his glasses to review his notes. "I had an opportunity to spend quite a bit of time talking with young Mr. Assali," the judge begins, his tone calm and controlled. "Although he was initially shy, I found him to be bright, open, and communicative. Despite the circumstances, you have both raised an impressive young man."

I can't help but smile with pride at the judge's compliment. I turn to see Sara pulling Scotty closer. She, too, has obviously been moved by the judge's kind words.

"I also had an opportunity to examine the contusions on the boy's upper body. While I'm not a trained medical practitioner, I have had considerable experience dealing with the victims of domestic and child abuse, and I believe these wounds are consistent with such."

"Your honor!" Sara's attorney leaps to his feet. At the same time, Martin grabs my right hand tightly.

"Sit down, counselor. Your time for raising objections is over." The judge taps his gavel on its sound block. "I rule Scott Assali shall be removed from his current domicile where he is clearly in danger, and that his father, Anthony Assali, shall be given full, permanent custody of said child until he reaches the age of majority."

I feel like crying out in joy, but Martin holds me back.

"I am granting his mother visitation rights every other Saturday," the judge continues. "These visitations will be no longer than four hours and must be conducted at a designated visitation facility under the supervision of a court-appointed monitor. The transfer of custody will take place immediately. Court is adjourned."

My body shakes so hard I have trouble standing. Still, I throw my arms around Martin. "Thank you. I couldn't have done this without you."

"I hope you're ready to be a full-time father."

"I am," I say confidently.

Turning, I see the bailiff towering over Sara while she holds Scotty in a crushing embrace. This must be heartbreaking for her, and I sympathize with her loss. But her passivity makes her equally culpable, and I feel no guilt in breaking up this destructive bond.

A moment later, the bailiff firmly removes Scotty from her arms and escorts him to our table. During all this, Frank has been gazing at the far wall with a 500-yard stare, refusing to acknowledge either me or the activity swirling around him. As far as I'm concerned, he can go to hell.

Now that Scotty is safely with me, I cross to the defendants' table to speak with Sara alone. "I'll call later to make arrangements to pick up Scotty's things."

"I never wanted this—"

"It's over now."

She wipes her eyes. "Please tell him I love him. So much."

"I'll see you in two weeks."

Over the next several months, things happen quickly. Scotty and I move into a two-bedroom apartment offering us plenty of space. Sara sends over his clothes, toys, books, and other possessions, so he can make his bedroom his own. The décor turns out to be an eclectic mélange of cartoon characters, racing cars, and posters featuring Red Sox baseball players. On our building's entranceway bulletin board, I put up a sign requesting nightly child-sitting services and am thrilled when a fifty-year-old widow who lives one floor up offers to take the job. Now I can continue going to work, confident my son is well supervised. *And safe.*

And then I meet Edie. Age twenty-five, she's a dispatcher for the Bedford, New Hampshire, Police Department, staying at the Sheraton Wayfarer as part of a local law enforcement convention. With short brown hair, deep brown eyes, and a trim physique, Edie is a restless, no-nonsense woman who knows what she wants and does not hesitate to pursue it. Happily, what she wants is me.

After dating for several weeks, I introduce her to Scotty. I had feared Scotty would resent me having another woman in my life, but he warms up to her immediately. The two find a common interest in baseball and they talk on and on about player trades and batting averages while I stand back and watch. Two weeks later, Edie moves in. She continues to commute to her job at the Bedford P.D., just five miles away. But she's dissatisfied with her current circumstances and eager for a change.

"I'm tired of Bedford. I'm tired of Manchester," she says to me as we lie in bed. "Small towns are filled with small opportunities and small-minded people. I want more than that."

"Where do you want to go?"

"Boston. I have friends there. One of them wants me to help her run her business."

"It sounds like a great opportunity," I say, already feeling she's slipping away.

"You should come with me." Edie turns over to look me in the face. "You've been here how long? Five years? It's time to move on. Get out of your rut. Go get your slice of the American dream."

Edie knows just how to push my buttons. The truth is, I have been feeling like I'm spinning my wheels, going nowhere fast. Moving to Boston could be the shot in the arm I need.

"Boston sounds good," I say with a smile.

Now all I need is a job. The next day I find Mr. Evans in his office.

"I have news," I tell him. "My girlfriend and I have decided to move to Boston. We're moving at the end of the month. I want to thank you for all the opportunities you've given me. I'm going to miss everyone here."

"Wow, that's too bad. We're going to miss you, too. You've been a model employee. One of the best I've ever had. If you need one, I'm happy to give you a glowing recommendation."

"Thank you. That's very kind."

"Do you have a job in Boston yet?"

"No, not yet. We just decided this yesterday."

"Then let me give you a referral. I know the restaurant manager at the Hotel Sonesta. You've heard of it?"

"It's on the Charles River. Five stars."

"Exactly. Their signature restaurant, The Rib Room, is one of the best in the state. You'd be an asset to their operation."

"I'm flattered."

"I'll give Mario a call. Go knock his socks off."

Later that week I meet with Sara. With some trepidation, I tell her I am moving to Boston—and will be taking Scotty with me. Although I expect a heated reaction, she does not seem at all upset.

"Frank and I have been thinking about moving, too. Going up to Vermont. There's lots of construction work up there."

"You realize you will have a much harder time seeing Scotty," I remind her, as if begging for a fight.

"Hey, I've got Jimmy, and he's a full-time job. Besides, Scotty was always closer to you than to me. Maybe this is the way things were meant to be."

Two weeks later, Edie, Scotty, and I move to a small apartment in Medford, Massachusetts, north of Boston. Mr. Evans has already put in a good word for me with Mario. An effusive Italian-American, he sports an all-too-obvious gray-tinged toupee and greets me like a long-absent family member.

"Brook tells me wonderful things about you," he says, referring to Mr. Evans. "You're a real charmer. A hustler. And you know how to upsell. I like that in a waiter. I have just one question: When can you start?"

"Right away."

"Great! We'll get you fitted for a uniform. And you'll need to fill out paperwork. You're legal, right?"

I assure him I am.

My job at The Rib Room keeps me busy seven nights a week. The demands are tough, but the pay is much better than it was in Manchester. Despite the added income, the long hours put a strain on my relationship with Edie. Though she looks after Scotty when he's not in daycare, she doesn't hesitate to tell me numerous times this is not why she moved to Boston. "Just how am I supposed to work on my business, acting as nanny to your child?"

Finally, after one particularly frustrating day with Scotty, she asks me point blank: "Tony, what do you see in our future?"

"What do you mean?"

"Do you see us getting married?"

I hesitate before answering. I've messed this up before. "I just got out of one marriage," I finally say. "I don't see the point of rushing into another."

That's all it takes. Edie is out of the apartment the next day. Now Scotty and I are on our own.

"Are you going to leave, too?" Scott asks fearfully as I tuck him into bed later that night.

"Never. I will never leave. You are my blood, and blood is forever."

Blood may indeed be forever, but with so much of my attention devoted to familial and professional issues, my thoughts of Lebanon have become less frequent. With each passing day I feel more and more American. Meanwhile, the land of my birth—of my ancestors—is becoming an increasingly distant memory. However, the reality of my situation comes crashing down on me when, on April 13, 1975, I see a news report that militant gunmen have attempted to assassinate a Maronite Christian leader leaving church. This immediately brings to mind dark memories of my friend Nabil's shooting on the steps of St. Joseph's.

Within a week, Lebanon succumbs to an all-out civil war. Night after night, the network TV newscasts show shaky film footage of once-beautiful office buildings and homes ablaze as local militias roll through debris-laden streets, firing high-powered weapons.

In a panic, I try to call my family back in Beirut, but the phone lines do not work. There is no way to contact them. There's no way to tell if they're alive or dead.

Chapter 19

DESPERATE TO CONTACT my family, I reach out to other Lebanese-Americans I know in both the Boston and Manchester metro areas. All tell a similar story. Phone service to Lebanon has been cut. Letters are not getting through, nor is mail from Lebanon getting to the United States. It seems my home country's infrastructure has collapsed in the wake of sectarian violence.

Anxiety triggered by these events impacts every aspect of my daily life. At work, my attention wavers. I make all-too-frequent mistakes with orders. At home, I fail to give Scotty the attention he needs as I find myself clicking through TV newscasts or poring over Lebanese civil war coverage in *Time, Newsweek, U.S. News & World Report,* and *The Boston Globe.* At night, though exhausted, I can only lie awake, staring at the ceiling, trying to devise ways to learn my family's fate.

Finally, in what I recognize as an act of desperation, I write a letter to Jack Kubisch, the American ambassador in Athens. (Greece is currently serving as a major way station for Lebanese refugees.)

"I only have you on Earth and God above," I begin. "For years, my father, Toufic Assali, served as an English-Arabic translator for Union 76. He has always had a great love for America and used what meager funds he had to send me to the U.S. so I could be safe. But now, because of his connections to American petroleum interests, as well as to members of the U.S. Embassy in Beirut, his life, and the lives of his wife and children, are in mortal danger. I beg you to find my family and provide them with the tourist visas they need to seek refuge in America. I can assure you their stay in the United States will only be temporary, as my parents have every intention of returning to Beirut once the situation stabilizes."

I include this last statement on the advice of my attorney, Martin Green. Martin believes the state department will be more receptive if I request temporary immigration status for my parents and siblings. The queue for permanent status, especially for refugees from the Middle East, is already years long. Even if my family wants to go home after the war, chances are there will be little, if anything, left to return to. From what I'm seeing on the *Nightly News*, the city long known as The Paris of the Middle East now looks more like Berlin did at the end of World War II.

Knowing this is the longest of long shots, I send my request as registered mail to the U.S. Embassy in Athens. I have nothing to lose by trying. All my life I have been lucky. Maybe God will once again bless me with good fortune.

Days go by. Then weeks. I continue writing letters to Ambassador Kubisch, each more anguished than the previous. I get few replies, but when they do arrive, they are merely form letters. "We understand the gravity of your situation…"; "Demands for American assistance continue to be overwhelming…"; "We are doing everything in our power to relieve the suffering of those currently in war- torn areas of Lebanon as well as in other areas of the Middle East…"

It's all bureaucratic BS. American diplomats won't venture into the chaos to help rescue foreign nationals. Despite its geographically strategic position, Lebanon is, in America's eyes, a small, unimportant country. We have no oil. Our armed forces are less than formidable. It is only the threat of our government falling to radical factions hostile to neighboring Israel that earns us any attention from Washington. To make matters worse, Syria, bordering Lebanon to the north, is now threatening invasion. The Syrians have been waiting for an opening like this for decades. Damascus never recognized Lebanon when it won its independence from France in 1943, and its leaders would like nothing more than to claim the land for themselves.

As I watch the tragedy in Lebanon unfold, I can't help but contrast the suffering there with the comforts I continue to enjoy in the United States. I have a good, paying job. I live in a comfortable two-bedroom apartment in a relatively crime-free area of metropolitan Boston. Access to food, water, medicine, and all the other necessities of life is never an issue. Whenever I reflect on my good fortune, my reaction is a confusing combination of gratitude and guilt.

The year 1975 rolls over into 1976 with little change in the Lebanese civil war. As for me, I'm seeing a new girl, Paula. We've been dating for a few weeks when, in mid-August, I take her to see The Platters perform at Copley Square. I love The Platters and their classic style of 1950s rock 'n' roll. After the concert, audience members are invited to the stage to compete in a dance contest. I'm just jazzed enough from the concert to participate. Backed by the pounding music, I shake off all my inhibitions and let loose.

Sweat pours down my face as I twirl Paula, twisting and turning to the beat. I look up for a moment to see a crowd forming as the disco ball lights bathe us in a rainbow of colors. The crowd cheers, and for a moment all of the tension from these last few years ebbs. Time disappears as I fling Paula faster and faster, kicking up my heels and throwing back my head. The shouting gets louder. Paula smiles back at the crowd as I sweep her off her feet and high into the air before dipping her back against my knee.

When I pull her up, everyone explodes into applause, and later on, the organizers find me to tell me I won first place.

"Thank you. Thank you," I say.

I've recently purchased a new orange Chevy Camaro convertible and, in my excited state, I can think of no better way to top the evening than to take it for a late-night spin. Although it's now well past midnight, the air is still hot and humid. With Paula riding beside me, I lower the roof, roll down the windows, and drive.

We're cruising up I-93 North toward Medford when I pull even with a late model red Corvette. As I glance over at the car, the driver looks at me and nods. This man wants to race! A second later, we both floor it. Paula laughs, cheering me on as the speedometer quickly climbs. Seventy miles per hour. Eighty miles per hour. Ninety miles per hour!

Suddenly, I notice two slower moving cars ahead in the far left and far right lanes. Only the center lane between them offers safe passage. The Corvette and I remain neck-and-neck. Only one of us is going to make it through. My fevered brain quickly makes a series of mathematical calculations; I'm going too fast to stop. Way too fast.

The Corvette and I continue to blast forward, jockeying for position. My heart is racing so fast I can feel it pounding in my ears. The slower-moving cars are coming up on us quickly, almost as if they're standing still. Paula screams.

Somehow, I turn at the last second and thread the needle between the two slower-moving cars. The red Corvette isn't so lucky. It hits the rear of the car in the right-hand lane. I'm confused. Terrified. I don't know what to do, so I just keep driving.

Easing my foot off the pedal, I struggle to breathe. Once again, something has rescued me from a near-certain disaster. Today is not something I am proud of. In fact, I feel ashamed. I put myself—and Paula—in mortal danger for no good reason. This is not the way a grown adult, let alone a responsible parent, is supposed to behave.

It's almost 4:00 a.m. by the time I arrive home. I check on Scotty. He's fast asleep. So is our babysitter, a high school girl who lives nearby. I gently wake her and, in light of the late hour, pay her overtime. Afterwards, Paula volunteers to drive the girl home.

A few minutes after Paula leaves, the phone rings. When a phone rings at 4:00 in the morning, it's never good news. Immediately, I fear Paula has gotten into an accident. I lift the handset, expecting the worst.

"Hello?"

There's a lot of static on the line. The voice at the other end is distant and scratchy. But I recognize it, and it takes my breath away.

Chapter 20

"TONY? CAN YOU hear me? It's your father."

Is this a dream? I lurch to my feet, struggling to control my emotions.

"*Dad?* What's going on? Where are you?"

"Athens," he says. "We're safe. Mom. Joey. Coco. Nunu. Josephine. All of us. We're okay."

"What are you doing in Athens? How did you get out of Lebanon?" I'm still struggling to grasp the reality of the situation.

"An officer from the U.S. Embassy found us. Roger Fortis. We were staying at Antoinette's house." Antoinette is my sister, just two years younger than me. My father tells me she and her husband had a house in one of the suburbs east of Beirut, out of the war zone. "Mr. Fortis said you were flooding the embassy mailbox with letters. They had to find us just to make you stop!"

When I join him in laughing, tears slide down my face. *They're safe. All of them.*

"He was able to get us out of the country by boat," my father continues. "Now we're in Athens waiting for our tourist visas to be processed."

"How soon will that be?"

"They say a few weeks. We could be in Boston by next month!"

This is fantastic news. Not only is my family alive, they're coming to America. *Could this really be possible?*

"You'll stay with me," I say without hesitation. "All of you. I have plenty of room."

Truth is, my two-bedroom apartment measures all of 1,000 square feet. Not exactly palatial. Even so, compared to the conditions my family has endured these past few months, this modest place will feel like the Taj Mahal.

After getting the embassy's phone number and saying my goodbyes, I drop to my knees and thank God for delivering my family to safety. As I do, I remember that, just an hour ago, I had literally come within inches of foolishly injuring—if not killing—myself in a high-speed car crash. I will never know if it was dumb luck or providence that brought me to this joyful moment; I decide I will never ever take my good fortune for granted again.

The next day, I send Ambassador Kubisch the biggest bouquet of flowers I can order. I have it shipped directly to the U.S. Embassy in Athens. The gift costs me a full week's salary, but it's worth it. Thanks to him and his staff, the Assali family will soon be reunited.

Over the next two weeks, I scramble to prepare for my family's arrival. In all, nine people are coming: My father, my mother, my brother, my three sisters, their spouses, and two children. I plan to meet them all at Logan Airport. But how am I going to fit nine people into my four-seat Camaro?

During a break at The Rib Room, I explain my situation to Paul, one of my fellow waiters. He's a native with a thick South Boston accent he tries to hide when chatting with customers.

"No problem," he says. "I got a van that seats six. You can borrow it if you want." With his accent, "borrow" comes out "bar-ah."

"Yeah, but if I drive, that only leaves room for five."

"My buddy Jake's got a van, too," Paul adds. "I'll talk to him. We'll make sure everyone in your family gets a ride. Trust me."

The day before my family is to land, I go to the supermarket to load up on groceries. I buy milk, ground beef, chicken, frozen pizzas, cold cuts, and a dozen loaves of bread. When the checkout girl sees all the bread, she looks at me like I'm nuts.

"My family's been through hell," I tell her. "I don't want them to go hungry."

Finally, the big day arrives: September 6, 1976. Paul and I drive the vans to Logan Airport. After parking in the short-term lot, we rush to the International Terminal. I can barely contain myself. The flight from Athens is scheduled to land at 5:15 p.m. Arriving outside the gate, I anxiously check my watch as I pace. It's already 5:20. I figure it's going to take at least a half-hour for my family to de-plane and get through Customs. So, I wait. And wait. Minutes pass. It's 5:30 p.m. Then 5:40. Finally, people from the Athens flight filter into the terminal. I crane my neck, trying to spot a familiar face. I don't see anyone familiar in the growing crowd. *Did something go wrong? Did they miss the flight? Was there a problem with their visas?*

And then, at the edge of the mob, I see my mother pushing my father in a wheelchair. I wave to them. At last she sees me.

"Tony!" she cries. We run to each other and embrace so tightly neither of us can breathe. Finally looking up, I notice my brother and sisters are right behind her.

"Joey. Coco. Nunu. Welcome to America!" I roar. There's a whole lot of hugging and crying and back-slapping and kissing. Then I rush over to where my father sits patiently in his chair. I bend down and kiss his rough, stubbled cheek. "Dad, you look great," I say. In truth, he looks much older than he did when I visited Beirut two years ago. His stroke has taken its toll on his body. His eyes are runny, and his cheekbones are unusually pronounced. Still, there is fire in those kind eyes.

With Paul's help, we claim everyone's luggage in the baggage area, then hurry to the parking structure. We're able to get everyone comfortably seated in the two vans. The drive to my apartment in Medford takes less than a half-hour, and we talk nonstop the whole way—about the war in Lebanon. About their escape to Greece. About the flight to Boston. About the Boston area traffic and my job at The Rib Room and my separation from Sara and the cost of apartment rentals in and around the city.

Arriving in Medford, we bound out of the vans and stream into my little two-bedroom apartment. Counting Scotty, there are now eleven of us here, but no one complains. We're all just happy to be together. Unable to sleep, we eat and talk well past midnight. Once again, the patriarch, my father, regales us all with tales of their numerous brushes with disaster these past few years.

"One night, four militia members broke into our house," he says. "They put a gun to my head and demanded to know where my daughters were. I told them I didn't have any daughters. One of them hit me with his gun, right here in my forehead. And then they left, thank God."

I try to pick my jaw up off the floor. "So, they never found anyone?"

"No. We were hiding in the house across the street," Coco says with her usual composure.

"But when the militants left, I was afraid they'd check the entire neighborhood," my father says with a grateful sigh. "About an hour later, our house was shelled. Totally blown apart. Your mother and I only survived by hiding in the bathtub."

"He lay on top of me," she says. "I could barely breathe. I didn't know what was going to kill me first, your father or the rockets."

"But you got out…"

"We all went to Nunu's house. We stayed there until the man from the U.S. Embassy came. Then we decided to leave together."

I'm so amazed my family survived, especially considering my father's condition. Somehow, they managed to not only get out but also find safety here, 6,000 miles from home. It's nearly three o'clock in the morning by the time our homecoming winds down. I give my bed to my parents and silently vow to give Paul my tips for a week for his kindness. Scotty keeps his bed. The rest of us either crash on the living room furniture or on mattresses I brought in for the occasion. Within a half-hour, everyone is asleep.

A half-hour later, a shrill siren wakes us. My mother screams.

"What's that?" Joe asks, instantly awake. "What's going on?"

"Fire truck," Scotty explains.

Still, I can't help noticing the terror I just heard in Joe's voice, the fear in everyone's eyes. I realize that while they left the civil war behind, the fear they've been living isn't far away.

"We hear them a lot," I try to explain. "There's a station a block away."

"What's on fire?" Coco asks. "Should we leave?"

"No, no, we're fine. Someone probably had an emergency. Like a heart attack. Firefighters are on call. They're usually the first to respond to 911 calls."

"911?"

"The emergency phone number."

Joe is still confused. "They send firemen to take care of heart attacks?"

"Welcome to America," I say with a smile.

Chapter 21

TRANSITIONING NINE LEBANESE refugees to life in America is no easy task. They have to be fed. They have to be clothed. They need transportation. Some of them need gainful employment. And as I know firsthand, securing employment can be hard with limited English language skills, no recognized educational degrees, and zero familiarity with the local geography, culture, and customs. In short, my family is exactly where I was when I came to America. Fortunately, my six-year head start as a resident of the United States has given me the knowledge and experience to guide my family. I will serve as their Virgil, escorting them safely through the exotic and wholly alien landscape that is metropolitan Boston.

My first challenge is transportation. To ferry everyone around town, I need something more formidable than my flashy orange Chevy Camaro. My solution is to trade in the sporty coupe for a less attractive, but more practical, used Ford station wagon. Just two years old, with only twenty thousand miles on its odometer, the green behemoth comfortably fits six adults and has a fold down rear seat that can accommodate another two. For getting everyone around town, the Ford is as efficient as it is aesthetically bland.

One of our first stops is to the offices of Martin Green who arranges to get everyone Social Security cards, critical to securing employment. Joe takes special pride in his new blue-and-white card. "Take my picture!"

Next on our itinerary is the Hotel Sonesta. Here I introduce Mario to Joe and Nunu's husband, Tony. (Yes, there are now two Tonys in the family.) Mario agrees to hire both as busboys on the spot. It's not glamorous work, but it will provide steady, predictable income.

"You are doing me a great favor," I tell Mario.

"Nonsense. If they work half as hard as you do, you're doing *me* a favor."

It's arranged that Joe and Tony will work the same hours I do so we can commute together. This way they can avoid the costs of public transportation that took such a bite out of my paycheck. Next, it's off to the Natick Mall to buy clothes for everyone. My family is awed by this magnificent indoor shopping center, having seen nothing like it in Lebanon. Of course, Beirut has—or had—fine department stores, but never has my family seen such stores under what is, for all intents and purposes, a single roof. Add to this dozens of high-end fashion boutiques for both men and women, jewelry stores, and two massive book sellers, and the impact is overwhelming.

The food choices blow their minds too. After all, the mall hosts a half-dozen traditional sit-down restaurants, cookie and snack shops, and the signature institution of all such modern shopping centers: a fast-food court.

"It's all hamburgers, Italian, and Chinese," says Joe. "Where's the Mediterranean food? The falafel? The kebabs?"

"People here don't know our kind of food," I explain. "There aren't enough of us here to support a Mediterranean restaurant."

"We should do something about that."

"Maybe we will," I say, half-jokingly. (Little do I realize how prophetic my off-handed remark actually is.)

Meanwhile, thanks to Paula, I secure Coco a job as a hairdresser at a salon in the city. Coco's English is far from perfect but she's a fast learner, and her natural charm and good looks help her overcome her lack of language skills. She is also more than adept with shears and a blow dryer and blessed with an innate sense of style.

Everything seems to be going well except for one thing: the matter of living accommodations. Obviously, my two-bedroom apartment cannot hold all eleven of us forever. Even after just a few days, the close quarters and single bathroom cause tensions to rise, and minor conflicts quickly escalate. If I don't find a solution fast, there is the distinct possibility someone will draw blood or the walls will burst at the seams. So, I check the local newspaper's real estate section and find a six-bedroom rental house in the city of Stoneham, just five miles to the north. The monthly rent is higher than I would like, but with Joe, Tony, and me all working, I believe we can comfortably manage payments.

"This is a mansion!" Nunu exclaims when we see the traditional two-story brown-and-white house for the first time. Twenty-six-hundred square feet spread over two levels, the house is twice the size of any in our old neighborhood in Beirut.

"No, it's a palace!" Coco cries. She seems genuinely nervous about entering the house, as if she'd be trespassing on forbidden ground.

Once inside, everyone's inhibitions vanish. Family members run from room to room trying to wrap their minds around how such luxury could be available to simple working people like us.

"Did you see? Three bathrooms?" my mother exclaims with tears in her eyes.

We all move into our new house in October 1976, just as the weather starts to turn. Coming from hot and dusty Beirut, this is my family's first exposure to a New England autumn. I'm reminded of my first fall in Manchester, how I was unprepared for the cold, damp winds that cut you straight to the bone. I make sure everyone has the heavy clothes, coats, and jackets needed to endure the autumn chill… and the deep freeze soon to come.

Winter comes early this year. We have our first snowfall in mid-November. It is just a light dusting, but for my family it is an early Christmas miracle. Everyone rushes out to play in it, just like they've seen people do in the movies.

"It's cold," Joey complains, as he grabs a handful of powdery snow, only to have it melt in his hands. "It's cold and it's wet."

"What did you expect?" I ask.

"I don't know. Something soft and fluffy?"

As everyone continues to play, I look back to the house and see my father in his wheelchair, watching us through the living room window. He looks at peace, content in the knowledge that his family can enjoy a safe and secure future far from the horrors of our war-ravaged homeland. He looks at me through the glass. We lock eyes. No words are spoken, but I know he is proud.

My work at The Rib Room continues swimmingly. To help pay for my family's upkeep, I have taken on expanded hours. Every day, I first work the lunch shift from 11:00 a.m. to 3:00 p.m., then the dinner shift, from 5:00 p.m. until closing, which is usually between 10:00 and 10:30. Daycare for Scotty is no longer an issue since he has started kindergarten. Afterwards, my mother, Coco, Nunu, and Josephine fight to watch over him.

I'm feeling good about things when I arrive at work just ahead of our lunch opening one day. I'm putting on my uniform when Mario calls to me.

"Tony," he says, waving me toward him. "Phone call."

Curious, I head out of the locker room to where Mario stands in his office doorway. As I do, I feel my stomach clench. Dread passes through me. Phone calls have often meant very good things—and very bad things. As Mario hands me the handset I notice he looks unusually pale and know it's the latter.

"Hello?" I hear myself say into the phone.

Chapter 22

"WE'RE AT THE hospital…" Joe says.

I can hear crying and sobbing in the background. It sounds like my mother. I think I hear my sisters. No doubt something terrible has happened. My imagination runs wild. I need more information. Now.

"Is it Dad?"

"It happened just after you left for work." Joe fights to keep his voice under control. "He started screaming. I think he was having another stroke. We didn't know what to do. Then Coco remembered you saying something about a special emergency phone number."

"911," I cut in, recalling my family's first night in America.

"Right. So, we called. The ambulance got here in five minutes. By then, Dad had stopped screaming. He wasn't even moving. They got him on a stretcher and put him in the ambulance…" Joe stops. The silence is intolerable. I want to speak up—to demand he continue. But I'm too terrified to hear what is sure to come next. "He died on the way here. They said there was nothing they could do…"

Again, Joe falls silent. All I hear now is crying in the background. One of these sobs turns into a mournful wail, a heart-breaking howl I have not heard since the day of the massacre at St. Joseph's church.

I try to imagine my father lying on a cold slab in the morgue. Here was a man who survived a home invasion, having his house shelled while he was inside, a paralyzing stroke, and a voyage around the world. Then, like Moses when he finally set eyes upon the Promised Land, he is struck down. The universe has a cold and wickedly cruel sense of irony.

"I have to go," I tell Mario as I hang up the phone, my breathing fast and shallow. "My father just died. I have to be with my family."

I feel like I'm carrying two hundred pounds on my back as I struggle to make it out of the hotel and into the parking lot. The pavement is slick with a thin sheet of fresh ice, just waiting for someone to slip. Carefully, I somehow manage to make it to my station wagon and climb in behind the wheel. But once inside, I don't start the engine. I just sit there. I can't move. Since Joe's call, I feel like my world has been turned upside down. I want to weep, but I cannot even muster the will to do that. I can only stare blankly into space.

I don't know how much time passes. Maybe a few minutes. Maybe more. I'm so unmoored I've lost the ability to grasp the concept of time. Somehow, I find the strength to dig for the car keys in my coat pocket, slide the key into the ignition, and pull onto the road.

I've only driven a half-mile when I have to pull over. My vision is blurry, and I can't make out the road. Idling on the shoulder, I look at my face in the mirror and realize I'm crying. The reality of my father's death is finally hitting me. Next to Scotty, he was the most important person in my life and I'm never going to see him again. The finality of this statement knocks the wind out of my chest, and I find myself gasping for breath.

Reminded that my family is waiting for me, I collect myself and head for the hospital. My arrival is greeted with more tears and lamentations. My poor mother is inconsolable. Joe, Coco, Nunu, and Josephine can barely hold it together. A young doctor explains my father did, indeed, suffer a massive stroke. In his weakened condition, he was beyond help. He offers his condolences, and I thank him for his kindness.

With nothing more to be done, I drive everyone home. This is going to be a long night.

The next day, I make arrangements for my father's funeral at one of the Eastern Catholic churches in the Boston area. When I go to discuss details with Joe, I find him in his bedroom, digging through his closet.

"What's wrong?" I ask.

"I can't do this. I can't go to the funeral."

"I know you're upset. We all are. But we have to show Dad our respects."

"Of course, I want to go, but I have nothing to wear. I don't own a suit."

I realize I am in the same position. I have plenty of nice clothes but no dark suits. The one I brought with me from Beirut no longer fits. I have not had occasion to even consider buying a new one. Until now.

With the funeral just forty-eight hours away, I call Mario for advice. "My brother and I need suits fast, and we don't have a lot of money. Do you have any suggestions?"

Mario doesn't hesitate. "Sallinger's. It's a men's clothing store on Washington Street. I know the owner, Louie Fagioli. Tell him I sent you."

"Thanks. I owe you."

"You just take care of yourself. And tell Louie I said 'hi.'"

The next day, I drive Joe into the city. We find Sallinger's in a large, four-story early twentieth century brick building. When we walk into the lobby, I get flashbacks of the months I spent as a salesman at the New Imperial in Beirut. The aroma is the same, a musky mixture of wool and leather. This triggers a twinge of nostalgia that, for a moment, makes me forget the real purpose of our visit.

"Can I help you gentlemen?" asks a slim, well-dressed salesman with prematurely gray hair.

"Our father just passed and we need suits for his funeral."

"I'm sorry for your loss. I'm sure we can find something you'll like."

"Actually, we were told to speak to the owner, Mr. Fagioli."

"So, *you're* the guy Mario sent."

I turn to find the source of the voice, but at first see nothing. Then I look down to see a diminutive, balding Italian-American man no more than 4½ feet tall and wearing a sharply tailored three-piece suit. My first impression is that he resembles the character actor Danny DeVito.

"I'm Louie." He extends his hand bearing several gold rings.

"Tony Assali."

Suddenly, Louie's expression changes. His smile drops away, and his eyes drill into mine. His grip tightens on my hand. What the hell is going on?

Chapter 23

THIS STANDOFF WITH Louie is becoming uncomfortable. His hand gripping mine like a vise, he continues staring at me as if I am either a long-lost relative or a freak of nature. Either way, he's making me self-conscious.

"Something wrong?" I finally ask.

This seems to break the spell. Louie abruptly releases my hand and at the same time, looks away with a slight nod of his head.

"No, no, it's all fine," Louie says, seemingly as shaken as I am. He gives his suit jacket a slight tug, then motions to the right. "Let's go upstairs."

"Upstairs?"

"It's where I keep my best suits."

Crossing through the store's main level, Joe and I join Louie in an old-fashioned elevator, the kind with a rolling metal gate. Louie presses a button on a wall-mounted panel, and we slowly ascend to the store's second floor, the car creaking all the way. As we rise, Joe and I share a quick but telling glance. It is obvious that he, too, noticed Louie's odd behavior when we arrived. Maybe coming here was a mistake.

On the second floor, I find row upon row of suits hanging under bright incandescent lamps. From my experience at the New Imperial, I recognize these as higher-end fashions from Europe, mostly France and Italy. The smoothness of the fabrics, the slimness of the cuts, and the detail in the stitching make their origins unmistakable.

"Take a look around." Louie gestures expansively. "Let me know if you find anything you like."

"These look great," I say. "But we don't have a lot of money. All our cash is going to pay for our father's funeral."

"I understand. Pick out a suit you like and, because you're a friend of Mario's, I'll give it to you wholesale. I won't make a penny. Let me see, you look like a forty-regular jacket, pants, thirty-two/thirty."

"That's right," I say, impressed. "How did you do that without measuring?"

"Kid, I've been in this business thirty years. If I can't size a man up on sight, I need to find another job. Here, try this on." He pulls a charcoal gray suit off the rack. It's an Italian designer three-piece. Obviously of high quality.

I take the suit into the dressing room and try it on. Louie gives Joe a suit in a similar style, which my brother puts on. When we emerge from the fitting room, it's clear Louie's eye was spot-on. We look sharp. Damned sharp.

"I like it," I say, I assessing myself from several angles in a three-sided mirror. "How much?"

When Louie doesn't answer, I turn and see him again staring with that same odd expression he wore when we shook hands downstairs. If he's trying to creep me out, he's doing an excellent job.

"Why do you keep looking at me like that?" I finally ask him flat out.

"Sorry. But, tell me, have you ever sold men's suits before?"

This is not the response I was expecting.

"When I was a teenager, back in Beirut I worked at a store called the New Imperial. We sold mostly European men's fashions. Like these."

"I knew it!" Louie says triumphantly. "After thirty years in this business, I can sense a natural salesman. Come on. Let's finish off those pants and get you out of here."

Louie calls over one of his tailors who measures and pins up our unfinished pants. He then takes them upstairs to the sewing room while Joe and I change back into our street clothes.

"I want to make you an offer," Louie says while we wait for the alterations to be completed.

"What kind of an offer?"

"My top salesman is retiring next month, and I need a new man on the floor. You have the right look. And you obviously also have the right experience. I know this is fast, but after three decades, I've learned to trust my gut. I can give you $100 a week, plus a 15 percent commission on everything you sell. Including accessories. That's gotta be more than you're making with Mario."

"I don't know what to say. I just came here looking for a suit for my father's funeral, not a new job."

"Of course, how rude of me. You're in mourning. Take your time. Think it over. Then call me back this afternoon."

He hands me his business card.

I don't bother to take it. I don't have to think this over. The fact is, $100 a week, plus commission is more than I make at The Rib Room. Plus, I'm tired of working evenings and weekends. I want to be able to spend more time with Scotty. My latest white tiger has just revealed itself, and I have to grab it before it disappears.

"Mr. Fagioli, you've got yourself a salesman."

"Great. When can you start?"

"I'll need to give two weeks' notice."

"Then I'll see you in two weeks. And sorry again about your father."

On the drive home, Joe and I can't stop talking about our bizarre afternoon.

"Dad dies and I need a suit. So, we go shopping and you get a job offer. How often does *that* happen?"

"I didn't plan it this way."

"No, you just got lucky. You've always been the lucky one. Things break your way."

The day of my father's funeral is frigid cold, with temperatures in the low teens. My mother spends the entire service weeping as the rest of our family tries to console her. The next day, I return to work and give Mario my two weeks' notice. I'm reminded of when I gave a similar notice to Mr. Evans two years ago. Like then, I expect to get resistance, only to be encouraged to leave.

"Louie is a great guy," Mario says. "You're going to enjoy working for him. Plus, I think you'll enjoy being in sales."

"If I go, Joe and Tony can still work here?" I ask, afraid my decision will trigger some form of retribution.

"Of course, they'll still have jobs. And if things don't work out with Louie, you can always come back and work for me."

"I appreciate that."

"Now let's get back to work. We have hungry customers to feed."

When I return to the dining room, nothing has changed. But everything has. I'm going through the motions—taking orders, flattering women, making dining recommendations—but part of me has already moved on. I can feel this chapter of my life drawing to a close, and I can't wait for the next one to begin.

Chapter 24

SO, I'M FINALLY getting back into sales. Mario says this is where I belong. Louie says he can tell I am a natural salesman just by looking at me. And he's been around a long time. The guy must know what he's talking about.

When I arrive at Sallinger's ten minutes before the company's official 9:00 a.m. opening, I am both nervous and excited. Nervous because my retail sales skills have gone rusty over these past seven years. Excited because I finally have an opportunity to earn an income commensurate with my efforts.

When you are a waiter, there is only so much food you can seduce a customer into ordering; no matter how hungry, a diner is not going to order two or three lobsters. On the other hand, a good retail salesman can convince a man shopping for clothes to buy multiple suits (especially if they're on sale), as well as a range of accessories such as shirts, ties, belts, and even shoes to achieve a particular "look." For a motivated salesman, the income potential is unlimited.

I try the front. Locked. I knock. No response. I knock again. Louie appears behind the tempered glass and unlocks the door from the inside.

"Right on time," he says with a smile as he ushers me inside. "I don't know about the suit, though. You look like you're going to a funeral."

In fact, I'm wearing the same charcoal gray suit I bought here two weeks ago. I wanted to look professional, and this is the only one in my wardrobe.

"A different tie will help," Louie says, sensing my discomfort. He takes me over to a display and finds one with a bright pattern of red and gold. "Try this. It'll give you some color."

I replace my simple black tie for the one Louie provides, and he's right—I look better. Certainly less mournful. Amazing what difference a simple accessory can make. I'll have to remember this when I'm working the floor.

For my orientation, Louie gives me a personal tour of his kingdom. The building's first floor serves as his main showroom. Here he displays his most- popular, lower-priced suits, sports coats, pants, shirts, shoes, and accessories. As he explains, many of the suits on display carry the Sallinger's label and are made right here on the premises.

"About 80 percent of my business is done here. People come here looking for bargains and that's just what we provide."

Done touring the first floor, we again take the rickety old elevator up to the second story. This is where Joe and I bought our suits. As Louie explains it, this floor is for his more "exclusive" customers, as it is where he displays and warehouses his finer French and Italian imports. "We carry stuff from all the big fashion houses. Loro Piana. Zegna. Rubinacci. Ungaro. Armani. Both with and without the designer labels. Without the labels, suits are half price."

"You mean adding a name label doubles the price?"

"That's the price of status."

Onto the elevator again, and we ascend to the third floor. Here Louie shows me the cutting room, a loftlike enclosure where wizened men and women, most of whom appear to be well into their sixties or beyond, work at cutting tables and sewing machines to create the Sallinger's-branded garments for the store below.

This is also where Louie's tailors perform their alterations, tightening or letting out waistbands, pant legs, and suit coats as necessary to match each customer's physique. Seeing this, I can't help but flash back to old black-and-white photos I've seen of turn-of-the-century seamstresses working row upon row of ancient sewing machines in sweatshops. At least Louie appears to keep this floor at a comfortable temperature.

"And what's on the fourth floor?" I ask as we finish our tour.

"Just offices and accounting. A lot of messy desks. Not worth the electricity to take the elevator up there."

So, back down to the first floor we go to meet our customers. It's now a bit after 9:30, and we have about a half-dozen men, most of whom appear to be young and middle-aged businessmen, perusing our merchandise.

"All I want you to do today is shadow me. Watch and learn."

So, this is exactly what I do. For the next eight hours, I follow Louie as he moves through the store closing customer after customer. Just as he described, most of his sales are made here on the first floor. Occasionally he takes a customer to the second floor to select from his exclusive merchandise.

I keep count and am impressed to see not one of Louie's prospects leaves without making a purchase. Twice he manages to sell a customer multiple suits, the final tab averaging more than $1,000. It doesn't take a mathematician to realize a 15 percent commission on just one of those sales is more than 50 percent higher than my base weekly salary. I now know for sure I made the right move.

After lunch, I tell Louie I'm ready to go to work.

"What? You sure? It's only been half a day."

"Let me have the next customer who comes through the door."

"You want it, you got it. Sink or swim."

Five minutes later, my test case strolls in. He looks to be in his late thirties. About five feet ten inches. Probably two hundred pounds. He wears a herringbone sports coat over an open-collared light-blue rayon shirt and has a gold chain around his neck.

"Good morning. Welcome to Sallinger's. How can I help you?"

"I'm just looking," the customer says with a forced smile.

I know this man's type. He hates "pushy" salesmen. He prefers to be left alone. I won't let this deter me. Instead, I tack from a different angle.

"I like your shoes" I point to his brown slip-ons. I can tell from the leather's sheen and lack of scuff marks near the soles that they are a recent purchase. "Florsheims?"

"That's right." There's still no warmth in his voice. "Got 'em last week."

"Those are good quality shoes. If you take care of them, they should last you for years. It always pays to buy quality."

The customer nods. He's not quite willing to connect with me.

"Do you work around here? I'm new to the area. Any restaurants you recommend?"

This appears to pique his interest. "The sandwich shop at the corner makes good hoagies. Barzini's has good Italian lunch specials. Spaghetti. Lasagna. But I'd pass on their pizza. If you want a good slice, go over to Leone's on Jefferson."

"Leone's. I'll remember that. Thanks. Now let me guess. You're a forty-six regular."

"Forty-four," the man corrects me with a frown.

"Are you looking for a suit or a sports jacket?"

"Sports jacket."

"We just got a new shipment in. Let's see what looks good on you."

I guide him over to a rack of sports coats. I pull out a navy blazer in size forty-four. "Let's try this on just for fit."

I hold the jacket while he slides his arms into the sleeves. He pulls the front taut and winces uncomfortably. "Bit tight. Especially in the armpits."

"Let's try a forty-six," I suggest, pulling out a jacket of a similar color. Again, I help him slip into the jacket. This time, as he adjusts it, he looks more comfortable.

"Feels good."

"Looks good, too." I can't help but smile. I was right about the size. Maybe Louie's skills are already rubbing off on me.

Half an hour later, my first customer leaves the store with a new sports coat and two matching ties. I look over to Louie, who's working on another sale. We catch each other's eye, and he gives me an approving nod. I'm off to a solid start.

Within two weeks, I have my rhythm down. A customer enters. I ask where he's from and how he heard about the store. I find something to compliment. His shirt. His shoes. His hat. It doesn't matter. I don't wait for him to tell me what he's looking for. I show him our newest merchandise or sale items. I tell him what will look good on him.

My enthusiasm is infectious, and he lets me take control. If he buys a suit, I throw in a free pocket square or lower-priced tie. He loves this. I tell him to send over his friends, to whom I will give a *special deal*. And nine times out of ten, he does. Customer volume increases. You can see it. You can hear it. The store is busy. Always buzzing. And my paycheck keeps increasing. I'm now making three times more than I ever have. It's a good feeling.

One Friday night, around my six-month anniversary, I check the store's sales records. Our dollar volume is up more than 100 percent. And I suspect it's virtually all because of me.

"Tony, I need to talk to you," Louie says a few weeks later after closing.

"Sure. What's up?"

"You're doing great. The truth is, you're the best salesman I've ever had."

"Thank you, Louie. It's great working here."

"My gut said I should hire you and my gut was right. In fact, my gut is almost always right. And you know what my gut is telling me now?

"What?"

"It's time I let you go."

I'm speechless. What the hell is going on? Louie just said I'm the best salesman he's ever had. Now he's firing me?

Chapter 25

LOUIE LAUGHS IN my face. "No, I'm not firing you," he says, scrunching his face in an expression of sheer incredulity. "I just said you're the best salesman I've ever had. Why would I fire you? You think I'm nuts?"

"You just said you're letting me go," I remind him.

"I am. I'm sending you to my other store."

I've long known that Louie owns a satellite store in Cambridge, just west of Boston. Close to Harvard University and the Massachusetts Institute of Technology (MIT), the location is perfect to cater to the professors, graduate students, and other upscale university employees who live and work in the area. I have never visited the Cambridge store, but I've always imagined it to be a busy—and profitable—establishment. So why is he sending me there?

"I think the people there are stealing from me. I want you to check the place out. Find out what's going on. Then report back. You know what I'm saying?"

"I know what you're saying," I reply, surprised to learn the Cambridge store is not the goldmine I imagined. "Should I tell them why I'm there?"

"Not right away," Louie says conspiratorially. "First I want you to case the joint."

"Case the joint?"

"You know, look around quiet-like. Pretend you're a customer. Watch how the staff behaves. Then, when you're ready, you can blow your cover."

"Blow my cover?"

"Reveal yourself. Jeez. Who the hell taught you English?"

After spending the weekend with Scotty, I arrive at the Cambridge Sallinger's around ten o'clock Monday morning. By now the store has been open for an hour, so my arrival should not attract undue attention.

The store itself is situated in the middle of a block of small commercial buildings, including men's and women's clothing stores, an art gallery, two trattoria-style restaurants, a jewelry store, a sporting goods store, a bookstore, and a pharmacy. Being close to two universities, the block has a lot of sidewalk traffic. I imagine it gets even busier during lunch hour. The front window contains a half-dozen suits and sports coats, as well as pairs of dress shoes and long-sleeved shirts. It's a generic display requiring little imagination or salesmanship.

Entering the Cambridge Sallinger's, I find it to be much smaller than our flagship store. It's perhaps a third the size of our main building's ground level. Strolling casually like I'm a typical looky-loo, I immediately notice that, organizationally, the place is a mess. Suits of different sizes hang together. Shirts on the table displays sit haphazardly and are not properly folded. The glass cases containing more expensive items, like men's jewelry and watches, look like they have not been cleaned or polished in months.

Standing by a rack of sports coats, I wait for a salesman to approach. No one does. I glance at the front counter to see two young employees talking animatedly. Dressed in sports coats and slacks, they don't appear to have noticed me or the other customer who entered after I did. If this is how this place is run, no wonder it's doing poorly. So much for casing the joint. Now it's time to blow my cover.

I walk up to the counter. "Hi there. Is one of you the manager?"

"Why?" The first one replies. He looks to be about twenty-five and has a thin face and slicked back hair. His complexion still bears scars from teenage acne.

"I'm here from the Washington Street store." I offer my business card. "Mr. Fagioli sent me. I'd like to speak to the manager."

"He's in the back," the other man says. He, too, appears to be in his late twenties but has about thirty pounds on his partner. His buttoned shirt collar looks to be about a size too small, causing his face to look perpetually flushed.

"Lead the way."

Clearly irritated by this interruption, the heavier salesman takes me through the store to a doorway beside the dressing room. Beyond it is a short, windowless corridor off which I see a supply room and a small manager's office. Here, surrounded by stacks of unorganized papers and lit by a single overhead fixture, sits a man in his late thirties. As he turns, I see he has short red hair and a bushy red mustache and wears thin, wire-rimmed glasses. A game show plays on a small black-and-white TV on the corner of his desk.

"Kenny, this guy wants to see you," my escort announces. "He's from the main store."

"Louie sent you?" Kenny says suspiciously, ignoring my hand. "He didn't say nothing to me about this."

"He wanted it to be a surprise," I say lightly, trying not to antagonize him.

"Yeah, well, I don't like surprises," Kenny says, a cold edge to his voice. Despite my best efforts, he's clearly antagonized. "So, what do you want?"

"Louie wants me to audit your operation. So, I'll need to take a look at your books."

"*What?*" Kenny sits back in his chair, his eyes boring into mine. "You walk in here, a complete stranger, and ask to look at my books? Screw you."

I had predicted some pushback from Kenny but am shocked by his outright hostility. "Maybe you should call Louie. Clear all this up," I suggest, my voice low and soothing.

"Or maybe you should just get the hell out of my store. And you can tell Louie I don't appreciate being spied on."

The heavier salesman exchanges a glance with Kenny, then wordlessly escorts me out onto the sidewalk like a bouncer ejecting an unruly barfly. Although I never get close to the store's ledgers, it's clear Louie has good reason to be suspicious; Kenny is a crook.

I head straight back to the Washington Street store where I tell Louie the story of my visit to Cambridge. He is not at all surprised. "I figured. I should have fired Kenny years ago. That store has been losing money forever. At this point, it's best to just shut it down."

"No."

"No?"

"Keep the store. It's a great location. It just needs better management." Suddenly, I realize I have just found my next white tiger. In a burst of confidence, I give Louie my pitch. "Let me run the place. Make me manager. I've already doubled sales here. If I can do even half that in Cambridge, I bet you'll be back in the black."

Louie is suddenly quiet. He's thinking it over. Before he can come up with any objections, I lay out my conditions.

"I want 100 percent control of the store. I will determine who gets hired and who gets fired. I will choose what merchandise to carry and in what volumes. I'll take full control—and full responsibility for the outcome."

I can't believe these words are coming out of my mouth. I haven't thought any of this through. I've never run a business before. I've never even managed other people. Who do I think I am to claim I can turn around a failing store? Especially one I visited for less than a half-hour.

"Fine. You want it, you got it. The store is yours. You'll have three months to turn it around. If you can't, I'm closing it for good. Sink or swim."

"Sink or swim," I reply.

I should be thrilled about this amazing opportunity, but I'm not. In fact, I'm scared. Maybe I have finally bitten off more than I can chew.

Chapter 26

I ARRIVE AT Sallinger's-Cambridge on Monday at 7:00 a.m. sharp, a full two hours before the store's scheduled opening. Louie has given me a key, so I have no trouble letting myself in. When I turn on the lights, I'm shocked—but not *that* shocked—to see the sales floor has been left in disarray from the previous weekend. Shirts are stacked haphazardly on display tables. Some even lie scattered on the linoleum floor. Clothes on the sales racks are painfully unorganized. Over in footwear, shoeboxes are stacked so randomly it looks like a toddler put it together.

With two full hours before anyone else is scheduled to arrive, I take the opportunity to straighten up the showroom to my professional standards. Starting with the suits, I make sure each is arranged neatly not only by size, but by color and shade. I do the same with the sports coats and slacks. Moving to the display tables, I neatly fold and stack the shirts, smaller sizes on top, larger ones on bottom. In the shoe department, I organize the boxes by manufacturer, style, color and size. Such attention to detail not only demonstrates pride and professionalism but also gives the shopper what will someday be known as a "user-friendly experience."

With a full half-hour remaining, I find my way to the supply room from which I grab a spray bottle of ammonia-based glass cleaner and several cloth rags I use to remove the thick layer of grime and grease from the glass display cases. Finally, I grab a mop, bucket and a bottle of floor cleaner and proceed to mop down the floor's linoleum tiles from wall to wall.

Shortly after nine o'clock, I hear a key click in the front door. I recognize the thin-faced salesman from my earlier visit. From Louie, I have learned his name is Jamil. Like me, he is a Lebanese immigrant, although his family came to America when he was ten years old, so any trace of an accent has long vanished. Jamil clearly recognizes me, too, for his reaction upon seeing me, mop still in hand, is one of concern rather than surprise.

"You again. What are you doing here?"

"Your job, it seems. This place was a mess."

Before Jamil can respond, Kenny, the red-haired manager with the bad attitude, enters. His reaction is as immediate as it is belligerent. "What the hell? Who let you in here?"

"I did. Louie gave me the key. I'm the new manager."

I pull an envelope from my pocket and hand it to Kenny, who immediately takes a step back, like it contains explosives. Steadying himself, he eyes me suspiciously, then fumbles with the envelope, removing the letter inside. Louie and I have debated whether to alert Kenny about this change in management beforehand or whether to spring it on him. We decided on the current strategy to avoid giving him time to cover his tracks—or seek retribution—before my arrival.

"This is bullshit," Kenny snarls, throwing the letter back in my face. "No way you're kicking me out."

He storms over to the front desk, picks up the phone, and punches in the number from memory.

"It's Kenny in Cambridge. I got some guinea here with a letter he claims you wrote naming him store manager…"

I recognize "guinea" as a slur word for Italian. With my dark, Mediterranean complexion, curly black hair, and vowel-ended last name, I've been mistaken for a son of Italy many times.

Whatever Louie is telling Kenny seems to be having the desired effect because the man's posture sags. His responses collapse into a series of quick "Yes, sirs" and "No, sirs." Finally, he lets the handset slip from his fingers back into the cradle, then turns back to me, seething.

"Fine. You want the store. It's yours. Enjoy."

"You still have a job if you want it. Right now, I just want everyone to carry on with business as usual. I'll be watching closely. If I decide to make changes, it'll be at the end of the week."

The sound of the door opening draws our attention to the entrance. It's the round-faced salesman—I have learned his name is Jeff—arriving a full ten minutes late.

Seeing the three of us gathered by the checkout counter, he walks over curiously. "What's going on?"

"Louie thinks we're not doing our jobs and we need a babysitter," Kenny says. "He's put this goomba in charge."

"First, my name is Tony Assali. You can call me *Mister* Assali." Usually, I prefer being called by my first time, but if I am to assume authority over these slackers, I'll need to take a tough approach. "Second, I'm Lebanese." I share a quick, knowing glance with Jamil. "And, finally, I'm your new manager. Kenny, can we speak in my office, please?"

"*Your* office?" Kenny sputters. I throw him a sharp, uncompromising look, and he immediately capitulates. "Fine."

Together, we retire to the manager's office. Once inside, I motion him to shut the door. "Let's pick this up where we left off last time. I want to see the store's books."

Kenny squirms like a student exposed for cheating on a test. Grumbling, he reaches onto a tall shelf to grab a thick leather-bound ledger.

"I think this is what you're looking for. If you have any questions, you let me know."

"Oh, I will," I assure him. I set the ledger on the desk and take a seat.

"So, what do you want me to do?"

"I want you to go out on the sales floor and sell some suits. You do know how to do that, don't you?"

"Sure. No problem."

Turning back to the desk, I finally allow myself to breathe. As uncomfortable as that confrontation was, it could have been much worse. At least no punches were thrown and no one is bleeding. Yet.

Over the next five days, I divide my time between trying to make sense of Kenny's convoluted bookkeeping and observing him and the two sales guys work the floor. At five o'clock, Jamil and Jeff leave and two new salespeople, Robert and Harold, replace them. Both are grad students from MIT using this job to help pay for their master's degrees. When not helping customers, their noses are deep in their textbooks. I can't help but admire their dedication to their studies; even so, by dividing their attention, they allow numerous sales opportunities to escape.

It quickly becomes obvious to me that while Kenny hasn't been embezzling, he's been a poor steward of the company's capital, buying volumes of high-margin merchandise, which has spent months on the showroom floor, while failing to keep the store's popular items in sufficient stock. He's also been spending lavishly on lunch and dinner food deliveries from the area's best restaurants, for which he cavalierly reimburses himself out of petty cash.

On Friday night, we close our doors at 8:00. I have asked Jamil and Jeff to stay, along with Robert, Harold, and Kenny. They're all aware this is when I plan to announce my personnel changes.

"This will just take a minute," I announce without fanfare. "As I said I would, I've been watching you closely over the past week, and I've decided—you're all fired."

"What? Why?"

"You're not salespeople. You're lazy, unmotivated, and rude, and you have no pride in yourselves or in this store. Jamil, you leave the shirt displays a mess and half the time you show up here unshaven. Jeff, you only talk to customers when they make an effort to ask for help, and you never even try to upsell. Rob, Harold, you are good kids, but you have to make a choice, do you want to earn master's degrees or do you want to sell clothes? You can't do both—or at least, you can't do both well. And Kenny, all these problems are a reflection of your poor leadership. You view this store as your personal fiefdom, to do with as you like. But this store doesn't belong to you. It belongs to Louie. You serve him. We all do. And in that respect, you have failed to live up to your side of the bargain. I have your final paychecks here, as well as severance checks equal to two weeks' pay. Good luck on your next ventures, wherever they may be."

Opening the front door, I hold it wide as my now ex-sales team shambles out, heads bowed. As he approaches me, Jamil stops to plead for mercy.

"Come on, Mr. Assali. I'm Lebanese, too. Gimme a break. We're family."

"I have my own family. And, frankly, if any of them produced your kind of sales numbers, I'd fire them, too. But I'll tell you what. Come back when you learn how to sell suits, and I'll think about giving you a job."

"You're an ass, you know that?"

"I've been called worse." I shrug.

Kenny is last to leave. Instead of being hostile, his manner is surprisingly contrite. "You probably did the right thing. I did what I could with these losers, but you can't get blood from a turnip. You know what I'm saying?"

Actually, I have no idea what he's saying. I've never tried to get blood from a turnip, nor am I ever likely to try.

"Anyway, so I was hoping, for my next job, could you at least write me a letter of recommendation?"

I don't even dignify Kenny's ludicrous request with a response.

The next morning, I meet with Louie at the flagship store on Washington Street. As soon as I enter, the little man goes ballistic.

"Tell me it's not true you fired everybody," he demands.

"It's true."

"Are you crazy? Are you *pazzo*? What are you going to do? Run the store by yourself? Or are you trying to bankrupt me?"

"It's okay, Louie. It's all under control. I'm going to hire new people. People I can trust. People I can train. People I can mold into super salesmen. Remember, you gave me total control."

"You're right, I did. Only here's the thing: If the store keeps losing money, there's going to be one more person fired, and that's *you*."

"That's not going to happen. Trust me."

That afternoon, I call my brother Joe, already at work at The Rib Room. "How'd you like to come work for me as a salesman?"

"Me? Why me?"

"Because you've got the right look. The right attitude. Business runs in the Assali blood, and I know you've got it. Besides, I know I can trust you."

"What about Little Tony?" Joe asks, referring to my brother-in-law who still works with Joe as a busboy.

"He's a nice guy, but his English is bad, and he just doesn't have the look."

When you're selling men's fashions, you have to have *the look*. This doesn't mean you have to have the chiseled features of a Hollywood movie star, but your posture, bearing, and attitude have to say, "I've got it all together, and I can teach you how you can, too." Ultimately, the role of a fashion salesman is to be the person the customer wants to become. Louie knew I had *the look* when he saw me. When dressed properly, Joe has *the look*, too. But Little Tony, while not unattractive, always comes across as mousy and beaten down. He doesn't have an appearance you'd want to emulate, so he's not going on my "hire" list.

My next call I make in person. It's to my mother. Being recently widowed, she spends far too much time alone, pining for joys of time gone by. She needs to get out, to apply her talents to something constructive. And I tell her as much.

"So, what do you want me to do, go work in a factory?"

"No. I want you to come work for me. You're good with figures. You can be my bookkeeper. Help with bills, tracking, and ordering inventory. You'll love it."

How can she say "no" to her first-born son? She agrees to give it a try.

I also need a cashier. Someone bright and attractive. As it happens, I've just moved in with another girl named Maria. She has a daughter Scotty's age, and they get along fine. I offer her the job and she's more than happy to take it.

"Now I'll know what you really do all day," she teases.

So, my small but mighty team is now in place. Can I make the store profitable? I have three months to find out. If not, I'm not only going to be out of a job, but I'll be taking my family and girlfriend down with me. Whoever said you should never mix business and family may have had a point. But it's too late for me to turn back now. As Louie said, it's sink or swim.

Chapter 27

I HAVE HEARD that in real estate, three factors contribute to a property's value: location, location, location. By that account, Sallinger's-Cambridge should be a cash machine. As noted earlier, the store is convenient to both Harvard University and MIT, two of America's most prestigious schools and training grounds for tomorrow's leaders in business, government, and science. Some of America's top families send their children to these institutions, not only for a world-class education but also for the cachet a degree from these schools provides. Their faculties are likewise world class.

And yet, as I slowly discover, most of the customers who frequent Sallinger's-Cambridge do not hail from either of these hallowed institutions. While we may sell to the occasional Harvard undergrad or MIT teaching assistant, the vast majority of my customers are workers from a nearby shoe factory. Most of these men are poor Portuguese immigrants who come to Sallinger's looking for suits to wear to church on Sundays. Such business wear is not part of their daily wardrobe, nor do these men see a need to invest heavily in suits and slacks they are likely to wear only a couple dozen times in any given year.

To make the situation more challenging, most of the store's customers don't have credit cards or even credit history. They deal in cash. The irony is, most of our merchandise is too expensive for them to buy without credit. No wonder this store has been losing money.

My first week as manager, I experience just how frustrating this can be. I'm working with a thirty-five-year-old Portuguese immigrant who has expressed an interest in one of our Sallinger's-branded suits. He's tried on the pants, vest, and jacket, and all will fit perfectly with minor alterations. Then he looks at the price tag: $250.

"Too expensive. I can't afford this."

"How much can you afford?" I ask, turning him at an angle so he can get a flattering view of himself in the full-length mirror, hoping to create a level of enthusiasm to overcome his price objection.

"One hundred dollars."

This puts me in an impossible situation. The wholesale cost of the suit is $150. To sell it for $100 would be to take a $50 loss. That's not how this store—*any* store—is going to stay in business.

At the same time, I see the man is not taking off the suit. He likes how he looks in it. He likes how he feels in it. This tells me that he wants to buy the suit; he's just waiting to see if he can get a good deal.

I make some quick mental calculations, devising what I believe is an attractive counteroffer. "Here's what I can do. I can give you the suit, plus a matching dress shirt and tie, all for just $300. All you have to do is put down $150 now, then come in and pay me $10 a week for fifteen weeks. I won't charge any interest. But there's one other condition. You have to tell your friends so I can give them the same deal."

I barely have time to blink before there's a wad of $20 bills in my hand.

So how was I able to make a $300 sale when the customer initially offered just a third of that? First, he knew he was buying quality merchandise. He had tried on the suit and knew it felt solidly tailored. And he understands it's better to buy a good

$250 suit he can wear for ten years than a cheap $100 suit he would be lucky to wear for two.

Second, by purchasing a matching dress shirt and tie, he has a full ensemble ready to wear. He has no more decisions to make. Third, the $10-per-week payment I have requested is money he may miss, but the sum is low enough he can afford it. It's not going to break him. But most important of all, I showed him trust. I showed him respect. I made him feel important. If he chooses not to ever come back and leaves me on the hook for $150, how am I going to find him? He knows this but does not want to violate the trust I put in him.

And what do I get out of this? Of course, there is the sale. Immediately receiving $150 in cash covers the wholesale cost of the suit. But more importantly, I now have a customer who is guaranteed to revisit the store every week for the next fifteen weeks! I am betting he will choose to make additional purchases as a result. And when he tells his friends about the deal I gave him, I'm likely to get even more customers. It's a win-win situation for both of us. And it works.

Two weeks later, when we open at 9:00 a.m. Monday, there is literally a line down the street, all Portuguese factory workers wanting to buy new suits for Sunday churchgoing. Back in Beirut, I rarely attended church, but I know everyone in a congregation judges everyone else, especially when it comes to attire. Perhaps it's not a very Christian thing to do, but it's human nature, and is part of what holds communities together. Apparently, the behavior is the same here in America.

As promised, I offer each of my new customers the same deal I offered the first one: 50 percent down, the rest on credit with $10 due in person every seven days. The customers are ready for this, so there's no resistance or haggling, just sale after sale after sale. I instructed Joe to make the same offer to the customers he serves, and he enjoys successes similar to mine.

When December 1 arrives, we are down to just 25 percent of our usual inventory. Shortly after lunch hour, the time when we do the most business, I get a phone call from Louie. "You did it, you crazy bastard."

"Did what?"

"I just finished going over your sales numbers for the quarter. Not only are you in the black, but also, you've sold more suits than I have in my entire life, including here in Boston."

Due to my success, I get to keep my job, and Louie gives me a generous holiday bonus. This year, Scotty will not be wanting for toys.

Christmas is two weeks away when a man I have never seen before enters the store. He's shorter than me and a bit gaunt in the face, with thinning brown hair streaked with gray. He wears corduroy pants and a heavy woolen coat appropriate for the season. He does not look like one of my Portuguese regulars although some degree of Mediterranean ancestry is obvious from his light olive complexion and pronounced nose.

"Welcome to Sallinger's. Are you looking for something for the holiday season?"

"Yes, for church," he says, his voice raspy. "I have a suit, but it's fifteen years old. It's time for something new."

"I'm sure I can find you just what you're looking for," I assure him, escorting him to the rack of suits at the back of the store. "By the way, how did you hear about us? Did someone refer you?"

"No. I got on the wrong bus. When I figured out I was going the wrong way, I got off right in front of your store." He points to the metro sign on the sidewalk beyond our display window. "The bus I need isn't due for another twenty minutes, so I figured I'd drop in and look around."

"Maybe it's God's will you buy a suit from me today," I say lightly.

"Father Caulder might agree."

"He's your priest?"

"Yes. At St. Anthony's."

"I've never been there. Is it close?"

"It's on the far east end of town, near East Cambridge. Not much to see. It's old. One of the oldest in this area. It's pretty much falling apart. And losing parishioners. So, there's not enough money to make repairs."

Suddenly, I'm hit with an epiphany. A vision as if God himself is speaking to me. This is another white tiger to pursue. Not just to do well. *But to do good.*

Chapter 28

AS SOON AS the Christmas season is over and 1976 prepares to turn into 1977, I arrange to meet with Father Caulder, the resident pastor of St. Anthony's church. Arriving, I can see the building does indeed need a serious facelift. The floor tiles are worn and cracked. The stone walls and ceiling bear evidence of serious leaks from the roof above. The wooden pews are faded and scarred. Many of the windows are missing pieces of stained glass that have been replaced with corrugated cardboard.

I meet Fr. Caulder in his office, located toward the rear of the failing building. The priest appears to be in his early fifties, with a round, friendly face, sparkling green eyes, and long, thick gray hair. He wears the traditional black clerical shirt and white collar. When he stands to shake my hand, I see he's a tall man, well over six feet.

"Welcome to St. Anthony's," he says in a voice I find surprisingly high-pitched for a man of his size. "How may I help you today?"

"As I said on the phone, I'm a friend of one of your parishioners, Vincent Montez," I explain, referring to the customer I served earlier this month. "I manage Sallinger's in Cambridge. I helped him buy the suit he wore to Christmas mass."

"Ah, yes, Vincent." Father Caulder's eyes stare off into space as his mind retrieves a memory. "I remember. He was quite proud of that suit."

"When we talked, he mentioned this building is in serious need of remodeling."

"That's not exactly a state secret," the priest says with a laugh. "Unfortunately, we're a small congregation and getting smaller every month. Our members tend to be working people, most of whom live paycheck to paycheck, so contributions to the building fund tend to be modest. Still, we make do with what we can."

"I'd like to help."

"You're a Catholic?"

"Lebanese Maronite."

"Close enough." He smiles.

"Here's how I can help," I say, beginning a speech I've now rehearsed in my head more than a dozen times. "I'll give every customer you send me a 10 percent discount on each suit he buys. I'll then donate that 10 percent difference to your church's building fund."

"You mean, you want me to refer customers to you? That's not exactly our mission here."

"As I understand it, an important part of your mission is to foster community," I counter, ready for this objection. "The customers you send will understand they are contributing to the church's rehabilitation, to keeping this congregation strong and healthy. And they'll just happen to do it at the same time they're getting a good deal on a quality suit."

"And you get more customers…"

"To contribute money, I have to make money. And, of course, my boss gets a big fat tax deduction at the end of the year. We all benefit."

My honesty appears to have the desired effect, as Fr. Caulder relaxes. "So how do we make this happen?"

"I will write a letter explaining the offer, which you can then distribute to your parishioners. They must bring the letter in to get the discount. And there will be a time limit. I can only run the promotion until Easter."

The priest is silent now as he runs the scenario through his mind. I decide to fill in the awkward silence by pointing to the cracked plaster above.

"Your ceiling will look so much better when it's repaired."

"Deal."

As soon as I get back to the store, I type up the promotional letter that will go over Fr. Caulder's signature and mail it to St. Anthony's church. On New Year's Day, I close down the Cambridge store and spend the next eight hours marking up the prices of our suits by 10 percent.

Is this cheating? Let's consider the situation. If Louie saw our profits suddenly drop by 10 percent, he would put the brakes on this promotion. Then we would get fewer sales, and the church would not get its money. Who gains from *that*? No one. This way, customers get the clothes they want, we get the profits we need to stay in business, and the church gets the funds it needs for repairs. Like I told Fr. Caulder, we all benefit.

On January 2, I open our doors at 9:00 a.m. sharp and am delighted to find four Portuguese men waiting on the sidewalk.

"Welcome to Sallinger's," I say, ushering them in. I see each carries a folded piece of paper, presumably their copy of Fr. Caulder's letter.

"Is it true you're offering 10 percent off your suits?" one asks. "And that you're donating that to St. Anthony's church?"

"Absolutely. You have that in writing."

I remind the group of my other offer: If they don't have credit, they can buy their suits for a down payment of just 50 percent of the total cost and then pay off the balance in $10 weekly installments.

"I haven't bought a new suit since my wedding twenty years ago," another man says. "I could really use this."

"Then come right this way." I motion them to the back of the store. "We'll make sure you get you a suit worth waiting for."

I'm fitting one of my new customers with a jacket when three more men walk through the front door, each carrying the telltale piece of paper. I send Joe over to help. He's just started talking to them when two more customers arrive. This is going to be a busy day.

In the weeks between New Year's Day and Easter, business explodes. The Catholic community in and around Cambridge is close-knit, and word of our store and its support of St. Anthony's grows far beyond the church's congregation. In mid-March, my mother, who has been keeping the store's books since I evicted Kenny and his crew, calls me into her office.

"We're running low on stock."

"You mean suits?"

"*Everything*. Suits. Shirts. Shoes. Ties. At the rate we're going, we soon won't have anything to sell."

"Have you talked to Louie about this?"

"He's got his tailors working overtime but there's only so much they can produce."

Having a supply that can't keep up with demand is a great problem to have. But it's still a problem. And problems require solutions. I get Louie on the phone to review our situation.

"Call other men's stores in the area," I suggest. "See if we can buy their overflow. Based on our numbers, we must be siphoning off a lot of their traffic, so I bet they have a lot of standing inventory they'd love to get rid of."

"We don't sell our competition's labels!"

"So, we'll change out the labels. How long can that take?"

Seeing we have no other choice, Louie agrees to call around. That afternoon, during our usual post-lunch hour slump, I leave the store in Joe's hands while I go across town to visit St. Anthony's. Entering, I'm thrilled to see a towering scaffold in place and workmen high above repairing the ceiling.

"Your contributions have been a true blessing," Fr. Caulder says, shaking my hand.

"The blessings have been all mine." With that, I reach into my pocket and pull out an envelope.

"Another check?"

"Business has been good."

Fr. Caulder opens the unsealed flap and looks inside. He smiles. Within is a check for $1,555.

"This will definitely help us get ready for Easter."

"Speaking of Easter, I talked to my boss, and he agreed we don't have to end the promotion on Easter Sunday." In reality, I haven't spoken to Louie at all about this, but am confident my numbers will more than satisfy any objections he may have. "We'd like to keep it going indefinitely. Make it permanent. Your parishioners will continue to get 10 percent off, and that 10 percent will continue to come back here to the church."

"Bless you. You—and your boss—are truly generous men."

"As ye sow, so shall ye reap," I say, quoting Galatians. "Or, how do they say it now? What goes around comes around."

Call it karma, kismet, or cosmic payback, my putting good vibes out into the universe has indeed yielded enormous dividends for me, the church, and my customers. The week after Easter, I receive a letter from Cardinal Bernard Francis Law, archbishop of the Boston archdiocese, personally thanking me for my donations to St. Anthony's. When I proudly show this letter to my mother and brother both are overwhelmed.

"It's like a blessing from God," my mother says.

Of course, in life, nothing is certain but change. And in early spring 1977, a call comes for me at the store. It's my immigration attorney, Martin Green.

"Hi, Martin. What's going on?"

"It's about your citizenship application," he says. I immediately tense up. It's been years since I filed for citizenship. A week hasn't gone by when I haven't wondered whether I'd be approved or have my visa revoked and be sent back to Lebanon.

"And?" I ask cautiously, wary of what the news might be.

"They've made a decision. I suggest you sit down."

Chapter 29

AS INSTRUCTED, I find a chair and sit. I'm ready for Martin to tell me my citizenship application has been delayed… or even rejected. If so, will my work visa be renewed? Will I even be able to stay in the United States? The greatest irony would be if I had to return to Lebanon while my family was allowed to stay in America.

"I come bearing good news," Martin says. "Your application was approved."

"But I thought you were gonna tell me something bad." My heart is beating so fast in my ears I can barely hear the rest of what Martin has to say.

"Not at all. You have an appointment on June 8, to take your citizenship test. There's a written portion, and then they'll ask you some questions. I'm sure you'll pass with flying colors. Then you're a U.S. citizen."

This is the best news I can possibly imagine. When I tell my mother and Joe, they are equally ecstatic. We jump and cry and laugh like we've just won the lottery. This is why I was sent to America.

For the rest of the day, I can barely tend to business. Even as I wait on customers, my mind wanders off to thoughts of the test ahead of me. What kind of questions will they ask? Will I be prepared? What happens if I don't pass? There is simply too much at stake for me to fail now.

Fortunately, Martin is kind enough to send me test preparation materials that I can study well ahead of the examination. Over the next several weeks, I get up early and stay up late studying American history, civics, government, the Constitution, and geography.

When did America declare its independence? July 4, 1776. *What European power was America's ally against Great Britain during the Revolutionary War?* France. *What are the three branches of the Federal Government?* The executive (president), legislative (Congress) and judicial (Supreme Court).

What do they call the system by which each branch can control and limit the powers of the other? Checks and balances. *When is federal Election Day?* The first Tuesday in November.

The more I read about the Constitution, the more I'm amazed this country works as well as it does. With power distributed among so many institutions, and with so many people having to agree before anything happens, it's amazing anything gets done at all. It's almost as if the Federal Government were designed to fail. As for the Electoral College, no matter how much I read about it, I still don't get it. Why not just elect the president by popular vote like every other country? On the other hand, the first ten amendments—the Bill of Rights—are magnificent. They ensure Americans far more freedoms than you'll find practically anywhere else in the world. This is why I love this country. This is what makes America great.

On June 8, 1977, I go downtown to the John F. Kennedy Federal Building on Sudbury Street to take my naturalization test. The written portion contains one hundred questions. My studying pays off. None of the questions pose a challenge, and I pass with a perfect score. Then I sit before an immigration officer who asks me ten more questions.

"How many U.S. senators are there?"

"One hundred."

"If the president can no longer serve, who assumes his office?"

"The vice president."

"What are the two major political parties in the United States?"

"The Republicans and the Democrats."

"How old do citizens have to be to vote for president?"

"Eighteen."

"What ocean is on the west coast of the United States?"

"The Pacific."

"Why does the American flag have fifty stars?"

"One for each state."

"The idea of self-government is contained in the first three words of the U.S. Constitution. What are they?

"We the people."

"What is the economic system of the United States?"

"Capitalism."

"We elect senators for how many years?"

"Six."

"How many justices sit on the U.S. Supreme Court?"

"Nine."

Another perfect score.

I'm ready to leave when the officer asks me another question.

"Mr. Assali, have you ever been convicted of a crime?"

"No," I answer honestly. But the officer can see I am nervous.

"Have you ever been *charged* with a crime?" he asks.

"No," I repeat, "not charged."

Now he seems suspicious. "Have you ever committed a crime for which you were not charged?"

I would make a terrible secret agent. In less than a minute, I crack.

"I'm living with a woman who is not my wife," I confess, then quickly add, "But there is no sex. We are like roommates."

"Jesus, Mary, and Joseph," the officer sighs, annoyed. I know living out of wedlock is not technically a crime, but there's nothing like being questioned by a man in uniform to make you feel guilty.

Having passed the test, I am ushered into a large room with fifty other immigrants who, like me, are ready to become citizens. Looking around, I see people of all kinds. Men. Women. White. Black. Brown. Asian. Some, like me, are dressed like typical Americans in suits and ties. Others wear attire from their native countries. I recognize fashions from Africa, the Caribbean, India, and South America. A true melting pot.

A female judge wearing her judicial robe appears at the front of the room. "Everyone, if you will please raise your right hand," she instructs. We all do so. "Now, repeat after me. I hereby declare, on oath, that I absolutely and entirely renounce and abjure all allegiance and fidelity to any foreign prince, potentate, state, or sovereignty of whom or which I have heretofore been a subject or citizen…"

As one, we repeat the words as they are spoken. I have no problem renouncing allegiance to Lebanon. What government previously existed there is now long gone.

"…that I will support and defend the Constitution and laws of the United States of America against all enemies foreign and domestic…"

As I repeat these words, my voice becomes stronger and more assured.

"…that I will bear true faith and allegiance to the same; that I will bear arms on behalf of the United States when required by the law; that I will perform noncombatant service in the armed forces of the United States when required by the law; and that I take this obligation freely without any mental reservation or purpose of evasion, so help me God."

"So, help me, God."

"Congratulations," says the judge. "You are now citizens of the United States of America."

A huge cheer erupts from the group. And then, spontaneously, someone begins to sing "The Star-Spangled Banner." Immediately, more people join in. By the end of the first verse, we are all singing our hearts out.

"Oh, say, does that star-spangled banner yet wave… O'er the land of the free/And the home of the brave!"

I have never felt prouder.

Following the ceremony, my mother, Joe, my sisters, and I go to a nearby Greek restaurant to celebrate. (In Boston, Greek cuisine is the closest we can find to Lebanese at this time.) I tell everyone why I am so glad to be an American.

"Here, as long as you follow the law and pay your taxes, you can do whatever you want. *Whatever* you want. There is no one stopping you. 'The pursuit of happiness,' says the Declaration of Independence. That is why I am here." I turn to my family members. "And now that I am an American citizen, I can officially sponsor the rest of you. You can all be Americans soon. We are children of Lebanon, but America is now our home."

Chapter 30

A MONTH AFTER acquiring my American citizenship, I take another major legal step that will forever change the course of my life: I formally divorce Sara. During our lengthy separation, I have been dating regularly, but now, at age twenty-seven, I can see the end of my third decade looming on the horizon and something is beginning to change. I realize I am not a teenager anymore. I'm a divorced man with a seven-year-old son whose welfare is my sole and sacred responsibility. I am also the manager of a successful menswear store, and I have employees who count on me and a boss who trusts me to protect his sizable investment. And I am now a legal American citizen, with all of the rights, privileges, and responsibilities that go with it.

I guess I'm growing up and feeling the need to settle down. This change of attitude does not go unnoticed by my family.

"I know just the girl for you," my brother-in-law Tony says one evening as we're eating dinner at my house. "Her name is Karla Baccash."

"Lebanese?" I ask.

"Her family, yes, but she was born here."

I shake my head wearily but Tony persists. "She's pretty and she's smart and she loves dancing…"

I cut him off. "Nope. I'm through dating Lebanese girls. When I date a Lebanese girl, it's like going out with one of my cousins."

"Well, I think she sounds wonderful," my mother interjects. "At least *meet* her. Take her out for coffee. What've you got to lose?"

I have no interest in Karla, but how can I say no to my mother? Tony arranges for me to meet her later that week at a coffee shop two blocks from Sallinger's- Cambridge. The way I imagine it, we'll exchange small talk for a half-hour or so, casually part ways, then never see each other again. I will have done my due diligence, my mother will be satisfied, and my romantic life will again be my own.

The appointed day arrives. Walking into the coffee shop, I scan the crowded seating area and immediately notice a young woman alone at a booth facing the entrance. If this is Karla, I'm impressed. She has dark hair and hazel eyes. She wears a designer blouse and jacket well-tailored to her elegantly slender frame.

"Karla?"

"Tony?"

We shake hands as I take a seat across from her. Immediately a waitress appears and I order coffee.

"So. How do you know the other Tony?"

"Tony's dating my roommate. He tells me you manage Sallinger's."

"That's right. It's all mine," I say proudly. "If you know anyone who needs a good deal on a quality suit, you know where to send them. I have nothing but happy customers."

"Tony said you were a great salesman." She laughs. It's a pretty laugh.

"And what do you do?"

"I work for my dad. He owns an engineering company. I'm his receptionist."

"Do you enjoy it?"

"I do. It's a good company. My hope is to work my way up and one day run it myself."

"That's ambitious."

"I don't pretend to understand the technical side of it, but I do understand the business aspects," she says, now engaged. "And I'm taking night courses to earn my business degree. I'm very serious about this."

Karla may be ethnic Lebanese, but the way she speaks is pure native-born American. There's not even a trace of an accent. That appeals to me. As do her ambition and self-confidence. To me, she is both familiar and exotic.

What I thought would be a half-hour turns into two. We agree to meet later that week for dinner. I suggest a local steakhouse, and she accepts. Our first official date is as smooth and effortless as our initial meeting. We are never at a loss for conversation. She knows I have a seven-year-old boy and asks to meet him.

"I think it may be too early. We've just started to know each other."

"And I'm looking forward to learning more. But it's important to see what I'm getting myself into."

So, we agree Karla will come to the apartment to meet Scott that Saturday. As soon as she arrives, he begins talking non-stop about the movie we saw three weeks earlier. Ever since we saw it, Scott has been obsessed with it.

"Have you seen *Star Wars*?"

"Actually, I have," she says. "What was your favorite part? The Millennium Falcon? The trash-compactor? The droids?"

"The jump to hyperspace!"

Karla makes a big "whooshing" sound, to his pure delight.

I'm no big science fiction fan. Actually, I kind of find space movies silly. Rubber monsters, circus costumes, and bad acting. But clearly, she and Scott are bonding. That I do like.

Over the next month, Karla and I agree to move in together. But first, she asks me to meet her parents.

"Your parents? Now, this is a serious step."

"Don't let them intimidate you." she says, which immediately warns me I am likely to be intimidated.

That Friday, we drive to her parents' house in Salem, forty miles north of Boston. We enter a neighborhood of sprawling estates comprised of vast, well- manicured lawns. After passing mansion after mansion, we pull into the long driveway of what can only be described as a European-style castle.

"You told me your father owned an engineering company…"

"A very *successful* engineering company."

We park in the large circular driveway behind a late model Mercedes-Benz sedan. We're not even to the front door when it opens and a tall man with a full head of curly brown hair and a bushy brown mustache steps out.

"Karla!" he cries as she runs into his open arms.

"Papa, I'd like you to meet Tony."

Her father offers his hand and grips mine firmly. "It's great to meet you," he says in an American-tinged Lebanese accent. "My girl has wonderful things to say about you. She says you're a real up-and-comer."

"I do my best," I say, with more than a touch of embarrassment.

"Come, let's go inside." Mr. Baccash throws one of his big arms over my shoulders. "I can guarantee tonight you will not go home hungry."

The interior of the Baccash house is tastefully decorated with traditional furniture attended by numerous mid-nineteenth century antiques. A large, formal portrait of the family hangs over the impressive stone fireplace. It gives the living room a stately, Old World ambiance.

Mr. Baccash introduces me to Karla's mother, a short, attractive Lebanese woman from whom Karla obviously inherited her infectious smile. The action quickly moves to the family room where I'm offered a glass of wine and a plateful of authentic Lebanese appetizers: pita and hummus, grape leaves, and charred eggplant.

"I feel like I'm in my mother's kitchen back in Beirut."

"Speaking of Beirut, what do you hear of things back home?" Mr. Baccash inquires.

I have little first-, second-, or even third-hand news to report since I get most of my info about the civil war from Walter Cronkite.

"You were lucky to get your whole family to America," he says. "Even with all my contacts, I still could not get all my family out. Many died."

"I'm so sorry," I say, genuinely moved.

The rest of the evening goes remarkably well. At her parents' urging, I go into great detail about my childhood, my parents' decision to send me to America, and the various jobs I've held over the past seven years. They seem impressed by my energy and entrepreneurial spirit, attributes Mr. Baccash credits for his own remarkable success. I believe he sees me as a kindred spirit, an impression Karla confirms as we drive home later that night.

"My parents like you. They think you will make a good husband."

"*Husband?* To anyone in particular?"

Karla laughs her delightful laugh. For the first time since divorcing, I can again see myself in the role of husband and father. Two weeks later, I move out of our family's big rental house in Stoneham and into the townhouse Karla rents. Scott joins us. Six months after that, Karla and I decide to get married.

For Karla's family, the wedding is a big deal—so big that, after our church wedding, we end up having two receptions. The first is at Bishop's, the only authentic Mediterranean restaurant in eastern Massachusetts. My family, deprived of Lebanese cuisine since leaving Beirut, goes crazy over the fresh, highly seasoned kebabs and other eastern Mediterranean specialties. The following day, there is a second reception at the Baccash mansion.

There the dinner features a main course of steak and lobster. Karla's father introduces me to several men who turn out to be prominent local politicians. Clearly, Mr. Baccash is well connected. And although he is nothing but smiles, he occasionally throws me a look that says, "Hurt my daughter and I will kill you." I suspect he would not hesitate to do so.

During this second reception, I notice Joe spending a lot of time with Karla's younger brother, David, a thin, gangly young man with sharp, delicate features. Joe is normally shy with strangers, but the two seem to hit it off.

Later that night, I take Joe aside.

"What were you and David talking about?" I ask.

"Stuff," Joe turns away, refusing to make eye contact. His evasiveness concerns me. Even as kids, Joe was always a terrible liar. Whenever he'd look away or become physically restless, I knew he was trying to evade responsibility for some kind of mischief. I mention my observations to Karla, and she shocks me with her response.

"David is gay," she explains. I don't know the meaning of this word. "Homosexual," she explains.

"Joe is not homosexual," I respond, perhaps a bit too forcefully. "Why would David be interested in him?"

"Maybe he just likes Joe as a friend. You've had female friends you weren't interested in sexually, didn't you?"

I have to think about this. The truth is, I've never had a girl *friend*. If I found a girl interesting, I usually tried to take her to bed. Not that I was going to admit this to Karla. It would only make her jealous. If her brother was anything like me, then Joe was best advised to stay clear of him.

The wedding and receptions behind us, Karla and I enjoy the next week, honeymooning in New York City. This is my first time in The Big Apple, and it turns out to be just as big and crazy and awesome as I dreamed it to be. We see two Broadway shows, *Annie* and *Man of La Mancha*, and I am inspired by Don

Quixote's call to "dream the impossible dream." You could say the song is the story of my life. We also dine at spectacular restaurants, several of which put Boston's fine cuisine to shame.

After the honeymoon, we spend several weeks house hunting, and eventually, I buy my first house, a two-story, four-bedroom home on five acres of land outside Salem, New Hampshire, a small city just north of the Massachusetts border. I'm able to buy the house for $40,000. My mortgage is $600 a month, which for me is a sizable commitment, especially since I'm still paying for the rental house in Stoneham. But I believe I can grow into it. And I am proud to finally own my little piece of the American dream.

Over the next month, Karla, Scott, and I set up house. Five days a week, I drive the thirty-three miles to Cambridge, manage the store from 9:00 a.m. until 8:00 p.m., then drive home, usually arriving just in time to put Scott to bed and have a late dinner with Karla. On Saturday, I go in at 9:00 a.m. but leave at 1:00 p.m., delegating Joe to manage the store so I can spend time with my family.

Life is good. Then, one summer day, my mother arrives late to work and informs me Joe will not be coming in.

"What's wrong? Is he sick?"

"I don't know," my mother confesses, shaking her head. "He was out late last night, and this morning he just refused to get out of bed."

"Probably hung over," I say with obvious disapproval. Joe is very much like I was at his age, a party animal. But he lacks discipline.

"It's more than that. He's been acting strange lately."

"What do you mean, strange?"

"He used to be happy and talk all the time. Now he's always gloomy and sad. You must have noticed this. You work with him every day."

The truth is, I've been so busy running the business I haven't paid much attention to Joe's demeanor. I did notice his sales numbers falling over the past few weeks, but I attributed that to the warm weather. You have to work twice as hard to sell suits when the temperature tops 80 degrees, and Joe has never had the kind of initiative to push it to the limit.

"Maybe you should talk to him," my mother suggests.

"I will."

"Today. After work."

Never one to disobey my mother—not about which women to date nor about intervening with my brother—I drive to the Stoneham house after work. There I find Joe in his bedroom playing a new Atari 2600 video game. I tell him about Mom's concerns.

"I'm fine," Joe says, never taking his eyes off the pixelated TV screen.

"You don't look fine," I say. And he doesn't. His skin is sallow. His eyes are ringed with red. There's an uncharacteristic twitchiness to his movements.

"Are you taking drugs?" I ask him straight-out.

"Screw you," he says, shocking me with sudden hostility. "Leave me alone."

Just then, I hear the jarring blare of a car horn. I turn to look out the window. Alarmed, Joe jumps out of bed and runs over. A late model jet-black Ford Mustang sits idling in the driveway. I recognize the driver as David.

"I have to go." Joe pushes me aside and heads for the door.

Red warning lights flashing wildly in my brain, I follow him down the stairs but I'm not as fast. By the time I reach the front door, he's already in the seat beside David, and they're peeling out of the driveway.

Later that night, I tell Karla what I saw. Her response adds to my anxiety.

"A year ago, David was caught dealing drugs. Nothing serious. Just pot and some prescription meds. But he stopped. He promised me."

"I don't believe it," I say, fighting to control my temper. "I think he is selling drugs to Joe."

"I'll talk to him about it."

I nod, but I doubt David will be forthcoming.

At work, Joe's performance continues deteriorating. He shows up late, if at all. When he does make an appearance, he ignores our customers, putting the full onus on me to drive sales. When I confront him, he either assaults me with profanity or just turns and sulks away in wounded silence.

I'm considering forcing Joe to get a medical evaluation when, at 3:00 a.m., I'm jarred awake by the ringing phone. This is the same time of night I got my father's call from Greece two years ago. Yet I already know in my gut this is not going to be good news.

"Hello?"

"Is this Antoine Assali?" the male voice at the other end asks.

"Yes. Who is this?"

"I'm Sgt. Owens with the Massachusetts State Police. Are you the brother of Joseph Assali?"

Now my mind is reeling. What has Joe done? Was he caught with drugs? Does he need me to bail him out of jail?

"Yes. What's wrong? What happened?"

"Sir, I'm sorry to have to tell you, but there's been an accident."

Chapter 31

IT IS COOL and crisp the afternoon of Joe's funeral. We bury him next to my father. I do my best to comfort my mom, but she can't stop crying throughout the whole service at the St. Patrick community church in Stoneham. She's only been in America for two years, yet she's already had to bury two family members. The irony is, this is where we were supposed to be safe.

The police filled me in on all of the details when I went to claim my brother. Joe fell asleep at the wheel of his car, swerved into the breakdown lane and crashed, snapping his neck. He was DOA to the hospital. When the coroner analyzed his blood, they found cocaine in his system.

Unlike my mother, I am not merely overcome by sadness. All through the graveside service, I glare across at David, standing with the rest of the Baccash family and staring blankly into the distance. I have no doubt he was the one who sold Joe the drugs. Now I want to snap *his* neck.

Only Karla gripping my hand prevents me from storming across the lawn and fulfilling my violent fantasy. Instead, I turn my rage inward, causing my heart to race, my stomach to twist. This experience is so excruciating I swear to myself I will never attend another funeral ever again.

Despite losing my only brother, I somehow will myself back to work. I put an ad in the local paper and find an experienced retail salesman to take Joe's place. His name is Randall Cross, a twenty-eight-year-old with an associate degree in business. He's punctual, dependable, and communicative. Though I believe he will be an asset to the business, I still have to push down my grief and rage to place him in my brother's old position.

Still, with Randall helping me on the floor, the daily routine becomes surprisingly therapeutic. The store continues to generate business, and at the end of each day, I have a happy home to return to. With no major crises demanding my attention, I can relax, or as Karla tells me, "Go with the flow."

Such serenity is foreign to me, a man who just ten years ago was working twenty-two-hour days and somehow surviving on two hours of sleep. Yet I find the less I allow my frustrations to determine my actions, the more pleasant my life becomes. Perhaps acceptance is the key to happiness. Maybe it's time to stop chasing white tigers and simply live life one day at a time.

Or maybe not.

It is now 1979. Our freelance window dresser, John Bolger, a rail-thin Boston native in his late forties, is working on a mannequin display when he motions me over.

"What's up, John?" I ask, assuming he wants to know which suit I want displayed this week.

"You ever hear of a place called Mr. George?"

"Of course."

Everyone in the Boston metro apparel industry knows about Mr. George, the high-end men's fashion store in Newton. I would call the store one of our chief competitors, but their well-heeled clientele is so different, no real competition is possible.

"I heard Mr. Pearlman's been asking about you."

"What?"

Mr. Pearlman *is* Mr. George, the owner of the shop. A real mover and shaker.

"You should give him a call. I do his displays too. Here."

John hands me a shiny, embossed business card bearing the familiar Mr. George logo and the name and phone number of the owner, Ivan Pearlman. Even though it's just the two of us, John leans in close to whisper. "I know you and Louie are close, but if you are ever want to move up in the world..."

I tell him thanks and slip the card into my pocket. For the rest of the day, I can feel it practically burning a hole in my side. Louie has been good to me. He trusted me with this store and gave me the opportunity to make more money than I ever could have imagined. At the same time, if Sallinger's is a college football team, then Mr. George is the NFL. If there's even a chance I can work there, I owe it to Karla and Scott to make the call.

Shortly before closing, I telephone the number on the card. Mr. Pearlman's secretary immediately puts me through to her boss.

"Tony, so glad you called," Mr. Pearlman says in a friendly, upbeat voice. "John says when it comes to fashion retail, you're a real miracle worker."

"I won't lie to you, Mr. Pearlman, it's been a challenge," I reply, never one to diminish my accomplishments. "But I've made it work."

"So, I've heard, which is why I think we should meet. Louie Fagioli is a great guy. He knows his product and knows his market. But his vision's limited. He doesn't see the potential in high-end retail like I do. And I suspect you do, too."

"I see the potential in everything."

"Then let's talk."

We agree to meet the following Saturday. Leaving Randall in charge, I head up to Newton, a tiny, upper-middle-class suburb seven miles west of downtown Boston. Founded in the late seventeenth century, Newton is actually a collection of thirteen villages, each with its own distinctive downtown business district. Mr. George is located on Centre Street in Newton Centre. I find a metered parking space and jog the half-block to the store.

As I enter, my jaw literally drops. The place is amazing. Huge. Luxurious. Like a menswear museum rather than a neighborhood clothing store. The displays are made of dark, polished hardwood, not the typical painted pressed wood. The floor is tile, not linoleum. Rather than fluorescent lighting, incandescent illumination emanates from frosted glass fixtures.

I'm approached by a handsome young man wearing a stylishly tailored suit. "You're Tony Assali. Mr. Pearlman is expecting you."

The salesman escorts me to a small suite of executive offices at the back of the building. There I'm introduced to Ivan Pearlman, a fortyish, slightly balding Jewish man with a big smile. Like his salesman, Mr. Pearlman is dressed in a perfectly tailored suit and wears a fine blue silk tie.

"Thanks for coming, Tony. Let me show you around." As Mr. Pearlman leads a tour amongst the various racks and displays, all of which are kept in immaculate condition, he tells me the history behind Mr. George. "I opened this place in 1967. Opening day also happened to be the day my first son was born. I figured that was a good omen and I was right. Twelve years later I've got two top men's fashion stores in New England. Can't beat that with a stick."

"You have the best reputation in the business, sir."

"It takes work. *A lot of work*. Not that I'm telling you anything you don't know. After a while, it wears you down. No pun intended. Which is why I'm looking for a full-time manager."

"Are you offering me a job?"

"Yeah, I'm offering you a job."

I look around. Mr. George is easily four times larger than Sallinger's Cambridge. At least a half-dozen salesmen work the floor, and an executive secretary and other assistants work in the back. For the first time in a long time, I feel intimidated. Out of my league.

"I'm flattered…"

Ivan's smile never falters. "Whatever Louie is paying you, I'll double it."

"Thank you. But I'm doing very well at Sallinger's."

The more I protest, the more Mr. Pearlman's grin expands. "I've asked around. I know you're the man for this job, and I'm going to have you, one way or another."

My confidence level rises. I feel emboldened by a white tiger lurking in these luxurious clothes racks.

"Louie lets me do whatever I want as long as the store is profitable. I don't like to be micromanaged."

"I understand. You have to know, I'm not Louie. I still intend to run this store. However, I'm willing to give you plenty of latitude so long as sales and profits stay strong. Let me show you something."

Mr. Pearlman takes me downstairs to a storage room in the basement. The space has a nearly identical footprint as the showroom upstairs, yet is mostly unused. Its bare, windowless brick walls remind me of a club I used to frequent back in Beirut.

And this gives me an idea.

"Mr. George should be more than just a place to shop for clothes," I say. "It should be a shopping *experience*. A place where men can be men." I move to the center of the room as ideas explode across my synapses. "We could put a pool table down here. No, no, not a *pool* table. A *billiard* table. This will be the *billiard room*. We could even serve wine and beer. The longer customers stay—the happier we'll make them—the more purchases they're likely to make."

"I suppose we could think about that," Mr. Pearlman says cautiously. "So long as I have your commitment you're coming onboard."

I put out my hand. "You can still run the business upstairs but I want full autonomy down here," I say, now operating on pure instinct and adrenalin. "It's my idea. I'll take full responsibility for its success or failure. Sink or swim." This is the same demand I made of Louie—even the same language. *Can lightning strike twice?*

"Sounds risky."

"It's risky *not* to do it. You can't stay king if you don't stay bold. If you don't innovate and grow."

I notice Mr. Pearlman's smile is long gone. The weight of our conversation seems to have depleted him, and he actually puts his arm on the banister to steady himself. At last, he turns to me. "If you can do for me what you did for Louie, it will be worth it."

That night, I discuss Mr. Pearlman's offer with Karla. She agrees it's a great opportunity. Now all I have to do is tell Louie. This won't be easy.

Chapter 32

"TONY, YOU'RE KILLING me."

As I anticipated, Louie is not at all happy with the news I am leaving him to manage Mr. George. We're sitting in a neighborhood restaurant. I invited him here for lunch, hoping the pleasures of a good meal would soften the blow of my departure. From the look on his face, I was clearly mistaken.

"I want you to know this is nothing personal," I assure him. "Working for you has been one of the great joys of my life. I appreciate the opportunities you've given me. And I think the return I've delivered on your investment has been substantial. I've made a lot of money for you."

"That's true. And I want to make more."

"So do I. Ivan offered to double my salary."

"That bastard." He shakes his head. "That's something I cannot do."

Louie looks even more defeated. I feel bad for him but I mustn't let that cloud my thinking. "I have to think about what's best for my family. Frankly, if I didn't take this job, Karla would kill me."

This almost gets a laugh from Louie. As a married man, he understands the power a wife can have over her husband's career choices.

I lean closer, putting my hand on his slumped shoulder. "Look. I'm not going to leave you high and dry. I've been training Randall to run the store. Teaching him everything I know. He's a hard worker. Conscientious. He's going to do well for you."

Louie puts his face in his hands. It looks like he's having a breakdown. People around us stare. Our server approaches out of concern, but I wave her away with a smile. *Everything is okay. I hope...*

At last Louie looks up. His lined face seems older. "Tony, I've been in this business thirty years. And if it's taught me anything, it's that nothing lasts." He sticks out his hand. "Good luck with Ivan. I know you'll do well there."

Just then, our server returns with the check. Before Louie can reach for it, I slap down a twenty. Louie doesn't object.

Two weeks later, I begin as the new general manager of Mr. George in Newton. Though I will miss working for Louie, I'm thrilled to be a part of this world-class operation. Unlike at Sallinger's-Cambridge, where most of the suits are lower-end products made onsite in the third-floor factory, the clothes here are all European imports of the finest quality. And the styles are exclusive to this store. The first thing I do upon arriving is have a suit tailored for myself. After all, if I'm going to sell Mr. George fashions, I have to show them off.

Next, I go to City Hall and apply for a wine and beer license for our new billiard room. There the frowning female clerk tells me it will take several months to approve our application. Middle-aged and stern, she looks beaten down by bureaucratic life and reminds me of the clerk Sylvia took me to all those years ago to get my visa. The only bright spot on her cluttered desk is a framed picture of what appears to be her grandson.

"Beautiful boy. Looks just like his mom."

"That's my grandchild," she says and blushes from my compliment.

"Is there any way you can possibly expedite this process? Please. I could really use the help."

She sighs. "I can't promise anything. But I'll see what I can do."

"Wonderful. I would really appreciate it."

In the meantime, Mr. Pearlman gives me a budget to renovate the store's basement, install a bar, and buy a pool table along with all the necessary accessories. I interview several architects and contractors for the remodel, ultimately choosing professionals I believe can deliver my vision at a price Mr. Pearlman can afford. Between this and managing the sales team above, I'm working fourteen-hour days. But I have to admit, I'm having the time of my life.

Mr. George customers are very different from Sallinger's customers. In Cambridge, most of my clientele were lower-middle-class factory workers, many first- or second-generation Portuguese. The men who come in and out of my new shop tend to be professionals: doctors, lawyers, accountants, business executives. Many are Jewish, which makes sense; Newton has a large Jewish population. Because the people we serve are busy during the week, they tend to shop on Saturdays. And they often come with their wives, who end up making the final decisions.

How can I attract more of these desirable customers to the store? Though they are financially better off than my previous customer base, everyone loves bargains—even top-level professionals who can afford to pay full retail. Also, like everyone, they like to eat, especially familiar foods of top quality. So, one week, I decide to advertise a free brunch buffet for the upcoming Saturday. I order bagels. Lox. Whitefish. Cream cheese. Traditional Jewish deli breakfast food. It's an investment of several hundred dollars, and if it fails, there's no way I can recoup the loss. The food will be no good by the end of the day.

But, lo and behold, the investment pays off. Husbands and wives come together for the culinary bounty—and stay to buy suits. The store has one of its best Saturdays in years. After that I make it a weekly tradition: Saturday brunch at Mr. George. It pays to know your customers.

Several weeks after submitting my application, we get our wine and beer license. I say a silent prayer to my female clerk friend. Within days we finish work on the billiard room. I put signs all over the store and advertise the new attraction in the local paper. It, too, becomes a big hit, especially when we bring in attractive servers. This enticement, plus the *man cave* aspect to our store can't help but draw in gobs of businessmen. They fill the place to standing-room capacity on their lunch hours, shooting pool and knocking back beers from the coterie of beautiful, smiling waitresses.

Importantly, almost no one leaves without buying something. A shirt. A tie. A watch. Soon after rebranding, Mr. George transforms from a high-end apparel store to a destination. *An experience*, just like I promised Ivan.

"Honey, I have great news," I announce one night. Since working at Mr. George, this type of announcement has become a new ritual.

"Tell me," Karla demands eagerly.

"We just made a deal with Delphi's Basement." Delphi's is a local discount clothing store known for its cut-rate prices on unsold merchandise from other local fashion stores. "You know we just had a big Father's Day sale, right? Well, we offered to sell the remainders to Delphi's for 50 cents on the dollar."

"Congratulations." She kisses me on the cheek and pushes me into my favorite chair for dinner.

"No, that's not the good part," I say, getting back up. "Before we sold the suits, we marked them up 20 percent. *And Delphi's was happy to buy them.* We made a nice profit, and Mr. Pearlman was ecstatic."

"I'm proud of you. And now I have some news for *you*."

"What is it?"

"I'm pregnant."

For a moment, I'm speechless. Karla and I have discussed having a child of our own for many months, but now the reality hits me like a ton of bricks. I fall back into my chair after all.

The experience I had with Scott is now going to start all over again. The sleepless nights. Diaper changes. The floors landmined with baby toys. The good stuff, too. Really good stuff. First steps. First words. The indescribable joy and pride that comes with ushering new life into the world. A broad grin breaks out across my face, and I pull Karla down into a passionate embrace.

Karla gives birth to our son on April 1, 1980. We name him Joseph after my late brother. At first, I'm afraid Scott, now nine, will be jealous, but he is happy to have a baby brother. He hovers over the infant like a protective parent, alerting us whenever the little guy seems uncomfortable or distressed.

When baby Joey is just six months old, we take him to church for the first time since his christening. This simple decision triggers a series of events that will change the course of my life forever —and rock the food world.

Chapter 33

CHURCH HAS ALWAYS been an important part of my life, not only for the moral and spiritual guidance it offers but also for the sense of inclusion it provides. Going on Sunday mornings gives me the opportunity to spend time with my neighbors, exchange family news, share our triumphs, and commiserate in our losses. Many sociologists contend a primary goal of organized religion is to create and sustain communities, to build trust and fellowship among people who would otherwise be strangers. I can't argue with this idea. Church is where I have found many of my closest friends. It's also the place that kindled the spark for one of my greatest ventures.

On this particular winter's day in early 1980, our entire family is attending Sunday services. Little Joey, now just six months old, is surprisingly quiet and content as Karla holds him in her arms throughout Mass. Afterwards, we run into Abe Hanna. Now in his late fifties, Abe knew my father back in Beirut. When my dad was still alive, Abe would drop in on occasion, so he already knows Scott. This is his first introduction to baby Joey. He is thrilled that my family is growing and, of course, that Joey's beautiful mother is Lebanese.

"We need to keep our bloodline strong," Abe tells me, one hand on my elbow. "In America, that can be hard. Our young men have so many other... *options*."

I get the none-too-subtle hint he is alluding to the many American women he's seen me date. To change the subject, I invite Abe out to lunch at a local Italian restaurant with Karla and me. Once again, he steers the conversation to how difficult it is to maintain our cultural identity.

"Do you realize there's not one Lebanese restaurant in the whole Boston area?" Abe grouses. "Everyone else has their restaurants. The Italians. The Chinese. The Mexicans. The Greeks. Even the Portuguese. How can we ever stay Lebanese if we can't even *eat* Lebanese?" He points his pinky finger in the direction of my sleeping boy in his stroller. "Little Joey here will never know about the old country growing up on pizza and French fries."

Karla and I exchange secret eyerolls but, in my heart, I sense he's right. All the way home, I can't get what Abe said out of my mind. It's true. Everywhere I look I see ethnic restaurants representing numerous immigrant populations. Yet there's not a Lebanese eatery in sight. And as someone who grew up on Lebanese cooking, I can tell you it is delicious. The people here don't know what they're missing.

Later that night, I can't sleep. For the first time in years, I feel like I'm hunting a white tiger. As the hours pass, pieces of the mental puzzle I'm constructing fall into place until, sometime around 2:00 a.m., an idea blooms.

The next morning—Monday—I call in sick to Mr. George. This is the first time I have missed a day on a job since starting at Sallinger's four years ago. At 9:00 a.m. sharp, I drive to a local print shop where I order labels for a new company I have decided to call Cedars Mediterranean Foods, the cedar tree being the symbol for Lebanon. Next, I drive to a local gourmet market where I buy a large quantity of garbanzo beans, olive oil, lemons, eggplant, parsley, wheat germ and tahini, a condiment made from toasted ground hulled sesame seeds. The latter is difficult to locate, but an accommodating salesperson helps me find this essential ingredient in their Middle Eastern section. Five bags of fresh pita bread later, and I'm ready to rock 'n' roll.

"What are you doing?" Karla asks as she watches me struggle to shove my recent purchases into our refrigerator.

"We're going into business."

She frowns. "Business doing what?"

"Selling Lebanese food."

"From where?"

"From here."

She puts her hands on her hips. "Hold on. You mean you're going to make it yourself?"

I race around her to get to our pots and pans, my mother's recipes bouncing around in my brain.

"Yep. Make it. Package it. Sell it."

She watches me combining ingredients in a bowl with growing irritation.

"And just when are you going to have time to do this?"

"It's going to be my new full-time job."

"You're going to leave Mr. George?"

"I have no choice."

She throws her hands up in the air, stomping in her high-heels. "You're crazy."

"Which is why you love me."

Saying nothing, she storms out of the kitchen. Hours later, I wipe my forehead with a towel and exhale. I haven't sat down since returning, and the sink and counters are covered with dirty dishes and food scraps. The sun went down long ago but I made up my mind not to stop until I whipped together my first batch of Cedars' hummus.

I call Karla's name from the bottom of the stairs. No response. I run up to our room to find Joey asleep in the baby swing. Beside him, his mom flicks through channels on the TV.

"Can you come downstairs for a moment?"

She acts like she doesn't hear me.

"Honey?"

Wordlessly, she turns off the set and accompanies me downstairs. I break off the first chunk of pita bread and offer her a taste. Skeptical, she dips the flatbread into the creamy tan concoction and slips it into her mouth.

Immediately, her eyes light up. She likes it. Scratch that. *She loves it.* Her lips spread into a wide grin.

"So, who's crazy now?"

She kisses me with garlic breath. I can't think of anything sweeter.

Exhausted, I fall into bed at midnight. But for the second night in a row, I can't sleep. What am I thinking? I'm twenty-nine years old. I have a mortgage and a wife, baby, and growing son to support. I have responsibilities. I can't pursue foolish get-rich-quick schemes like some dumb teenager. Still, I resolve not to give up.

When I arrive at Mr. George the next morning, Ivan assumes I'm still sick because, after two sleepless nights, I look like a mess.

"Um, maybe you should go home," he advises. "I don't want you infecting the rest of my staff. Or our customers."

"I'm not sick. I've just been... I have this... I want to... I'm giving my two weeks' notice."

"What? Why? What's wrong?"

"Nothing's wrong. I have an idea for a food company."

"What kind of food company?" His pinched face reminds me of Karla's the moment I told her my plan.

"Lebanese."

"But no one eats Lebanese food."

"Exactly. It's a wide-open market."

"Do you have any experience in the food business?"

"No. But I had no experience in men's fashion either, until I did."

He leans in close. "Why are you doing this? Did I do something wrong? Tell me. I will fix it."

"It's not that at all. It's because I have to. I'm compelled. Like a calling."

He paces, literally wringing his hands together. "I want you to stay. I'll double your salary."

"You already did that."

His pacing speeds up. His hands are flying back and forth now. "Well, then, I'm doing it again. I'm doubling your salary on top of what I doubled it to already. You're worth it."

I want to stop him in his tracks. His insatiable fidgeting is making me crazy. "Please. There's nothing you can do that will convince me to stay. It's one thing to make a living, another to create a legacy."

He finally stops to glare at me. "And that's what you think you're doing?"

"I hope so."

"Aren't you even just a little bit afraid?"

I consider his question for a tense moment. "There's no room for fear."

But I'm lying. I'm scared out of my mind.

That Saturday, I make additions to Mr. George's weekly brunch buffet. Beyond our traditional bagels, lox and whitefish, I present my homemade hummus, and tabbouleh. This will be my first field test. Will New England Jews even consider eating *exotic* Lebanese cuisine? As it turns out, they will, and they do. *Joyfully.* By noon, all of my samples are gone. Even Ivan looks like he sees the wisdom of my decision.

During my last two weeks with him, I find a local wholesaler from whom I buy commercial-grade mixing equipment and plastic lidded containers. From a local grocery wholesaler, I order fresh vegetables to be delivered to my home. My kitchen becomes my factory. My mom and Coco help me create the finished product before placing it into plastic containers. Even Scott assists by putting labels on the lids. Still, I double-check to make sure he has labeled each properly.

My first batch consists of forty-eight eight-ounce containers, including twenty-four hummus, twelve tabbouleh, and twelve baba ghanoush. The operation produces a lot of organic waste, too much for our regular residential garbage cans, so I put all the refuse into heavy-duty plastic bags and, at midnight, drive to the rear of our local supermarket where I drop them into their industrial waste dumpster. Not my proudest moment, but what's a struggling entrepreneur to do?

Less than two weeks after my initial brainstorm, Cedars Mediterranean Foods is in business. Now all I need are customers.

Chapter 34

WHEN YOU ARE starting a business from scratch, prepare to wear many hats. Besides being the founder, owner, and CEO of Cedars Mediterranean Foods, I am also its chief chef and senior VP of sales. In this latter capacity, it is up to me to find prospects and close sales. Fortunately, selling is in my DNA. Having produced sufficient quantities of my three principal products—hummus, tabbouleh, and baba ghanoush—I pack them into boxes of forty-eight items each and load them into large coolers I purchased expressly for this purpose. I then load the coolers into the back of my station wagon.

Map in hand, I drive to the first local, independently owned grocery store I identified as a potential buyer. It's just after eight o'clock when I arrive, and the parking lot is mostly empty. I take a smaller cooler containing sample containers from the back of the car and head inside, my heart in my throat.

Entering, I approach a cashier and politely ask to see the manager.

"Do you have a complaint?" the girl asks with concern.

"Not at all. I represent a new line of food products—"

She cuts me off. "Sorry. We don't take solicitations—"

"I would like him to consider carrying in his store."

"Yeah, we don't accept those kinds of offers. They need to go through corporate."

I flash her my most winning smile. "This is my first time doing this and I'm a little nervous."

Her hardened face softens. A little. "It's not me. It's company policy."

"Have you ever tried hummus before?"

"What's that?"

"It's delicious."

I open the lid to a small plastic tub so she can smell it. She says nothing, making me worry she's going to show me to the door.

At last, she picks up a telephone handset. "Let me call Jeff."

A moment later, a stocky man in his mid-forties wearing a blue short-sleeved shirt approaches with an extended hand. "Jeff Banner, Manager" reads the plastic tag pinned to his chest.

"How can I help you?" he asks.

"I'm president of Cedars Mediterranean Foods," I say, offering him my business card. "I just opened my company here in Salem. I'm selling a new line of authentic Lebanese food products I believe your customers will fall in love with."

I pick the small cooler off the floor, set it down on the counter, and open it to reveal my three plastic sample tubs.

"This is hummus, this is tabbouleh, and this is baba ghanoush," I say, pointing to each label. I look up to see Banner's reaction. Like the girl at the counter, his face is a complete blank. I realize he has never heard these words before. To him, they must sound like pure gibberish. He looks to the cashier. She nods for me to continue. I have a small window of attention. If I don't get this right, he will surely give me the boot.

"Hummus is like a dip or spread made from cooked, mashed garbanzo beans, blended with olive oil, lemon juice and spices. Tabbouleh is a vegetarian salad of finely chopped parsley, tomatoes, mint, onion, bulger, and other fresh ingredients. Baba ghanoush comes from fresh eggplant mixed with tahini, olive oil and seasonings."

Again, Jeff stares at me like I'm speaking Martian. Undeterred, I open a packet of pita bread—made locally at Abe Hanna's bakery—and motion for him to take a piece. He does so with obvious trepidation.

"Tear off some bread," I coax. "Dip it in the hummus. And enjoy."

Like a wary child being asked to sample his first brussels sprout, Jeff tears off a piece of pita bread, touches an edge to the hummus, then oh-so-gently brings it to his tongue. He lets the flavor register for a moment, realizes my odd-sounding concoction is quite flavorful, then returns for a second, more generous sample.

Less inhibited, the girl dips her bread in next. "This is good," she says between bites. "I mean, really good."

"Like I need you to tell me that," says Jeff, taking another piece of bread, this time *submerging* it in the hummus. "Don't you have aisles to stock?"

Swishing her hair back with attitude, she gets up to leave. Now it's just him and me at the front of the store.

"Everything here is 100 percent homemade, using only natural ingredients. Nothing artificial," I say as Jeff continues sampling my products with increasing vigor. I notice he's making a real dent in the sample tub. "Once your customers try these, they'll keep coming back for more." Just to seal the deal, I add, "And because I know this is a brand-new food line and represents a degree of risk for you, I will buy back anything you don't sell after the first week. You can't lose."

"Let's go back to my office," Jeff says, smacking his lips. Fifteen minutes later, I walk out with a signed order. High as a kite, I return to my car and grab a pre- packaged forty-eight-product pack from a cooler. I carry it to the refrigerated shelves of the store's deli section.

"One week," Jeff reminds me.

"One week."

I visit six more small, independently owned supermarkets that first day and make the same pitch. Each time, I convince the manager to sample my products. Each time, I offer to buy back any unsold merchandise after one week. And each time, I sell the full forty-eight-piece package.

When I return home an hour past sunset, the back of my station wagon is empty. I've done it. Cedars Mediterranean Foods is off and running. The following Sunday, I again see Abe Hanna at church.

"I did it," I tell him. "I brought Lebanon to America."

His eyes widen. "Huh?"

His bony hand grips my elbow harder and harder the more I explain my new venture. But I save the best piece of news for last. "And if it weren't for you, I never would have done it. You inspired me."

Abe looks like he will die of a heart attack on the spot. He's swaying, his big eyes blinking profusely. "Well," he says, at last. "I got just one question for you: How can I help?"

Much to his surprise, I have a prepared answer. "Your bakery sells pita bread all over the Boston area," I say as a preamble. "How about I follow your delivery truck around and your driver introduces me to the manager at each store? Since they know you, they'll trust me. While your driver is dropping off bread, I'll be selling the humus to spread on it."

"Anything for you," Abe says. We shake hands on the deal.

And so, starting that Monday, I'm on the road day after day, store after store, breathing exhaust from Abe's truck and selling and selling and selling. It's exhausting work, but every sale gives me the courage I need to push on.

Within a month, the business I've risked everything on has taken over our whole house. With so much commercial equipment crowding the counters, we can't use the kitchen to make our own meals. It's obvious I need real space. Yet no sooner do I decide to look for larger accommodations than a nearby salon goes out of business. I contact the listed agent, rent it, buy a commercial-size refrigerator, and move all our equipment into the new building. I also make sure everything is as neat and clean as possible. I don't want trouble with the Health Department.

However, a week after moving to our new digs, there's a knock on my door. When I open it, a serious-looking man in a brown suit flashes an ID card. "Mr. Assali, I'm with the State Department of Weights and Measures. We have a problem."

Chapter 35

"A PROBLEM?" I ask the agent, struggling to keep the tremor from my voice.

"This one of your products?" He holds up a container of hummus bearing my label. My heart skips a beat. Immediately, I imagine the worst-case scenario. My food has spoiled. It's contaminated. Customers are sick—dying. I begin to sweat. There will be lawsuits. *Oh God.* I never bought liability insurance. I'm personally on the hook for damages. Claims could run into the thousands. *Millions.* I'll have to sell my house. All my possessions. I'll have to declare bankruptcy. *What will my wife do? My children?*

"Yes, that's mine," I respond, trying to keep an even tone. "What's the problem?"

He points to a tub. "You sell all of your products in these containers?"

"Y-yes."

"These *eight-ounce* containers?"

"Um, yes. Eight ounces."

"And just how do you know they contain eight ounces?"

I'm not sure where this is going but answer him all the same. "Because those are eight-ounce containers. It says so on the package."

This conversation has taken a turn for the bizarre. Here I was terrified I might have killed somebody, yet this man from the government is grilling me about my plastic container size. It's like something out of a Kafka novel.

"That's not sufficient. You have to actually *weigh* each container and verify it contains the volume of product you claim it does. That's the law." He cites the number of the code in question, but I don't bother to write it down. I'll take his word for it.

"So, what should I do now, sir?"

"First, you must recall all your products still in stores."

"Excuse me?"

"Take them off the shelves. Then buy a digital scale with an automatic label maker. When you package each product, weigh the container and put the label on it."

"Wait a minute. What about the food I need to recall?"

"You'll have to throw it out. And make sure that in the future, all your containers are properly weighed and labeled, or you will be cited and fined. *Capiche?*"

"I understand."

Again, my mind races. If I have to throw out all the food I've already sold, it could cost me thousands of dollars. I have to move fast. First, I direct Karla to buy the kind of digital scale the agent described. Then I drive to each grocery store I've sold to, talk to each manager, explain the situation, and apologize for my error. Then I pick up any and all unsold merchandise, put it in my coolers and drive it home. There, with Karla's help, we weigh each container digitally, add or remove product as necessary, and attach the labels the scale produces. Fortunately, my foods are selling so fast most of the containers I recall have only been on the shelves a few days so I can safely return them to the stores stamped with their original expiration dates.

By day's end, I have repackaged and restocked about 90 percent of my recalled products, sending only 10 percent to the trash. Quick action helped me turn what could have been a disaster into a minor, short-lived inconvenience. I'm still recovering from this averted crisis when my phone rings.

It's Karla's father. "Tony, there's something I would like to discuss with you," he says.

"Sure. What's going on?"

He sounds mysterious. "I can't do this over the phone. Can I come over to your house right now?"

"Sure, come over," I reply, wondering what could be so sensitive it can't be discussed over the phone. Part of me worries my new food enterprise has upset him, too. In my haste to conquer grocery stores with Lebanese cuisine, I may have committed some other grievous error.

Half an hour later, Mr. Baccash arrives, carrying a leather briefcase. This is getting weird, yet I say nothing. I'm eager to see where it goes. After gingerly carrying the briefcase into the kitchen, he sets it on the table. Then, very businesslike, he snaps the locks and opens the lid to reveal an interior stuffed with bound bundles of one-hundred-dollar bills. I've seen this kind of scene in movies but never believed it could happen in real life.

"One hundred thousand dollars," he announces.

"For what?"

"I'm impressed with what you've done with Cedars. I want to invest in your company. I want to be your partner. You can use this money to expand. Buy more equipment. Hire workers and salespeople. Turn Cedars into a major regional powerhouse."

It takes a few seconds to process this. Truth be told, Karla's dad is an intimidating man. Kind of like Don Corleone. It is difficult to say no to him. Plus, $100,000 in cash staring you in the face is equally difficult to reject. But I know in my heart of hearts accepting his proposition would be unwise.

"I'm tempted. Very tempted. But I've always believed it's dangerous to mix business and family." I leave out the fact I got many of my relatives jobs—first at Sallinger's, now my mom and Coco at Cedars. What I really mean to say is I distrust working with *in-laws*. From the look on his disbelieving face, I can see Mr.

Baccash doesn't like what he's hearing, so I try to explain. "What if the business fails? It could affect things between Karla and me."

"So, you're telling me no?" He looks more than disappointed, he seems downright offended. "You'll be sorry."

"I'm already sorry. I love you, you know that. But I think any kind of business relationship between us would be a bad idea."

"Fine." He closes the lid and snaps it shut. Without a further word, he takes his briefcase and quickly exits the house, not bothering to look back. I hadn't noticed Karla watching from the shadows of the den until now. Once he's gone, she throws me a dark look that speaks volumes.

I have a feeling this decision will come back to haunt me.

Chapter 36

WHEN SOMEONE OFFERS you a briefcase containing $100,000 in cash, it makes an impression. Such a dramatic display of wealth can easily undermine your self-confidence, causing you to second-guess the most well-considered decision. Even though I still believe I did the right thing by rejecting Mr. Baccash's offer, I can't help but replay the encounter over and over in my mind, wondering if I should have handled the situation differently. Oddly, I keep drifting back not to the money and the potential for exponential growth it represented, but to something I thought at the time but did not say.

The truth is I need a partner, a *working* partner. Someone like Abe. Why Abe? It's not like I'd been thinking about partnering with the man before. At least not consciously. But it wasn't a bad idea the more I gave it thought. Not bad at all. Perhaps my confrontation with Karla's father crystallized a notion swimming inchoate at the back of my mind ever since Abe let me follow his truck from store to store.

The morning after I send Mr. Baccash packing, I walk confidently into Abe's bakery. I find him on his dock, supervising the loading of his truck.

"Tony," he says and smiles as he sees me approach. "What ya doing here?"

"You got a second?"

"For you, always. So, what's up?"

I wait until his workers leave us alone, then say, "Someone just offered me $100,000 to become partners in Cedars."

"Holy shit. Who?"

"That's not important. What *is* important is that I turned him down."

"You turned him down? Are you crazy? How do you turn down $100,000?"

"That kind of money expects control and I don't want to be controlled. I told the guy point blank, right now, I don't need an investor. What I need to grow is a working partner. Someone like Abe Hanna."

Abe staggers to his feet. "Me? Wait a minute, what are you saying?"

"I'm saying I would like you to be my partner."

Abe looks around as if he's expecting someone to burst in on us any minute. "That's kind, but I don't have this kind of money to invest."

I put a hand on his shoulder. "I'm not asking for money. What's of value to me right now is your knowledge, your relationships—your infrastructure. I spend half of each day driving around delivering product to the same stores you're servicing, too. It would make more sense if your trucks could deliver my food containers at the same time you're delivering your bread. That would free me up to make more sales. Which is how I should be spending my time."

"And the terms?" Abe asks, now clearly intrigued.

"We split the profits right down the middle, fifty-fifty," I offer without reservation.

Abe is struck dumb for several seconds. It's obvious he can't believe I'm offering him so much for so little. I can't believe it, either. But it feels like the right thing to do. And if I've learned anything during my three decades on earth, it's to trust my gut.

"You've got yourself a deal." Abe extends his hand. I take it, and he grips me tightly, pulling me into a full-body hug. "Your father would be so proud!" he says into my ear. "You, me, together, bringing Lebanese food to America."

Until now, I have been selling my products only to small, independent grocery stores. The first thing Abe does as my partner is advise me to shoot higher. "We need to get into the big supermarket chains," he says between bites of cantaloupe days later at his loading docks. He eats it like a bowl of cereal, scooping orange fruit right out of the center of the melon, enunciating each word with his spoon. "DeMoulas. First National. Stop and Shop. Purity Supreme. That's where the money is. We get into one of those chains, we'll have it made."

I watch his spoon slice the air like a sword as I contemplate his words. DeMoulas is one of the major supermarket chains in the area. I know of at least four or five of its stores in the north Boston suburbs alone. They're owned by a Greek-American family that went into the grocery business early in the twentieth century. The story is that the founder's two sons, Mike and George Demoulas, bought the original struggling mom-and-pop shop from their father in the mid- 1950s and, by 1970, grew it out of near-bankruptcy to become a thriving forty- store chain. One of the brothers, George, died of a heart attack while vacationing in Greece in 1971, leaving Mike in charge of the family operation. Today, he runs the company while his eldest son, Jack, manages operations.

Abe, who counts DeMoulas among his many customers, gives me the number for the headquarters in Tewksbury, Massachusetts.

"I'd like to speak to the person in charge of deli products," I say to the woman who answers the corporate number.

"What's this about?"

"I have a line of Mediterranean food products I'm interested in getting into your stores."

There's a long pause. "For that, you'd have to speak with Jack. He makes our buying decisions."

"Can I make an appointment to see him?"

"I'll connect you with his secretary."

Moments later I have an appointment to meet with Jack this week. I spend the next several days rehearsing my pitch, making sure my samples are as impressive as possible. At last, the day arrives for our meeting. I get to the company offices five minutes early, carrying a cooler containing my very best hummus, tabbouleh, and baba ghanoush. Expecting to receive the same cool reception I usually get when presenting these exotic dishes to American buyers, I explain their origins in a way I believe a man with the last name of Demoulas can understand.

"Lebanese food is like Greek food," I begin. "We use many of the same ingredients. And I recommend these spreads be eaten with pita bread, which is also Greek."

"I'm familiar with all of these," Jack grunts. The man is in his late thirties, olive skinned, and wearing an expertly tailored Ralph Lauren suit. "May I have a taste?"

"Of course." I place my samples before him, offering him a bag of pita bread.

"From my partner, Abe Hanna. You carry his bread in your stores."

Jack tears off a piece of pita and dips it into the hummus. I can feel my legs shaking and fight to keep them under control. The next ten seconds could make or break me. I can just picture Karla shaking her head if I were to walk in the door empty-handed. How she will say, "I told you. You should have trusted Daddy." Then again, if this man likes what he's eating, I could become a millionaire.

As Jack lifts the pita to his mouth, I can't breathe. My fate is in his hands.

Chapter 37

"DELICIOUS," JACK DEMOULAS pronounces with a satisfying lip smack. "Now let's try the baba ghanoush."

Fifteen minutes later, Jack has sampled—and re-sampled—and re-re-sampled all three of my products. Halfway through his extensive taste test, he calls in his secretary and two other nearby staff employees to join us. Between the four of them, they polish off my samples as well as my pita bread supply.

"I have only one problem with this product," Jack finally says, wiping his mouth with a cloth handkerchief. "…And that's that I didn't think of making it first."

Smiles flash all around, mine the biggest.

"Having grown up on Greek cooking," he continues. "It's about time our customers had a chance to enjoy the pleasures of this remarkable cuisine."

"I couldn't agree more," I concur, along with the heads bobbing beside me.

Then Jack drops the bomb. "I'd like to carry your line in all forty of my stores."

I'm stunned. I was only aware of the four or five DeMoulas markets in the north Boston area. What he's asking me to deliver is on a whole different order of magnitude.

"Can you do that, Tony?"

All eyes turn to me. I can feel the blood pumping in my head. This is crazy. This is big-time. *This may be impossible to pull off.* The seconds draw out as I can sense Jack sizing me up, determining just what kind of man I am.

"Of course," I reply, doing my best to keep my smile plastered to my face. "I'll just need to scale up my production." Another idea hits me as adrenaline courses through my body. "I can even send people into each store to offer free samples."

"More samples?" one of Jack's employees, an accountant-type guy with pita crumbs on his shoulders asks. "Why?"

I keep my eyes on Jack since he's the decision-maker. "Most of your customers will have no idea what these products are. We'll need to introduce them in a dramatic way."

The accountant-guy and the others look to Jack for his response.

"Excellent idea," he says, standing up. "How much time will you need?"

I try to work out the logistics on the spot, but I'm so supercharged I can't think straight and blurt out an answer. "A month."

"A month?"

Does he honestly think I can go faster than that? Already, it's pushing us way out of our comfort zone. "Yes. We can't rush quality."

"Right. Yes. I'll send out a memo to our store managers alerting them to get ready for your deliveries." He grips my hand so hard it pinches my wedding ring into my knuckle. "Tony, I want to thank you for thinking of us first. I have a feeling we're going to make a lot of money together."

As I leave Jack's office, my legs shake so badly I feel like I'm walking on the deck of a storm-tossed ship. Yet somehow, I manage to stumble my way to my station wagon and climb inside. Once behind the wheel, I scream into my shirt sleeve. This was the biggest test of my life and I passed. I look at my smile in the rearview mirror. It's ear to ear.

Although I asked Jack for four weeks, I pull it off in three. The hustling part of my nature won't let me think about anything else but putting out this order. I have to crack the whip on my sleep-deprived people, double-timing our production to make this happen. I also buy a refrigerated delivery van while Abe hires two more cooks. Together we plan a route allowing us to hit six to seven DeMoulas locations per day every six days. This ambitious schedule allows us to cover all forty locations inside a week.

"I want to make these deliveries myself," I tell Abe a few days before beginning.

"I can do it, Tony. This is what I do after all."

"At least at first, you gotta let me in there. Please."

"Fine." He throws up his hands in mock defeat. "What do I care? I'm busy enough with my own customers. You want the headache? It's yours."

"Yes, my friend. I do want the headache."

What I don't say is I *need* the headache. Just like every other job I've ever held, I must know how to do it all, inside and out. Otherwise, I can't catch mistakes. I can't improve. I can't track my white tiger.

With our production line now operating at full capacity, I arrive at our warehouse at 5:00 a.m. to load up the van for our first run on game day. I pull up to the first store on our list at 6:30 a.m. Immediately there's a problem.

"Just who are you?" asks the meaty dock foreman with the fading tattoos on his wrists.

When I explain what I'm delivering, he claims to have no shipments from Cedars Mediterranean Foods on his manifest. Finally, he calls for the manager to resolve the situation. The word *fat* doesn't do this next guy justice. Rolls of flab spill over his waistline, and it sounds like someone's stepping on his chest when he speaks.

"Oh, right, you're the Greek guy."

I correct him. "Lebanese."

"I got the note from Jack. You got some kind of Greek appetizers."

I correct him again. "Lebanese." I haul out a box of my product and show him a container.

"Why is your yogurt yellow?" the foreman asks, his nose screwed up at the mere thought of spoiled dairy.

"It's not yogurt. It's *hummus*."

"Hoomis?"

"*Hummus*."

"What the hell is a *hummus*?" asks the manager.

I'm now used to this. I explain it's a dip made from pureed garbanzo beans and olive oil, but they still don't get it so I crack open a container.

"Try it," I say. "This one is yours."

The manager approaches cautiously while the other guy looks on with actual fear in his eyes like his boss might keel over any second from contamination. Just like all the others, though, the manager melts. I witness it in slow motion. His watery eyes dilate. His shoulder relaxes. He makes a kind of grunting sound between bites that could almost be described as sexual. When I throw the foreman an I-told-you-so look he rolls his eyes and walks away.

I'm not bummed. Fifteen minutes later, my containers command half a shelf at eye-level in Jack's hallowed refrigerated deli section. On this first day, I select two stores to stage free-sample giveaways for deli customers.

"These are authentic, traditional Lebanese delicacies," I announce as part of my pitch. "Handmade from only fresh, all-natural ingredients. Garbanzo beans. Eggplant. Olive oil. Native herbs and spices. A healthy, all-natural appetizer, snack, or side dish. Your family will love them."

Inevitably, I attract a small number of adventurous epicureans and their *oohs* and *ahhhs* when they taste my samples, attracting even more shoppers. My product all but flies off the shelves.

It's a beautiful thing when the managers begin calling in to double their orders.

I am proud and feel vindicated by the reaction I receive. In my heart I knew if I offered the public a good, clean, delicious ethnic food product they had never tried before, they would buy it. And buy it they do. My challenge now is to produce enough supply to meet the demand I have created. Yes, it will take effort, but I have never been afraid of hard work.

Ironically, the more my business grows, the more strained my marriage becomes. This is a pattern I'm sure has been repeated thousands, if not millions of times, since the institution's invention. Wives want their husbands to be providers, to deliver security in the form of money and material goods. But achieving success requires time and effort, and focusing on business matters leaves less time to spend with one's wife and children. So, the wife complains she is being ignored. Perhaps the man heeds his wife's grievances and steps away from his business activities, in which case the business suffers, income drops, and the cycle repeats itself.

I love Karla, but I can't let that happen. *I won't let that happen.*

"I barely see you anymore," she complains during one of our increasingly brief meals together.

"I know. But this is what it takes to be a success."

She hasn't touched any of the food on her plate. Now she lays her fork down. "You were already a success at Mr. George. Why couldn't you have stayed there?"

I rub my eyes. This is not the way I wanted to spend the evening. "Because no one gets rich working for somebody else. If you want to do more than just get by, you have to start your own company. Be your own boss." I look her straight in the eye, unflinching. "This is what I was meant to do."

She walks out on me. After finishing my meal, I do all of the dishes. By the time I get upstairs both boys are sleeping, so I climb into bed. When I reach for Karla to apologize, she pulls away.

My marriage may be rocky, but things are really happening with my company. With each new success, my ambition only grows. After six months, we move our kitchen operations from the old hairdressing shop that served as our first factory into a 25,000-square-foot commercial building. We hire more workers, generating even more product. At Abe's prompting, I contact a buyer for Purity Supreme. With more than two hundred stores throughout New England, Purity is by far the largest and most successful supermarket chain in the area. Not long ago I thought winning Jack over was my biggest test, but now the stakes have skyrocketed.

I arrive at the company's North Billerica, Massachusetts, headquarters bearing my usual collection of samples. When I offer the VP of purchasing one, he demurs. "I'm familiar with your product. You sell to DeMoulas, right?"

"That's right. They've been carrying us for the last six months."

"Six months," the man repeats, letting the words settle on his tongue like a dollop of baba ghanoush. "I'm surprised. Why didn't you come to us first?"

"If I hadn't already sold to DeMoulas, would you even have talked to me?"

The man laughs. "You have a point,." Then he says, "I'd like to start with sixty stores. If that goes well, we can expand. How soon can you be ready?"

I give him the same answer I gave Jack. "A month."

"And, for the first month, we want you to do demonstrations, just like you do for DeMoulas. Not some hired model. You. You're the key to your company's success. You personally. Can you do that for us?"

"I wouldn't have it any other way."

Once again, Abe and I ramp up production. We hire more employees. We buy another truck. Now I deliver only to Purity Supreme while another driver handles DeMoulas. My schedule is grueling. I'm on the road from 5:00 a.m. to 5:00 p.m., six days a week. Then I stay late at the warehouse to manage the company and help with bookkeeping.

"I can't take this anymore," Karla tells me five weeks into my Purity Supreme contract. "This has to stop. You're killing yourself. You're killing *us*."

"I can't stop," I insist. "If I stop, the company dies. I have dozens of people who depend on me now. Families rely on the income I produce." I'm on a roll now. I can't even stop arguing though I see her inching away. "How do you think your father got rich? By sitting on his butt? By waiting for money to just come to him? No. He worked. Just like me. Because that's what it takes to be a success." Then I blurt out something that's been at the back of my mind for weeks. "You know, I bet if I had taken your father's money, if I had made him a partner, none of this would be an issue. You never liked Abe. What you really resent is he's my partner and your father's not."

"You're crazy," she finally says. "And I don't want to live this way. I'm sorry, but I can't."

Karla and I have known each other for three years. We have been married only one. We have a child. It doesn't matter. The next day, Scott and I move out.

Chapter 38

SCOTT AND I move into a two-bedroom apartment near the Cedars Mediterranean Foods factory/warehouse. Karla and little Joey remain in the house in New Hampshire. Going from a single-family house back to a rental apartment represents a jarring reversal of fortune, but I tell myself our circumstances are only temporary. If I apply myself, I can make enough money to buy comfortable homes for both parts of our now-divided family.

Karla was right about one thing: I truly am obsessed with success. As I see it, I really have no other choice. Americans have an expression: Money is power. And they are right. Money gives you choices. It gives you options. *Opportunities*. True, even with money, life can be unpredictable and capricious, but without it, you're like a cork cast into a raging river, condemned to float wherever fate's currents take you.

At least with money, you can steer. You can turn. You can resist. As I have painfully learned, money comes with a price, usually the loss of personal relationships, but I also believe that, in most cases, money merely accelerates processes in play. Many relationships follow the same infatuation/love/contentment/boredom/repulsion curve, regardless of financial circumstances; having money in the equation just speeds things up. Unless, of course, you have found that special someone to buck this trend—and so far, I have not.

So now, with Karla and I formally separated, I work harder than ever. I hire a professional nanny to watch Scott after school and in the evenings as I usually don't come home until 9:00, or sometimes even 10:00 p.m. I miss spending time with my son but am convinced the company's future—and therefore our own—depends on me giving it my full attention.

My dedication yields quantifiable results. Through my dealings with Purity Supreme, I connect with a distributor who provides food for dozens of Jewish delicatessens throughout New York City. My product is already kosher, meaning it meets the strict dietary dictates for cleanliness and purity set forth in the Old Testament, so it satisfies all of his buyers' requirements.

At this time, kosher delis are still extremely common throughout New York's five boroughs. Rather than deliver packaged food to each deli individually, my contract calls for me to truck several dozen cases of product to a central warehouse in Manhattan. From there, the distributor transports the cases to their destinations. To meet the contract, I buy a refrigerated semi-truck and hire a driver whom I take once a week on the 430-mile-round-trip. Each journey takes a full ten-hour day, but earns the business $40,000, $10,000 of which is pure profit.

And the other five business days? We use the truck to make deliveries to grocery stores and supermarkets in the surrounding states: Connecticut, Rhode Island, and Pennsylvania. Altogether, I'm doing $300,000 a month in volume. This is more money than I have ever seen in my life. Some mornings I have to pinch myself that I came here with $28 in my pocket. And just a few years ago I was earning several cents an hour making doughnuts.

Responding to popular demand, I decide to add other Lebanese and Greek dishes to our Mediterranean food line. These include *dolmakadia*, grape leaves stuffed with rice and spices; and *baklava*, a delicious dessert made from flaky phyllo dough, chopped nuts, and honey. Thanks to the success of my company I become a kind of hero in Boston's Lebanese community. Letters pour in from Lebanese-Americans all over New England, telling me how thrilled they are to go into an American supermarket and find products offering them a taste of back home.

And there is other good news. My younger sister, Josephine, is getting married. Her fiancé, Jamil, is also Lebanese. Although they met here in the Boston area, Jamil's extended family now lives in Orange County, California. At the wedding, as our families dance to traditional Lebanese folk songs played by a live band, Jamil takes me aside.

"Tony, I have something to ask of you."

"What is it?" I ask, feeling pleasantly loose from the three glasses of wine I've had so far. "Do you need money? What I have is yours."

"No, no, nothing like that," Jamil says, embarrassed. "It's about Josephine and me. We're thinking of moving West. To be with the rest of my family in California. I know how close the two of you are, and I respect your relationship, so I wanted to ask for your permission."

I am moved by Jamil's show of respect, but still I have to laugh. "Of course. Who wouldn't want to move to California?"

"Then we have your permission?"

"You have my permission," I assure him, adding, "On one condition."

"What is it?"

"If I ever decide to visit, you let me stay with you."

Jamil pulls me into a big hug. I'm going to miss Josephine, but how could I deny her happiness?

It is now 1983. Jamil and Josephine do indeed move to Orange County. I fear it will be many years before I see them again. Although the three-thousand-mile distance can be covered in half a day by jet airplane, my crushing work schedule makes it impossible for me to consider even a short trip.

This is also the time I formally divorce Karla. I have now dissolved two marriages, something I could never have imagined just ten years ago. In the settlement, I give her the house, monthly alimony, and child support for Joey, who she wants to keep for herself. Letting go of my little boy is difficult. We named him after my little brother, and Joey always reminded me of the good times we shared. It feels like losing my brother twice.

A year later, I begin dating a girl named Maria. Fun and high-spirited, she suggests I take a weekend off and take her to Las Vegas.

"I'd love to, but I don't have the time."

"Of course, you do. Aren't you the boss? We can leave late on a Friday and come back late Sunday night. The company will survive. Trust me."

"But Las Vegas is far away. Atlantic City is so much closer."

"Atlantic City wants to be Las Vegas. But there's nothing like the real thing."

I have to admit, I'm tempted. From what I have seen in the movies, Vegas has everything I enjoy: luxurious hotels, great food, and world-class entertainment. I've been working my fingers to the bone for years. Don't I deserve a break?

"Sounds like fun," I say with a smile. "And while we're at it, we can take a side trip to visit Jamil and Josephine in California." (At this time, I imagine Las Vegas and Orange County being in close proximity. Which, compared to Boston and O.C. they are. The fact that this *side trip* will add two days to my *weekend getaway* does not yet register with me.)

Maria books the airline and hotel reservations both in Las Vegas and in Huntington Beach, the largest city close to Jamil and Josephine's home in smaller Westminster. The more I read about Southern California, the more intrigued I become. Compared to Boston, much of which dates back to the late nineteenth and early twentieth centuries, everything in the area seems fresh, new. And the weather? I'm getting older now, and every autumn the threat of coming winter fills me with dread. I did not grow up with subzero temperatures, and they are becoming increasingly hard on me. They also wreak havoc on my truck drivers. Truth be told, I envy the life my little sister and her husband must be living.

Before I leave, I meet with Abe at the warehouse. "I'm taking a few days off," I announce. "Maria and I are going to Vegas, then to California to visit my sister."

"Good for you. Drop me a postcard from the beach."

"While I'm there, I'm going to check around for business opportunities. I've been thinking about it, and if I like what I see, I may decide to move there. Start fresh, you know?"

"You mean open a West Coast subsidiary?" Abe asks cautiously, thrown by my sudden announcement.

"No, if I do this, I want to start from scratch so I may need you to buy me out."

His jaw drops but I continue unfazed.

"While I'm gone, talk to our lawyers," I say. "See what needs to be done. If I decide to make this move, things could happen quickly."

I have no idea how right I am.

Chapter 39

I NOW BELIEVE in love at first sight. From the moment I emerge from our American Airlines Boeing 737 into the bright sunlight of Southern California, I am smitten. Maria and I left a bone-chilling and windy Boston six hours earlier. When we changed planes at Chicago's O'Hare Airport, the outside temperature had fallen another 5 degrees, with icy rains and high winds making our landing a stomach-turning excursion into vertiginous hell. But here, even on April 8, 1984, the sky is blue, the sun is clear, and the air is a delightful 75 degrees. I don't even need the windbreaker I brought along.

As we descend the metal steps to the tarmac of the Santa Ana/John Wayne Airport—they actually named this airport after a movie star—I can see palm trees standing tall around the airport's perimeter. This is the first time I have seen palm trees in person, and the sight fills me with visions of tropical luaus, surfers, and grass-skirted island beauties. I really feel like I've just stepped onto the set of a Hollywood movie.

Once we claim our luggage inside the tiny brick terminal, we grab a taxi and drive fifteen minutes up the crowded I-405 north to the City of Westminster, population eighty thousand. As we leave the freeway for the surface streets, I notice many of the storefronts bear signs in an unfamiliar Asian language. I ask our cabbie about this.

"It's all Vietnamese," the driver, a fiftyish Caucasian explains. "Came here after Saigon fell. They call this whole area Little Saigon."

"Little Saigon?"

He nods. "Remember their president? Little guy? Nguyen Cao Ky? Now he runs a liquor store a few blocks from here."

Maria looks at me. "That's a come-down."

When America was fighting the Vietnam War, I was still a teen chasing girls on the streets of Beirut, so my memories of the conflict are thin. But the idea that a former national president and military leader is now reduced to the role of liquor store owner on a distant continent makes me realize there are many sides to the American dream. Still, I suppose, in many ways, the man is lucky. Most deposed leaders, especially despots, end up losing far more than just wealth and privilege. They lose their heads. At least Ky is still alive in a country offering him constitutional protections and due process. Who knows? Perhaps with some hard work he can grow that one liquor store into a huge, multimillion-dollar chain. In America, a person can always dream.

Arriving at my sister's address, Maria and I are greeted warmly by Josephine and Jamil in the driveway of their five-year-old, 1,700-square-foot, single-story home. Its white-painted rough stucco exterior makes a strong impression on me, as I am accustomed to houses with facades of brick or wood siding.

"It's because of earthquakes," Jamil explains. "If the earth moves, stucco will crack, but bricks will collapse."

I get it. Form follows function.

As soon as we enter Josephine's, my mind turns to business. "What are the biggest chains in the area?" I ask.

Josephine doesn't seem to mind. She knows my workaholic personality. "Vons. Ralphs. Alpha Beta. Lucky. Stater Brothers. Hughes. Which ones do you want to see?"

Maria knows me too. "He wants to see them all."

"We're only here for two days," I put in. "So, we should get going now."

Maria joins me on my impromptu scouting expedition. With Josephine at the wheel, we spend the next two days casing supermarkets in Westminster and the nearby cities of Seal Beach, Huntington Beach, Fountain Valley, Costa Mesa, Newport Beach, and Santa Ana. We even visit small, independent neighborhood stores we happen upon. Much to my delight, not a single one sells Mediterranean food. No hummus. No tabbouleh. No grape leaves. No baba ghanoush. Just like Boston a few years ago, Orange County is open territory.

That Sunday, as we prepare to leave for Vegas, I hand Josephine a blank check drawn on my personal account.

Confused, she stares back at me. "What's this for?"

"I want you to rent me a house. Three bedrooms, two baths, preferably."

"You mean, you're moving here?" she gasps.

"I've had it with Boston. It's cold and crowded. It also holds a lot of bad memories. Here everything is fresh and new. A whole new frontier."

Suddenly, I have a vision of myself as an American cowboy leading a wagon train across the great plains. Perhaps it's that oversized statue of John Wayne in full western regalia I saw at the airport.

"How soon are you going to do this?" Josephine asks.

"As soon as I can. Next month, I hope."

"That fast?"

"When something feels right, do it. Why wait?"

From Orange County, Maria and I fly to our original destination, Las Vegas, a mere forty-five minutes by air. We spend the next two days at the legendary Sands Hotel. I'm not much of a gambler, but I manage to win a grand total of $35 at casino's slot machines. We also enjoy several scrumptious buffets as well as a delightful stage show complete with dancing girls. Maria was right for suggesting this place. It's like Disneyland for adults.

Upon returning to Boston, I call Abe and tell him of my decision. "Get ready to buy me out."

And buy me out he does. Seeing the check's impressive array of zeros, I again can't help recalling how I left Beirut with all of $28 in my pocket. Now, not even fifteen years later, I am rich. Literally rich. America has truly been kind. Nowhere else in the world could I have enjoyed such success so quickly.

"I want to take you to California," I tell my other sister Coco even as she reels from my decision to move three thousand miles across the country.

"I thought you'd never ask," she says gratefully. Coco has never gotten used to Boston. She always complains it is too crowded and chilly. According to the travel books, Orange County has a Mediterranean climate, which, of course, she says sounds a lot more like home.

To facilitate the move, I rent a massive Penske truck, the largest in their local inventory. Its 26-foot bed is large enough to accommodate all of Coco's possessions as well as mine, along with the black 1984 Chevy Monte Carlo I recently purchased. In early May, we hit the road. I drive. Coco rides shotgun. Wedged between us is Scott. He sees this move as a great adventure and can't wait to see magical Disneyland.

From Boston we drive west over ten days, taking our time to see America. Except for my recent flight to the West Coast, I have never been farther west than eastern Pennsylvania, and the size and variety of this vast country amazes me. After leaving the green hills of western Pennsylvania midway through day two, the land becomes completely flat for a good thousand miles. When we pass through Kansas, the topography is so empty the highway appears to stretch straight and unbroken clear to the horizon. In central Colorado we enter the Rocky Mountains, which are visually spectacular but difficult to navigate driving such a big, heavy vehicle.

Riding up into the mountains I can feel the engine straining as I grind my foot into the pedal to keep our speed at thirty miles per hour.

Peering into my side-view mirror, I glimpse a long line of cars and their frustrated drivers stuck behind me, wishing they could pass. Coming down the other side, I have to keep the truck in low gear and use the engine like a brake just to keep our behemoth of a vehicle from careening out of control. I literally sigh with relief when we finally return to level ground.

On the other side of the Rockies we encounter nothing but empty desert for hundreds of miles. This part of the country reminds me of pictures I've seen of deserts in the Middle East, especially in Iraq and Iran, with its low, rocky hills and parched plains. In Utah, we stop at Bryce and Zion national parks, where we marvel at the incredible natural canyons and rock formations.

Finally, on May 21, 1984, we cruise out of the San Bernardino Mountains and into Orange County, California. Before us lies a grid of crisscrossing freeways, palm tree-lined streets and picturesque neighborhoods stretching mile after mile beneath the baking sun. Beyond our squinting eyeline the sparkling waters of the Pacific Ocean lap the shore. This is as far west as America goes. End of the line.

This is where I will make my stake. As far as I'm concerned, there's no going back. In Boston, I made a small fortune selling foods from my distant homeland. This new location is even more distant still. Am I crazy for starting over in a place I've only visited once? Can lightning really strike twice?

Chapter 40

WHEN I STARTED Cedars Mediterranean Foods back in Salem, it was just my kitchen, my family, and me. Yet, within a few years, we grew to occupy a small warehouse, employing dozens of people. We were serving customers in several states, including Massachusetts, New York, Pennsylvania, and New Hampshire. Now, here in Southern California, I am back where I started. It's just my kitchen, my family, and me. Only now, my company has a new name: Coco's Mediterranean Foods, Inc. Yes, my sister Coco is my partner. And I wanted her name on our product. Of course, with several years of experience behind me, I now have a formula for success I intend to follow. Why mess with what works?

As I did in Salem, I begin by preparing sample batches of hummus, tabbouleh, and baba ghanoush, placing them in plastic tubs featuring our new company label. (This time, I weigh and label each container carefully. I don't need another visit from the state Board of Weights and Measures.) These I place in large coolers I bought specifically for this venture.

My first stop is Mother's Market, a health food store with locations in Huntington Beach and Newport Beach. My brother-in-law Jamil shops here often and has assured me they will be receptive to my exotic food products.

Entering the Huntington Beach location, I see large displays of fresh fruit and vegetables, all of which are stacked loosely and lack the uniform packaging and appearance of produce grown by large agri-businesses. The setup reminds me of a local farmer's market—which I am sure is exactly the effect they're going for. The first thing I smell is vitamins. I don't know what chemical produces that strong, almost acrid odor, but I find it to be all too common in shops catering to the health food community.

Carrying my sample cooler, I ask a cashier to point me to the manager. I'm introduced to a lean, almost gaunt man who could be anywhere from thirty to fifty years of age. He wears faded jeans, a checkered long-sleeve shirt and full-length apron with the store's logo printed on its coarse fabric. He looks like he stepped out of a West Coast hippie commune.

After giving my name and introducing myself with a firm handshake, I go into my spiel. "I just moved to California from the East Coast where I ran a successful Mediterranean food company. We supplied some of the top supermarket chains in New England, including Purity Supreme and DeMoulas. You may have heard of them."

Despite the manager's blank expression, it still feels great to rattle off my track record. Being able to name-drop offers instant credibility—even if the person you're talking to is as oblivious as this manager appears to be. "I recently sold my half of the business so I could move out here and introduce these amazing recipes to a whole new market. Have you ever carried any Lebanese or Mediterranean foods?"

"No, that's not really our thing," he says. "We carry Hispanic and Asian stuff, but otherwise we don't do ethnic cuisine." I watch as his eyes drift to the samples in my open cooler. I sense that despite his objections, he's intrigued.

"People just love this," I say, removing a container from the plastic cooler. "It's called hummus. If your customers enjoy vegetable dips, they'll *adore* this."

I offer him a piece of pita bread, but he steps backward like I'm peer-pressuring him into trying his first cigarette. "Like I said, man, we don't really carry ethnic foods…"

"You know your customers better than I do," I say, appearing for a moment to concede. "If you don't think they'll buy it, I understand. But why not give it a try? You might change your mind. Hey, this could be the next big thing."

A long and strange silence passes. At last, with obvious reluctance, the man accepts the pita, dips it into the hummus… and freezes.

"Hey. You said this is all-natural, right?"

"No chemicals. No artificial ingredients. Made by hand following my mother's original recipe."

This seems to do the trick. He pops the pita into his mouth and savors the dip's flavor. Then, in what has become a predictable reaction, he breaks into a big smile. Good taste is universal. In the days that follow, I visit more small stores and receive a similarly positive response. At each, I leave behind a full complement of products, personally displaying them in the refrigerated sections. I'm off and running, baby.

Based on experience, I know I won't be able to keep up with demand by making food in my home kitchen. I'm going to need a real commercial space like the one I had back in Salem. It takes me several hours, but I draft an intricate sketch of what I want in my dream facility, including appliances, shelving, and ovens. It's unlikely I will get just what I am looking for, but from past experience I know it's important to be specific when preparing. Going through the want ads in *The Orange County Register,* I find a listing for a 10,000-square-foot building on Hoover Street in Westminster that looks promising.

However, when I visit the building, I find it's little more than four walls and a roof—a far cry from the sketch I drew. It will require a lot of improvements to become a functioning manufacturing facility. I'll need to buy and install refrigerators and freezers. I'll need machines to chop, puree, and blend our various ingredients. I'll need to create storage areas for packing materials, work tables, and benches, and to partition off and furnish spaces for executive and sales offices. This is all going to take major time and money.

Fortunately, fate once again steps in to help me in a baffling way.

"Attaboy, Scotty," I shout from the grandstand. "Let's hit a homer!"

It's a beautiful day in early June. Here in Fountain Valley we're enjoying clear blue skies and noontime highs in the mid-70s with refreshing breezes blowing off the nearby Pacific. In other words, perfect weather for a baseball game.

Scott is now thirteen years old and has become an excellent ballplayer in the local Little League. Or so I'm told. Although I have been in America for fifteen years, I still don't quite understand the rules of America's pastime. Yes, I do know the object of the game is to use the bat to hit the ball as far as you can, then run around the diamond before someone on the other team touches you with the ball. That much I can follow. But when it comes to hitting the ball…

Crack!

A big cheer goes up as Scott sends it sailing into the outfield. Tossing the bat aside, he dashes full-out to first base where he stops several seconds before a member of the other team throws the ball to the boy guarding second base. My son is smart enough to stop before getting tagged out.

"Way to go," I shout. "Great hit."

"Is that your son?" a man seated behind me asks. I turn to see he's in his late thirties, light skinned, with wavy, sandy-blond hair. He wears khaki Dockers slacks and a collared polo shirt with a little alligator logo sewn onto its chest. His attire screams Orange County.

"Yes, it is."

"He's a great player. I've been watching. By the way, I'm Danny."

"Tony," I offer my hand. "Your son is on the team, too?"

"Number eighteen. Right field." Danny points to a skinny blond kid sitting pensively on the bench with the other members of the Cubs.

Minutes go by with us chatting about typical dad stuff until my business mind, as usual, kicks in.

"So, what do you do?" I ask.

"I'm a baker for Panera Bread."

I immediately light up.

"You been to one of our stores?"

"No. But I happen to be looking for a baker."

"You?"

"Yeah. I own a Mediterranean food company. Coco's."

"You mean like the restaurant?"

Since coming to Orange County, I've noticed a chain of coffee shops with the same name.

"It's my sister's name. She's my partner."

"A family business. I like that."

"So, how long have you been a baker?"

"I grew up in it. My father owned a bakery in Fullerton. I worked for him when I was in high school but he sold it when he retired."

"He didn't give it to you?"

"Back then, I didn't want it. What can I say? I was young and stupid. I wanted to be an actor. Now I'm back to pounding dough."

I laugh along with him. "Hey, Danny. If you don't mind my asking, how much is Panera paying you?"

He hesitates. "That's kind of a personal question."

"Sorry."

We both go back to watching the game. Another kid steps up to bat.

Before the pitch comes, Danny blurts out, "Six hundred a week."

I turn to him. "I can pay you seven hundred. Here's my card."

He studies it for a moment. "I don't usually make deals at my son's baseball game," he says. Still, I notice him pocket it.

"And how do I contact you?"

Suddenly, I'm distracted by a cheer from the crowd. I turn to see a flurry of activity on the ballfield. I'm not quite sure what's going on, but the kid at bat must have really smacked the ball because he's sprinting like the devil himself is chasing him. At third base he makes a sharp left turn and runs full-out for home plate. Someone from the other team throws the ball to the catcher, which reaches him well ahead of our player.

I'm on my feet now. "Go, go!"

The catcher fumbles, and the ball goes rolling behind him. The kid darts across home plate, pumping his arms victoriously.

"Safe!" the umpire shouts. Scott turns to find me in the stands. I whistle back at him.

"Exciting game," I tell Danny.

He hands me a piece of paper back with his number on it.

The next day, I begin searching for an architect to help me design the space I need in the Hoover Street building. In the Yellow Pages, I find an ad for an architect named Michael Maynard. I call the number, explain I have a growing food business, and ask if he can design a facility for food preparation.

"Absolutely," Maynard says. "I've done about a dozen buildings just like it." He rattles off a list of names I don't recognize. But, like I said, name-dropping always helps establish credibility.

I arrange to meet him at the Hoover Street building at 10:00 a.m. the following day.

I then call Danny at the number he gave me. "I'm meeting an architect at my new building tomorrow morning. I'd like you to come."

"Me? Why?"

"You're a baker. I could use your input."

"I'm really kind of busy…"

"I'm not asking this as a favor. I'll pay for your time. How does a hundred dollars for one hour sound?"

"Let me give you my address."

Coco and I pick Danny up at his house in Fountain Valley at 9:45, and together we drive to the Hoover Street building, just ten minutes away. Maynard and the building's owner are waiting for us when we arrive.

The owner unlocks the door, and the five of us begin exploring the cavernous space. I walk Maynard around, explaining my vision for where the equipment needs to go and what we need to do to meet local health codes. Danny chimes in with suggestions of his own. They make sense. The man knows what he's talking about, and I'm glad to have him along. After ten minutes, Maynard stops writing notes and motions me aside.

"Have you signed the lease for this place yet?" he asks.

"No, not yet," I admit. "We're still haggling about price."

"Good. I want you to follow me."

"Where?"

"Tustin"

Tustin is another city about twenty minutes away. Its most notable feature is the sprawling U.S. Marine Corps helicopter base occupying the southern portion of the city and its two giant concrete airship hangars, relics from a time when the Navy flew blimps from here to scout the coast for Japanese submarines. Following along in our car, Coco, Danny, and I tail Maynard to a one-story light industrial building in a large office park blocks from the Marine base. As we step into the parking lot, I hear the thunder of nearby transport helicopters practicing take-offs and landings.

Maynard Opens the door and ushers us into what appears to be a turnkey food factory. One wall is lined with gleaming stainless-steel refrigerators and freezers. Four large white linoleum-topped worktables stand in the center of the room, two pizza ovens occupy another wall, and in the far corner are several rows of storage shelves.

I'm speechless and dizzy. I have to hold onto the wall or I will fall over.

"What is it?" asks Maynard with concern. "You're not having a heart attack, are you?"

I manage to pull out my sketch from my pocket. "Look."

Inexplicably, this setup matches the exact blueprints I drew days ago. I mean *identical*. Down to the placement of the shelves. It's as if this building were custom–designed just for me.

Maynard shakes his head. "This is nuts. My partner and I were going to start our own business making sandwiches here. We sunk our life savings into this place, then the project died. The building's been sitting empty for months. If you're interested," he continues. "I'm sure we can work out a deal."

I'm most certainly interested. After all, it's not every day you manifest the facility of your dreams. And we do indeed work out a deal. Afterwards, I hire Danny to be my chief baker and buy a refrigerated van so I can make deliveries anywhere in Orange County.

"You know, if you really want to sell, you've got to go up to L.A.," Danny insists soon after. "*That's* the health food capital of America."

Using the Los Angeles Yellow Pages, I write down a dozen addresses and buy a *Thomas Guide* map. Before Waze, before Google Maps, before TomTom, there was the *Thomas Guide*, a thick, spiral-bound book of indexed neighborhood maps, a lifesaver for urban exploration before GPS.

Almost giddy with excitement, I fill my new refrigerated truck with samples and head north up the 405. Leaving Orange County behind, I head into Long Beach and new, foreign territory. I'm looking for the Culver City exit, but when I pull off the freeway, I realize I have gotten off too soon. This is not cheery and affluent Orange County. This is the seedy part of L.A. you hear about on the news, the rundown section where drive-bys go down. Sad small houses with faded paint and bars on their windows glower at me. Turning onto a commercial street, I notice an inordinate number of liquor stores, pawn shops, and Payday Loan offices. Billboards advertise malt liquor and accident attorney services. As I roll by, pedestrians give me the stink eye.

I begin to sweat. Maybe coming up here wasn't such a good idea after all.

Chapter 41

INCREASINGLY AGITATED AND yes, somewhat frightened, I veer away from the shady characters giving me dirty looks, pulling my truck into a strip mall parking lot. After checking my rearview mirror to make sure no one's followed me, I consult my *Thomas Guide* for a way back to the 405.

The strip center is just as seedy as the neighborhood it serves. It's anchored by a rundown convenience store, next to which is a laundromat, a gun shop, a liquor store, and a Payday Loan center. My paranoid mind imagines a scenario in which a guy borrows money from Payday, then walks next door and uses that cash to buy a bottle of booze. Fueled with liquid courage, he next goes to the gun shop and gets a pistol that he then uses to rob the convenience store. And the laundromat? He can double back to that to wash any blood out of his shirt if he gets shot during the robbery. Now that's one-stop shopping.

My heart still racing, I try to shake these morbid thoughts and get practical. Flipping open the thick guide, I search for my current street index. What street is this? Inglewood? Edgewood? I'm not at all familiar with Los Angeles, and without any visible street signs, I don't know where to start.

Bang! Bang!

Startling noises cause me to jerk upright so fast I drop the guide to my feet. Spinning to my left, I see a man leering through my driver's side window. He's old, with craggy, furrowed skin, curly white hair, patchy white whiskers, and a twisted mouth revealing several missing teeth. His eyes are narrow and bloodshot. Although the outside temperature must be in the low 80s, he wears a heavy woolen coat marked by dark stains. My window is tightly closed, but I can almost smell the alcohol on his breath.

The man gestures to me, obviously asking for money. Again, he bangs on my door and extends an open palm. I pull my wallet from my jacket pocket and find a $5 bill. I lower the window to slide the bill through the opening. My visitor reaches up and snaps the money from my fingers, smiles broadly, nods, and trundles toward the convenience store.

Sighing relief, I turn the key and fire up my engine. "Screw the *Thomas Guide*. I'll figure this out on my own."

Backing out of the parking space, I turn toward the main road. Just then, a commercial milk truck bearing the logo of a local dairy rolls by. Then it hits me: *Milk trucks deliver to grocery stores*. I'm trying to find a grocery store. Not wanting to lose sight of the dairy truck, I force my way into heavy traffic. There are three cars between me and my quarry but the dairy truck is large enough I can follow it easily even at this distance. That is, until it roars through a yellow traffic light.

The cars ahead, obviously driven by locals who have no desire to waste time idling at a red light, also blast through the intersection in quick succession. By the time I arrive, the light has been burning crimson for at least two seconds. Once again in pursuit of my white tiger, I speed through it too, keeping as tight on the tail of the car ahead of me as I dare. Nervously, I look around for any flashing police lights. Fortunately, my traffic violation has gone undetected. I now feel like a true Southern Californian.

Three blocks later, the truck turns into the parking lot of a large grocery store called Glenn's Market. Energized, I throw the gear shift into park and grab a sample case from the refrigerated bay in the back. I take a deep breath, steady myself, and march through the entrance doors, ready for battle.

"Tony Assali? Do I know you?" asks the manager, identified by his nametag as Jack Daouk. His accent is obvious and as "Daouk" is a fairly common Lebanese name, I have every reason to believe I am dealing with a fellow countryman.

"I'm new to the area. Just moved here from Boston. But I was born and raised in Beirut."

"And I thought I knew all the Lebanese in the city."

"Actually, I live in Orange County. Westminster."

"Ah. Then welcome to the big city," Jack says with a smile. "What have you brought for me?"

"Food from the old country," I announce, removing the top of my cooler to reveal labeled containers beneath.

"Hummus. Baba ghanoush. Tabbouleh," Jack's voice has a hint of wistful nostalgia, like he's identifying old friends in a photo album. I'm relieved to talk to someone who already knows what I'm selling and tempted to pull out a contract on the spot. But then Jack turns to me, shaking his head. "I tried selling hummus two years ago. *Couldn't give the stuff away.* No one here is interested in our kind of food."

This throws me for a loop. Of all the prospects I've spoken to, I figured Jack would be the most receptive. How can a Lebanese grocery store manager not want to sell Lebanese food?

"Maybe you had the wrong recipe."

Jack looks like I just insulted his mother. "How the hell can you mess up hummus?"

I pull a container from my cooler, crack open the lid and show Jack its buttery contents. "You tell me. Was it as good as this?"

In what is quickly becoming a familiar experience, I pull out a bag of pita bread and offer Jack a piece. He tears off a slice and with the smoothness of a seasoned pro and scoops out the hummus. His reaction upon tasting the smooth, creamy concoction is, surprisingly, one of concern.

I'm instantly on red alert. *Did my samples spoil in transit?*

"What's wrong?" I inquire, wondering if the product I recently sold in Orange County was also accidentally tainted.

"Nothing. Nothing at all." But Jack still looks troubled. "I just can't figure out why this tastes so much better than the hummus I tried to sell two years ago."

"So, you'll sell mine," I say, more of a statement than a question. "Put it on your shelves for a week. What you don't sell, I'll buy back. You have nothing to lose."

"Okay, okay, you made your sale. Just show me your price list," Jack says, then turns away, muttering to himself. "How do you frickin' mess up hummus?"

In addition to Glenn's, my trip to L.A. takes me to the owner of Erewhon, a chain of health food stores, as well to the offices of Mrs. Gooch's and Quinn's. Each encounter begins the same: with skepticism and resistance. Yet each ends with me carrying out an empty cooler—and a signed contract.

Back in Orange County, I arrive with more product to restock Mother's Market in Huntington Beach, only to find the shelf where they sell Coco's Mediterranean Foods bare except for one sole container of baba ghanoush.

I quickly track down the store manager. Again, I fear the worst. Did I somehow screw up the recipe?

"What happened? Did something go wrong? Did you have to throw it all out?" I ask, my palms sweating.

He shakes his head. "No. No. Relax. I didn't throw it out."

"Then what happened?"

He grins. "It sold out."

"Sold out?"

"I was going to call you. I need to double my order. Can you handle it?"

"Let me go back to my truck," I respond without hesitation.

It's crazy. After one month in business, I'm selling two thousand units per week. My growth curve here is far steeper than in Boston, and while it's doing wonders for my bank account, it's taking a toll on my body. Every day, my muscles ache. I pop multiple aspirin to deal with the headaches, but still I find my concentration drifting as I drive. Sometimes I fear I'm going to fall asleep at the wheel and cause an accident. That would not be good for business.

Still, I keep hustling. I can't stop. It's my nature. While on another midafternoon run to restock my growing list of local customers, I pull into a parking lot to grab a cup of coffee. As I step out of my truck, a sign above a grocery store catches my eye. Trader Joe's. I've never seen this name before, but the attractive, South Seas-style logo appeals to me. I decide to check it out.

Entering through the automatic sliding doors, I find the place to be decked out in a tropical motif. All the aisles are trimmed with bamboo, palm fronds, and tiki statues. Staff members hurry about in khaki pants and colorful Hawaiian-print shirts. It's only 11:30 a.m., yet I have an urge to order a Mai Tai.

Recognizing yet another business opportunity, I locate the manager and introduce myself. "I see you already sell a variety of ethnic foods. I think my unique product line would fit perfectly here."

"You'll need to talk to our corporate office," the manager explains. He's a fortyish looking man with a receding hairline, thick mustache and black horn-rimmed glasses. Like the rest of the staff, he, too, wears a Hawaiian shirt. "It's in the City of Commerce. We have a lot of people trying to sell to us. We're growing fast."

"Fast? How fast?"

"We have more than twenty stores in L.A. and Orange County. And we're looking at Arizona."

I can barely contain my excitement. California is truly the land of opportunity—and white tigers. I soon discover the City of Commerce, like its neighbor, Vernon, is an oddity among Southern California municipalities. The city encompasses only a few square miles, is composed mostly of manufacturing and light-industrial buildings, and has only a minimal number of actual homes and apartment buildings within its boundaries. Its most notable attraction is the Commerce Casino, a legal gambling establishment where gaming is limited to card games such as poker, blackjack and pai gow. I find Trader Joe's corporate headquarters to be a three-story office building five minutes off the I-5 freeway.

There I meet with Harold Coretti, the company's senior vice president. "You won't be able to sell under your own name," Coretti tells me straight away. "Everything we buy from third parties carries our in-house brand."

"That won't be a problem."

"Also, what's your product's shelf life?"

"Thirty days."

He cracks an eyebrow up. "You're sure about that?"

"I guarantee it."

"All right. Give me two of your hummus and two of your bab—*What did you call it?*"

"Baba ghanoush."

"Sounds like the name of a wise guy I knew in Hoboken. Fine. Give me two of each."

I reach into my cooler and remove two containers of each product. He opens one hummus and one baba ghanoush, then uses a plastic spoon to sample each.

"You say these are all natural?"

"The ingredients are right on the label."

"That's important to our customers."

"It's important to me, too."

Coretti reseals the two containers.

"Here. You can have these back."

"What about the other two?"

"I'm going to keep them for thirty days," Coretti explains. "And I'll try them again. If they taste just as good as these first ones did, you have yourself a customer."

I smile in appreciation. But behind that smile, I know these are going to be the longest thirty days of my life.

Chapter 42

"TONY? IT'S HAROLD Coretti."

I hold my breath the moment I hear Coretti's voice on the phone. It's been exactly thirty days since I visited the Trader Joe's vice president at his office, and since then a day hasn't gone by when I haven't visualized my two-pound containers of hummus and baba ghanoush sitting in the back of his refrigerator, their contents slowly but inevitably breaking by the hand of time.

The truth is I have never actually tested to see if my products could remain fresh for an entire month. None had actually stayed on a grocer's shelf that long. This was going to be the first real-world challenge to my bold claim; if it turns out I am wrong, my reputation—and therefore, my fledgling company's entire future—could be in serious jeopardy.

"Good to hear from you." I feign an air of relaxed confidence. "I take it you tested my products?"

Long pause.

"I did," he finally says.

I don't ask for his verdict. I assume it will come soon enough. There is nothing I can do at this point to change it. My future—my company's future—my family's future—will be determined by whatever happens next.

"To tell you the truth, I was disappointed," Coretti continues.

I put my head in my hand. There's suddenly no saliva in my mouth. The ingredients must have spoiled. Maybe there was mold in the containers. Was the refrigerator even set at the proper temperature? When it comes to preserving food, there are dozens of ways for things to go horribly wrong.

"We just finished composing our latest *Fearless Flyer*, and the last thing I wanted to have to do was revise it," he goes on.

Having used these last thirty days to study Trader Joe's and its operations, I know the *Fearless Flyer* is the company's monthly newsletter. Incorporating humorous turn-of-the-century fonts and illustrations, the flyer devotes large sections to new product introductions, waxing enthusiastically about the exotic origins and top-quality ingredients of its latest frozen fish fillets or vegetable chips.

But what does this have to do with my hummus and baba ghanoush?

"But now I have no choice," Coretti says with a forced sigh. "We'll have to add another story about our new, *delicious* Lebanese food products."

Blood rushes to my face. I can't control my grinning.

"We'll be carrying you in all thirty-seven of our stores starting in two weeks. You can deliver by then?"

"Absolutely!" I assure him. In my mind, I'm already composing the help-wanted ad I'll have to place to hire more workers for our Tustin factory.

"Great. I'll have legal draw up the contract. Oh, and one other thing."

"Yes?"

"Can you send over two pounds of hummus? It's my wife's birthday this weekend, and I'd love to serve it at our party."

"It's on its way," I say happily. "No charge."

Over the next year, Coco's Mediterranean Foods continues to conquer the Southern California market. My non-stop, take-no-prisoners, don't-take-no-for-an-answer sales formula gets us into Vons, one of the area's largest retail supermarket chains, then into Price Club, the membership warehouse giant that will eventually become Costco.

Through a contact I develop in Greece, I am able to get regular shipments of authentic grape leaves. It makes me happy that I can satisfy even native Greeks. We also add *spanakopita*: savory pies made with phyllo dough and fresh spinach, to our catalog. Price Club loves these and orders them in huge twelve-inch trays. (As I quickly discover, everything that Price Club does is huge.)

For some people, the kind of success I am enjoying with Coco's Mediterranean Foods would give them license to relax, to take time off to enjoy the fruits of their labors. Not me. Instead of providing relief, my good fortune only makes me more restless, more eager to find more mountains to climb. It has come to the point that I can't drive down the street, go grocery shopping, or enjoy a meal out without searching for more white tigers.

For example, it's now 1986. One of my box suppliers, Kevin, takes me to lunch at a restaurant called Avila's El Ranchito. I have been living in Southern California for nearly two years and, amazingly, this is my first visit to a Mexican restaurant. At his direction, we both order a Corona and, as I am told is the custom at such establishments, are served a basket of fried tortilla chips along with a bowl of spicy tomato and pepper puree called salsa.

Always eager to try new ethnic foods, I dip a chip into the salsa. I love the combination of crunch and spice. After washing it down with the refreshing beer I can see why this stuff is so popular. The salsa *and the beer*. And it gives me an idea. When I return to the factory in Tustin, I call a meeting with my staff, many of whom are Mexican.

"Does anyone know how to make salsa?" I ask.

This gets a big laugh. Apparently, this is like asking Jewish people if anyone knows how to make chicken soup. Or asking a bunch of Lebanese if anyone knows how to make hummus. Several volunteers raise their hands.

Working together, my newly recruited team and I devise a recipe that blends just the right amount of tomatoes, jalapeno peppers, onions, garlic, and salt. No expert at Mexican fare, I insist my experts test-taste our concoction with their relatives. The last thing I want is to be seen as a phony.

"*Muy bueno*," is the reaction I get again and again. "*Delicioso*."

Once I am satisfied with the product, I find a company in Florida that can manufacture customized beer mugs with plastic lids. Anyone can make salsa. It's practically California's version of ketchup. What I intend to do is bank on the popularity of the tasty beer I tried that day at Avilla's. Two months later, Corona Salsa hits the market. I take samples to buyers for supermarkets all over Southern California. They're blown away by the creative packaging: fresh salsa sold in Corona-style glass beer mugs. They order them by the hundreds.

(Side note: three years later, I will receive a cease-and-desist letter from the lawyers for Constellation Brands, the company producing Corona beer for export to the United States. I had never licensed the Corona name or symbol for use on my product, hence the scary letter. So, yes, I ceased and desisted. Still, I sold a lot of salsa in those three years.)

Around the same time I invent Corona Salsa, I happen to be playing golf with a buyer for Vons supermarkets. Midway through the round, we stop at a hot dog stand run by a country club concessioner. I notice the stand provides four condiments for customers to dress up their frankfurters: ketchup, mustard, chopped onions, and pickle relish. The thing is, the ketchup and mustard come in plastic squeeze bottles but the onions and pickle relish sit in open containers with flies buzzing all around them.

This is horrible! *Why can't the condiments all come in a single bottle?* I wonder. Indeed, why not?

So again, I go to work. White tiger city.

The next day I get on the phone and, after asking around, find a supplier who can create the kind of squeeze bottle I'm imagining.

"It needs to have four compartments," I explain. "One for each of the ingredients, but they can't touch. All four must have separate nozzles."

"Sure, we can do that," the supplier assures me. "Not a problem."

A few weeks later, I offer Grand Slam hotdog toppings to my growing list of food distributors. Once again, sales explode. Thousands of bottles fly out the door every month. I'm on a roll.

Why Grand Slam? Well, as I learned from Scott, grand slam is a well-known baseball term, and hot dogs are popular foods at baseball games. Also, when a player hits a grand slam, meaning a home run with three players already on base, then the team scores four points. And there are four ingredients in my product. So, it's the perfect name, right?

Maybe not. A few months after my product hits the shelves, I get another C&D letter—this one from the lawyers for Denny's, the popular chain of coffee shop- style diners. Apparently, Denny's claims to own the name Grand Slam, which they use to promote their breakfast combinations. They want all my profits. I write them a polite letter explaining I was unaware of their trademark claim and promise to stop using it for my condiments. Happily, I never hear from them again.

Also, later that year, I am visiting Las Vegas when I stop off at a coffee shop (definitely not Denny's) for lunch. Coleslaw comes with my meal. My fevered white tiger mind can't help but notice the salad comes heavily laden with mayonnaise, which is clearly highly caloric and unhealthy. Still, as I look around, I notice people digging into their coleslaw sides to their meals. The fact is people love coleslaw. This gets me thinking: *Could coleslaw be dressed with another ingredient? Perhaps apple juice concentrate, to make it healthier?*

Immediately upon my return to Tustin, I begin working on my healthy coleslaw recipe. We try various types and concentrations of ingredients until I find one that provides just the right combination of sweetness and tartness. I then source a local supplier who can provide fresh cabbage in large quantities. I offer my healthy coleslaw to my Vons buyer, who takes one taste and immediately orders it in ten- pound tubs to sell in his deli counters. The name of my product? Slim Slaw.

One hundred percent original. And this time, I don't get any C&Ds from anybody.

I have been so busy with my various businesses I have barely noticed my son's slow decline. It's crept up little by little. Over the last few years as I have flourished, my boy has become listless. Distracted. According to Coco, he quit Little League and his grades are way, way down. I have seen this pattern of behavior before and I'm worried.

I followed Scott to his bedroom to have a conversation. "Scott, we need to talk."

"I'm busy right now," Scott says, slipping headphones over his ears.

"Are you doing drugs?" I ask him point blank.

He stares at me like I've just asked him the dumbest question in the world. "No."

"I don't believe you," I pull the headphones off. "You remember what happened to your Uncle Joe?"

He rolls his eyes at me.

"He kept denying he was taking drugs. . . until he crashed his car into a lane divider and broke his neck."

"So?"

"Is that what you want to happen to you?"

He puts his hand out. "Can I have my headphones back now?"

I stare at this young man, realizing I barely know him. He's almost my size and possesses the same curly dark hair and dark eyes. But our resemblance ends there. I would never talk to my father this way.

"Scotty…" I try again.

"I'm not taking cocaine, okay?" he blurts out. "Just leave me alone."

"I can't do that," I say softly. "I don't want anything to happen to you. You're the most important thing in my life. I've already lost enough people. I can't lose you too."

"Look, I won't do drugs. I promise."

I want to believe him. I do.

"I believe you," I say.

This is a terrible mistake I will live to regret.

Chapter 43

"TONY, I HAVE a girl I'd like you to meet."

This suggestion feels oddly familiar. How many times has someone tried to set me up with a date? Often, it goes well—at first. But then I usually end up marrying the person and then—well, it's all downhill after that. Still, I am lonely. Ever since moving to Orange County, my love life has been nonexistent. Not only have I been maniacally focused on building my business, but also, the AIDS epidemic has made the very idea of dating too scary.

I became aware of AIDS—Acquired Immune Deficiency Syndrome—a year ago. In the early 1980s, it was a rare disease that seemed to infect only gay men and intravenous drug users in big cities like New York and L.A. At the time, I gave it little thought. But in recent months, a flood of news stories on AIDS has spread. It's now affecting the heterosexual community, making lots of people worry.

Some articles characterize AIDS as the modern equivalent of the Black Death, predicting it will decimate major swaths of the world's population by the end of the century. From what I've heard, an AIDS diagnosis is tantamount to a death sentence. For this reason, I'm reluctant to get back into the dating game, steering clear of any encounters that could lead to my untimely end. And because I have always conflated sexual activity with romance, Antoinette's invitation holds little interest.

"Sorry, Nunu," I say, using her nickname. "I've taken myself off the market. I got too many other things to worry about right now."

"I'm not asking you to *marry the girl*, just meet her. Come over for dinner. And bring Scott. You still eat, don't you?"

"Yes, I still eat," I admit, glancing down at my not insignificant belly. Maybe this girl will find me unattractive and the whole dating issue will be moot. Then I will have satisfied my sister and gotten a free meal.

Scott and I arrive at Josephine and Jamil's in Westminster that Friday night as planned. Josephine greets us at the door, planting a kiss on each of our cheeks, then escorts us into the living room. There I find Jamil talking with a young, comely woman whose olive skin and straight black hair suggests a Latina. She wears a pastel blue dress with frilly sleeves. Very feminine.

"Ah, Tony, we were just talking about you," Jamil rises to his feet. "Meet Lucy."

Lucy stands, straightens her dress, and extends her hand. "Nice to meet you, Tony," she says in slightly accented English. Then she turns to my son. "And you must be Scotty."

"Scott," my son says sharply.

"Scott. I'm sorry," Lucy's dark eyes turn back to me. "You've raised quite a handsome young man."

Instead of looking pleased by the compliment, Scott lowers his eyes, acting like he didn't hear her.

Jamil breaks the tension. "Let me get you a drink. Beer, Tony?"

"Sure."

"And a Coke for Scotty—er, Scott?"

"Whatever." Scott shrugs.

Lucy returns to her chair and I sit on the sofa. Scott disappears to the bathroom without excusing himself.

"Well, this is awkward," she says with a nervous laugh. "Your sister really wanted us to get together."

"How do you know her?"

"We go to the same beauty salon. She can't stop talking about her handsome and successful brother. *Her* words," she adds even though I see the faintest beginning of a smile.

"As you can see, she exaggerates."

Her grin expands, but I want to temper her expectations, especially before Scott returns. "Look, the truth is, I'm not really looking for anything now. Between raising him and working on my business, I don't have time for…"

"For fun?" She's full-on smirking now. "No hobbies?"

Hobbies? "Not really."

She leans closer. "That's sad. If you're not having any fun, then what are you working for?"

I have to stop to think about this. When I was young, making money was a way to get girls. Fast cars and fancy clothes made me more attractive to women. Now that I'm in my thirties, chasing the almighty dollar has become an end unto itself. *What am I working for?*

Scott returns, plopping himself down onto the sofa. He finds the remote and flicks on the TV. Ignoring it, I keep my attention on Lucy.

"Why does anyone work?" I reply, perhaps too defensively. "To have a nice home. Security. So, when Scott gets sick, I have money to pay the doctor. So someday I can send him to a good college."

Scott doesn't acknowledge any of this. He's fixated on *Sports Center*.

"You don't have to convince me money is good," Lucy says. "My mother and father still live in Mexico. They've spent their entire lives scraping by. I have four brothers and sisters. I know what it's like to go to bed hungry, to not have shoes to wear to school…"

"I'm sorry. I didn't mean…"

She softens, lowering her voice so it's hard to hear her over the TV. "I didn't either. I'm just saying a person's life can't be just one thing. Even when we had no money, we could still enjoy nature. Sing songs. Play games. Tell stories. Sometimes, it helps to just step back and enjoy life."

"That's why we have beer." Jamil interrupts the moment by handing me a Corona. I'm actually annoyed by this intrusion. Things were getting interesting.

Jamil raises a toast. I do the same. Lucy raises her wine glass and touches it to my bottle. This is the first conversation in a long time I've had with a woman who wasn't an employee or corporate buyer. And much to my surprise, I enjoy it. After dinner, I invite her to join me for dinner the next weekend.

"But you're so *busy*." She draws the word out so it's nearly three syllables. "You sure you can spare the time?"

"Life has to be about more than just making money."

Her mouth forms that little half smile I like. "Then I guess it's a date."

The following Saturday, I take Lucy to an Italian restaurant in Huntington Beach. Again, I find I'm comfortable and surprisingly open in her presence. We share stories about coming to America. I tell her about fleeing Beirut before the outbreak of civil war. She tells me how her parents brought her across the border when she was just two so they could work in the San Joaquin Valley fields. Her parents returned to Mexico five years ago to tend to her ailing grandmother, but being in high school at the time, she chose to remain in America and move in with her older cousins who, like Jamil and Josephine, live in Westminster.

"So, you're not an American citizen?"

"Not yet," she admits. "But this is the only country I know. I went back to Mexico once, when I was thirteen, and it was completely foreign to me."

"What if the government finds you? They could deport you."

Her face darkens. "That's a danger we live with every day. That's why we keep a low profile. Work hard. Follow the law. Pay our taxes. Try not to cause trouble."

"It still sounds risky. I wish there was something I could do." I realize this sounds like a come-on, so I quickly backtrack. "Don't think I'm trying to get you into bed," I say hurriedly.

"I didn't think that..."

"I'm not thinking about having sex with you."

"Excuse me?"

Now I'm even more embarrassed.

"It's not that I don't think you're attractive. I think you're very attractive..." I think she's enjoying watching me squirm. "It's just that, I'm not having sex with anybody. It's too dangerous right now."

She leans in close. "What do you mean?" she asks, mock-serious. "Are you a secret agent or something?"

I chuckle, feeling more ridiculous. "No, I mean AIDS."

"Well, you don't have to worry about me. I'm still a virgin."

My jaw drops. Now I really don't know what to say.

"My two sisters got pregnant when they were very young. I saw how it changed their lives. I want to have children someday, too, but not until I'm older. So, I'm not going to do anything I might regret."

"That's smart thinking," I say, secretly relieved. "That takes a lot of discipline."

"Tell me about it," she says with a sigh.

We continue talking freely for the rest of the evening, after which we agree to go out again the following weekend. This pattern continues for another six weeks. We enjoy each other's company. And without the pressure of intimacy getting in the way, we're able to speak honestly about our hopes, our fears, and our dreams. At one point, Lucy reveals she wants to go to nursing school and is saving money for the tuition. When I hear this, I offer to pay her way.

She shakes her head. "Thank you, but I can't take your money."

"You asked me what I was working for," I remind her. "Well, this is one of the reasons—to help people who need it."

"That's very generous, but…"

"I have one condition."

"What?" she asks warily.

"If you don't graduate, you have to pay the money back. With interest. You have to be serious about this."

Her eyes light up. "Of course, I'm serious."

"Then we have a deal?"

Finding herself in a corner, Lucy realizes she has no choice but to agree. Two weeks later, she enrolls in a private vocational nursing program. A month after that, I ask her to marry me.

"I told you, I don't want children right now," she protests.

"Neither do I. I already have children. And raising one alone as a single father is no fun, believe me."

"So, you want a full-time babysitter?"

"No. I want someone I can come home to. Someone I can talk to."

"And what about sex?"

Even after going out for two months, we haven't kissed, let alone gone to bed.

"I think that would just get in the way. Why wreck a good thing?"

She nearly falls out of her chair with surprise. Still, two weeks later, Lucy and I marry in a simple civil ceremony at the Westminster City Hall. Our witnesses are Jamil and Josephine, plus Lucy's cousin and her husband. Before the wedding, she signs a prenuptial agreement that protects my business in the event of divorce. After two failed marriages, I'm going into my third with my eyes wide open.

Lucy moves in with me. When not at nursing school, she prepares meals and looks after Scott. In the evenings, I help her study, or we unwind together watching TV. As roommates go, I couldn't ask for a better one.

It's now 1989. Scott's behavior is getting worse. Rousing him from bed in the morning is a daily chore, and on weekends he sleeps until 1:00 in the afternoon. I get regular reports of him skipping classes. He stays out late. Almost every night I have to call local police stations and hospitals to see if he's been in some kind of trouble. He's rarely disrespectful, but it's clear he has emotional problems... and may be doing drugs.

At last, I sit him down and give him an ultimatum.

"Scott, you're a man now and you obviously have no interest in school," I start. "So, I'm going to give you two choices. Choice one: I will rent you an apartment in L.A. for one year, give you $100 in spending money, and then disown you. You will be on your own. Choice two: You can quit school now and enlist in the Army. You have one minute to decide."

Chapter 44

SCOTT BREAKS DOWN in tears. "I love you. I don't want you to disown me. Please. I'll do whatever you say."

"You'll enlist in the Army?"

"I will. Whatever you want."

This is as difficult for me as it is for Scott, but I know I'm doing the right thing. He needs to learn discipline, something I no longer have the ability to teach. It's something only an institution as strong as the army can provide. Fortunately, the United States is at peace and likely to remain so for the foreseeable future, so there is little chance of Scott actually seeing combat. Military training alone will be a good thing for him. For us.

The next day, I drive him to the local Army recruiting office, and he signs the paperwork. Being eighteen years old, he is legally an adult and does not need my permission. I am here only for moral support—and to stop him if tries to back out.

"I'm proud of you," I tell him as we leave.

"Okay, whatever." Scott sighs, still convinced this is some form of punishment rather than an opportunity for self-improvement.

One week later, I watch him board the bus that will take him to Fort Leavenworth, Kansas, for boot camp. I am both saddened and relieved as he pauses on the steps to wave, then disappears inside to join his fellow recruits. I am going to miss coming home to him every night. But, hopefully, this means I won't have to attend another funeral for someone I love, someone who died before their time.

Fed up with New England winters, my mother finally leaves New Hampshire to move in with Coco in Huntington Beach. Lucy and I are living in a rental house in Fountain Valley, just to the south. In the few weeks she's been here, my mother has made friends with a fellow Lebanese-American woman named Rose. She and her husband, Farid, have three sons and a daughter, all of my generation, all married. The daughter, Marlene, is married with two kids, Lorraine, six years old, and Michael, two years old. Marlene and her husband Steve live with her mom and dad, Rose and Farid. Not a strange arrangement at all in Lebanese culture.

"You should really meet this family," my mother tells me one day as we share lunch.

"I'm busy right now. I have to work late all week," I say.

"Then come over for breakfast. They'll be happy to have you."

Eager to get my mother to change the subject, I agree to join Rose and Farid later this week. When I arrive, Rose greets me at the door. She introduces me to her husband, Farid, and daughter, Marlene, then leads me to the kitchen counter where a traditional Lebanese breakfast has been laid out. The spread is impressive. There are meat pies, *za'atar* and spinach pies, *labneh*, olives, mint, several types of cheese, and green tea.

I would like to strike up a conversation with Rose's daughter so I ask her, "Is your name pronounced Madeline or Marlene?"

"The one you have a problem pronouncing," Marlene replies, then hurries off to the living room. I am both shocked and amused by her response. No one has ever remarked on how I pronounce my R's before. I find her attitude to be quite… bold.

Over the course of the meal, I quickly take a liking to Marlene's father, Farid. He's tall, medium built, and has a very confident personality, much like my late father. As we sip Turkish coffee, we discuss business, the economy, and international politics. The more we chat, the more I feel like I'm back home with my dad.

In August of 1990, I am at the Tustin factory when I get a phone call out of the blue from my mother. This concerns me because when she calls, she normally waits until after 8:00 at night. As usual, phone calls portend tragedy.

"What's wrong?" I ask.

"It's Farid. He's dead," my mother sobs.

"How? What happened?"

"A stroke," she chokes back tears. "He just collapsed."

It's only been a few months since I had breakfast with Rose and Farid, but during this time, I forged a strong connection with the man. I helped him after Rose also suffered a stroke that left her confined to a wheelchair. Now, Farid has passed away. Uncannily, it feels like losing my father all over again.

"Is there going to be a funeral?" I ask.

"On Monday."

"Who's taking you?"

"Marlene."

"I'll take you."

"But I thought you don't go to funerals."

This is true. Ever since Joe died, I swore I'd never attend another one. "But this is different. Farid was such a good man. I must pay him my respects."

"You're sure you want to go?"

"I'm sure."

That Monday, I drive my mother to the cemetery where Farid is to be buried. Rose is not present. Because of her recent stroke and incapacitation, it's been decided she should stay home with one of her sisters. During the service, the priest asks me to read a passage from the Bible in Arabic. As I step forward, I see Marlene and the rest of the family. She looks devastated. As I peer at her I can't help but wonder why I have been given this honor. After all, I didn't know Farid very long. Fortunately, my Arabic is still good, so I am able to read the verse smoothly and with emotion. As I do, I see Marlene staring at me, studying me. It occurs to me she probably has no idea who I am or what I'm doing at her father's funeral. This makes me slightly uncomfortable.

Later, we all return to Rose's house for food and drinks. There, I meet Marlene's husband, Steve, and her brothers, Wally and Bill, who I learn own an automotive repair and body shop in Huntington Beach.

"Maybe we can do business together," I offer. "I have a fleet of six trucks that need regular maintenance and repair."

"Happy to get the work," Bill says with a smile.

"And we'll give you our best rate," Wally adds.

The next day, even though all my trucks are running perfectly, I feel a sudden need to go to the brothers' body shop and check it out. I arrive just before 6:00 p.m. and find them closing up for the night.

"Why don't you come over for dinner?" Wally asks. "We still have all that food from the funeral."

"Can I use your phone?"

"Sure," Bill says. "There's one in our office."

I call Lucy and tell her about the brothers' invitation.

"Go, have fun," she says. "I can take care of myself."

I rejoin the brothers, and together we drive back to Rose's house. There, I again introduce myself to Marlene and Steve.

"I didn't know you and Dad were that close," Marlene says.

"We only knew each other for a few months, but I thought he was a great guy. He reminded me a lot of my father, who died about ten years ago."

"I'm sorry. He must have been special."

"He was. They both were."

Without knowing anything about the family's seating arrangements, I casually sit at the head of the table when dinner is served. As soon as I do, I see Marlene's eyes go wide with shock.

"What's the matter?" I ask.

"That's Dad's chair."

I immediately jump up. "Sorry."

"It's okay. You can sit there. He's not coming back."

Dinner continues, and to my surprise, Marlene and I end up talking until midnight. There is a connection between us I cannot explain. For the next two years, I join her and her family for dinner every night. I become part of their circle in everything but name. Back at home, Lucy develops her own group of friends and social life. Having finished nursing school, she gets a job at a local clinic. While I continue to pay the rent, she can now cover her personal expenses. We see each other in the morning, trade stories about the previous evening, then go our separate ways. Even as roommates go, our relationship is ultra-casual. I know this cannot be permanent.

One Saturday night, while having dinner with Marlene, Steve, and her brothers, Wally says, "You know what? We should go down to Newport to go dancing."

We all agree. After dinner, we pile into two cars and head down to Newport Beach, twenty minutes away. There, at the Balboa Peninsula's carnival-like Fun Zone, we board a large harbor cruiser with its own bar and dance band. For the next two hours, we slowly encircle the massive harbor, dancing, drinking, and generally having a wonderful time. We've been partying for about two hours when Marlene finally pauses dancing with her husband to sit down at the table where I'm nursing a draught beer.

"You see those guys at the bar?" she says, pointing to two casually dressed men who appear to be in their early thirties. "They've been looking at me all night."

"Thank you," I say with a smile.

Marlene looks at me curiously. "What do you mean, 'Thank you'? I'm talking about the guys at the bar."

"I know. Thank you," I repeat, still smiling broadly.

She shakes her head in exasperation. "You're drunk," she says, then turns to talk to Wally.

But I'm not drunk. I truly am thankful to her. Thankful for the opportunity to be part of her family for the last two years. The fact is, I am madly in love with her, but I dare not admit such a thing aloud, not unless she admits she's unhappy in her current marriage—which I suspect she is.

In fact, the more I think about this situation, the more I am convinced she wants to leave Steve. Whenever they're together, she always looks at him warily, as if she's afraid. When they dance, her body looks stiff. I've spent my entire professional life reading people's body language, and this woman is telling me she's not happy with the man she wed. I can only assume she doesn't want to appear to be the villain in this story by making the first move.

So, I decide to make it for her. The next Monday morning, I call her at work and invite her to meet me at a local coffee shop that evening.

"Why?" she asks.

"I just want to talk to you."

"If there's an issue between you and my brothers, I'd rather stay out of it."

"This isn't about them," I assure her. "I just want to talk to you."

She's unusually silent for the next few seconds, obviously trying to figure out what could be so urgent I need to speak to her in private.

"Fine," she finally says. "I'll meet you there at four o'clock."

I arrive at the restaurant a half-hour early and wait for her to join me. When she arrives, I notice I have mixed emotions. I begin to second guess myself, thinking perhaps I have misread the situation. There is only one way to be sure.

We find a booth, sit down, and order coffee.

"So, what did you want to talk to me about?" she asks.

"Last night, when we went dancing, you noticed those two men watching you."

"So what?" she asks a bit defensively.

"You pretended to be offended, but I think you were actually happy they were paying attention to you."

This seems to throw her off guard.

"Well, yeah," she admits. "After having two kids, I still turn heads. I take that as a compliment. That's what you needed to talk to me about?"

"All the happily married people I know don't see anyone else but their spouse," I say calmly. "The rest of the world doesn't exist."

"That's silly."

"So, my question to you is, are you happily married?"

As soon as I ask this, I can feel my heart pounding. I sense I've overstepped my boundaries. I may have even just lost the friendship we have built.

"That is none of your business," Marlene says sharply. "I don't even share my personal life with my family. I'm certainly not going to share it with you."

Her answer both shocks and amuses me. I don't want to be misunderstood, so I say, "I still don't have an answer to my question. Are you happily married?"

A full minute passes as I await her answer. I can see her mind working as she attempts to process a wave of conflicting emotions. Finally, she breaks her silence. "Whatever I say to you needs to stay in this restaurant," she says quietly, her voice taut. "I don't want my family involved with my personal life."

"Absolutely. I understand," I assure her. "I treasure our friendship and would never do anything to endanger it. I won't repeat a word you say."

With some hesitation, she tells me she has not been happy with her marriage for a long time, that she and Steve are seeing a marriage counselor twice a week, and that her father's death has only deepened her depression and put more strain on their marriage.

"But it's important that my family believes there are no problems," she tells me.

Listening to this, I struggle to keep a straight poker face, but inside I'm secretly smiling. This woman is my white tiger. I would have remained silently in love with her had she been happily married, but now all I can think about is a life with her. At the same time, I don't want to be the villain in this story, either. I don't want to do anything that might destroy what chance for reconciliation still exists between her and Steve.

So, I decide to keep my feelings to myself. For now.

"I'm here whenever you need me," I offer. "We can meet here whenever you want, and I can be your sounding board. Sometimes it just helps to have someone to talk to."

"Thank you. I appreciate that."

As we leave the coffee shop, I struggle to understand the emotions still roiling inside me. On one hand, I want to spend as much time with Marlene as I can. On the other, I want to see her have a happy life.

Soon, Marlene and I begin meeting at the same place every day after work. Within a few weeks, her mood noticeably improves, and she tells me about a new business venture she's considering.

"We've been renting a house I'm going to fix up and turn into a senior care facility. I took care of Dad before he died, and I'm taking care of Mom now, so I know what's involved. A lot of people need this service and I want to take a professional training course. I think I can make a go of it."

"I'd love to see it when you're done fixing it up."

A few weeks later, we meet at the property in Fountain Valley. It's a two-story house that she's spent more than $75,000 to improve. A city health inspector also arrives. He spends the next two hours studying the property before ultimately giving it a five-star rating.

"You're clear to begin operating at any time," he tells her.

That night, at the usual family dinner, Marlene can barely contain her excitement. "We just passed inspection. Five stars!" she announces. "I'm going to open the house next week."

Everyone stands and showers Marlene with congratulations. Everyone except Steve. "No, you're not," he says. "I rented that house in my name. And I'm going to break the lease. No way you're starting that business."

Immediately, the room becomes eerily silent.

I study Marlene. Over the past few months, she's become far stronger than she was following Farid's death. She's more confident. But I fear she still doesn't have the fortitude to stand up to her bullying husband. As it turns out, I'm wrong.

"Well, I've made a decision, too," she says, straightening up to her full height. "I don't want to be married to you anymore."

The shockwave that travels through the room is almost visible. Everyone stares in utter disbelief, eyes wide. Until now, no one had an inkling that this marriage was in trouble. No one but me. Steaming, Steve storms out of the house. While I can see looks of sadness on everyone's face, Marlene looks relieved.

In the weeks that follow, I continue spending time with Marlene, providing what guidance and emotional support I can. Ironically, my experience with multiple divorces now works to my benefit as I'm able to help her navigate the treacherous legal terrain she must cross before her separation from Steve becomes official. I'm now also able to spend time with Marlene's children. Both are young and sweet and need special emotional support now that her father and mother are no longer living together. I have plenty of experience raising a boy, so I have no trouble relating to young Michael. But Lorraine is another story. I am afraid to say the wrong thing and hurt her feelings.

I'm equally wary of how I speak to Marlene herself. This is one white tiger I dare not lose. I must be very careful not to offend her. And while I am helping her start her new life, I realize I must also get my own house in order.

One night I return home to find Lucy getting ready to see a movie with friends. I ask her to wait a few minutes.

"You know I'm proud of what you've done," I tell her. "You went to nursing school. Got your certificate. Found a great job. You're on your way."

"I hear a 'but' coming…" she says warily.

"You and I know this isn't a real marriage. We were lonely. I needed someone to look after Scott. But Scott's gone. There's no reason for us to stay together."

Her eyes get misty. "You've found somebody?"

"No. Not *somebody*. I've found the love of my life."

Chapter 45

I EXPECT SOME kind of explosive reaction from Lucy—I have heard many tales about the so-called "hot" Latina temper—but it never comes. In fact, she takes my announcement with surprising equanimity.

"If that's true, then congratulations. I'm happy for you. And, you're right. If this woman is the love of your life, then it's time I go. I can be out of here tomorrow, if that's all right with you."

"You don't have to leave *that* fast," I say, still somewhat ashamed by the way I sprung this news on her.

"It's not a problem. I have a friend I can stay with until I find a place of my own. It's not like we're really together or anything."

This last remark stings a bit. True, we have never been romantically involved. There has been no sex, no kissing, not even hugs. Still, I always thought we had a strong, meaningful friendship. We have enjoyed spending time together. We have looked out for each other's interests, and parting feels bittersweet.

When I come home from work the following day, Lucy has, indeed, departed. I check her room, and she has left nothing behind. The closet is empty. Her bathroom is barren. It is like she never existed. I take a moment to feel the emptiness. There had never been any love between us, but like the professor says at the end of the musical *My Fair Lady*, I had grown accustomed to her being here. Now that she has left, her absence is palpable.

I wonder how she will do on her own. Whether she will be happy with her nursing career. If she will ever find a true love of her own and perhaps marry again. As it turns out, I will never know the answer to any of these questions, for I will never hear from her again.

I soon find myself spending every free minute at Marlene's house. I am becoming a fixture. We are the best of friends, and I leave her house at midnight seven days a week. I do this because even though I want to offer support for her and the kids throughout the divorce, I never want to overstep bounds. A divorce is challenging enough for children to experience. The last thing I want to do is confuse or upset them by seeming to take the place of their dad.

It so happens that one day I charter a private boat to take my biggest clients on a fishing trip. Onboard, our chef makes delicious sashimi from the afternoon's catches, only adding to the enjoyment of our outing. However, by the time I arrive at Marlene's house later that evening, I've come to think twice about dining on raw fish.

The truth is, I'm suffering from acute food poisoning. It's so bad I can do little besides collapse on the couch between sprints back and forth to the bathroom. I cannot remember the last time I felt so ill and pled for the gut-wrenching nausea to end.

Sometime around 8:00 p.m., Lorraine comes over to me. "Tony," she says.

Delirious and miserable, she appears to me like an angel for a second. She takes me by the hand and walks me to the refrigerator door. Opening it she says, "It's okay. You can eat anything from here."

I'm so stunned I can barely eke out a "thank you" before she leads me again, this time to her mom's bedroom. I have never been to this inner sanctum before and am touched to see Marlene and her son curled up together beneath the covers of the large bed.

"Mom, Michael, and me sleep here," she says. Then she takes a pillow and puts it sideways at the foot of the bed. "You can sleep here 'til you feel better."

I've never raised girls, or had the opportunity to spend extensive time with Marlene's children, but tonight she has made her way into my heart faster than lightning. From this moment on, my heart melts whenever I see her. If she happens to ask for a certain toy, I go out of my way to get for her. I can honestly say being with Lorraine begins to change my personality. She brings out the gentle, caring side of me.

This night and the several nights that follow I accept Lorraine's invitation to sleep at the foot of the bed. As the minutes pass during the first evening, I start to feel better just listening to all of them breathing beside me. I come to realize this is where I've always belonged. Before long, Marlene, Lorraine, and Michael became my world.

"I want you to see Miss Mary," Marlene tells me one day soon after. "I really want to know what she has to say about us."

"You know what I think of Miss Mary…"

Miss Mary is a local psychic Marlene has been seeing for several years. I don't believe in psychics or ghosts or ESP or any of that supernatural hocus pocus, and I have told Marlene on multiple occasions I think she is wasting her money. Even so, Marlene continues to see her. Clearly, we don't agree on everything.

"Come on, Tony, what could it hurt? You might even learn something. She's very good."

"Can she tell me this week's winning lottery numbers? Those I would pay for."

She gives me an indulgent grin. "If it's about the money, I'll pay for the session. Please see her? Please? For me?"

"Fine. And I'll pay for it."

I leave out the fact that I think she's already wasted enough money on this fake.

Marlene makes the appointment by phone. The following day, we go to the suburban strip mall in Westminster where Miss Mary has her "office" on the second floor. I expect to find the space decked out like a Gypsy tea room, complete with frilly tapestries and beaded doorways, but I'm surprised to find it decorated like a doctor's or dentist's office. The furniture is simple and modern, the décor mostly paintings of natural landscapes. It's clearly a space designed to promote relaxation.

"Tony? It's great to meet you. I'm Miss Mary," says a woman in her early forties as she steps out. Like her office, Miss Mary does not conform to my preconceived notions. Instead of wearing a feathered headband, beaded shawl, and strings of gaudy beads, she's attired in a simple pastel blouse and slacks ensemble. A small gold cross hangs from a chain around her neck.

"So how do we do this? Are you going to read my palm? Look into a crystal ball?"

Miss Mary doesn't seem put out in the slightest by my comment. "That's not the way I work, but I do like to do my readings individually. Who wants to go first?"

"After you," I say with mock gallantry, motioning Marlene to the open door.

"Great. Take a seat. Make yourself comfortable." Miss Mary indicates for me to retire to her lobby. "This will take a few minutes."

"You better be here when I get back," Marlene teases as she follows Miss Mary into her inner sanctum. The door closes and I find a chair. There are several magazines lying about. I find an issue of *Entrepreneur* with an interesting article about new fast-food franchises. Fifteen minutes later, Marlene emerges looking badly shaken.

I don't like the looks of this. "What did she say?"

"We'll talk about it later. I don't want to mess up your reading."

"Ready, Tony?" Miss Mary calls.

My eyes flit back and forth between her and Marlene. I'm torn, wondering what kind of nonsense this quack has just said.

"Tony?" Miss Mary indicates me with her finger.

"Go," says Marlene. "It's fine. I'll be here."

With another quick glance back to Marlene, I enter Miss Mary's office. There's a small modern desk in the corner. In the center stands a small stone-topped table surrounded by two chairs facing each other. She motions me to one chair, then sits in the other. We stare at each other for a few seconds, then she reaches for my hands. "Let me hold them."

I do as she says. She grips my fingers, then lowers them onto the table. She closes her eyes and takes a deep breath. Oddly, I find myself mirroring her breathing patterns.

"Your heart is full of love." She smiles, her eyes still pressed shut. "You are totally in love with Marlene."

Then her expression changes, like she is struggling with an uncomfortable thought. This sets me on edge, and I squirm in my chair.

"But I feel sorry for you."

"Sorry for me?"

"She will go back to her husband. There will be no altar for you."

This sets something off in me. I yank my hands free and leap to my feet.

"That's a lie! I was right. You are a phony. We are done."

I storm out of the office, grab Marlene by the hand and drag her outside.

"Tony, wait. Slow down."

But I'm in no mood. All I want is to get as far away from Miss Mary as I can. Not until we are back in my car do I allow myself to speak.

"Are you really going back to Steve?" I ask her accusingly.

"What? Is that what she told you?"

I can barely think straight I'm so mad. "How can you do that after the way he's treated you?"

The way Marlene puts her hands on mine reminds me of Miss Mary for a moment.

"I'm not going back to Steve. I don't care what she said. We're done. I'm going to marry you as soon as I get the divorce papers."

This shocks me as if I've touched a live wire. We have never discussed marriage. It is something I had thought about—a lot—but the "M" word has never been mentioned. Not until now.

"You mean that? You're serious?"

A sweetness comes over her face, making her even more beautiful. Her eyes twinkle as she delivers a heart-stopping smile. "Yes. I'm going to marry you."

I want to believe her. But Miss Mary's words haunt me: *There will be no altar* for you.

"Tony, we need to meet," my new lawyer, Franklin Powell, says over the phone.

It is now 1992. With Franklin's help, I have been able to secure a divorce from Lucy. *My third divorce.* Even I can't believe it. However, once again, I am officially single.

Franklin brokered and set up the distribution deals for Coco's Mediterranean Foods throughout California, Oregon, Arizona, and Nevada. Business has been good and expanding rapidly. Yet, something in Franklin's voice concerns me.

"Is there a problem?"

"Just the opposite," Franklin assures me. "Coco's is one of my best-selling brands."

"So why do we need to meet?"

"Because I want to buy you out."

I have never considered this. A few years ago, I read a business book in which the author stated, "The only reason to start a company is to sell it." Yet, the idea of selling Coco's has never crossed my mind. I just enjoy running it way too much.

"But I like this business. This is my legacy."

"I know. Which is why I'm going to make you an offer you can't refuse."

I've seen *The Godfather.* Does this mean that if I don't sell, he's going to put a horse head in my bed?

Brushing away any silly apprehensions, I agree to meet Franklin at a local restaurant. As we wait for our food, he pulls a piece of paper from his pocket and slides it over to me. Very dramatic. Intrigued, I turn the paper over and look at the number he has written. My eyes almost pop out of my head. I can't even find the words to respond.

"I—uh—I need to talk this over with my partner." I haven't even told Coco about this meeting. Now I wonder how she will react. "Please. Give me a few days."

Franklin is so calm his thin face reminds me of a wax statue. Even his voice is measured and controlled. "This offer is good for forty-eight hours. But I don't think you'll wait that long."

That evening, I sit down with Coco and show her Franklin's offer. Seeing the number, she screams like she's just seen a mouse run by her feet.

"So, what do you want to do?" she asks, finally catching her breath.

"I've been thinking about it. Truth is, I'm getting tired of working. I am in love with Marlene, and I want to be able to spend more time with her. With this money, we can live well for the rest of our lives."

"*And then some.*"

"But it has to be a mutual decision."

"Don't worry about me. For me, this is all found money. I say, take it. *Today.* Before he comes to his senses and changes his mind."

Franklin was right. I don't need forty-eight hours. The next day, we have a handshake deal, and two weeks after that, we sign paperwork. I have sold my company.

Now I am forty-one years old. Single. And again, a millionaire. A few months later, Marlene officially gets her divorce from Steve. Immediately, I propose marriage. Marlene accepts. This is going to be my fourth marriage. No need for anything fancy. I rent a Cadillac, and we head north on I-15 to Las Vegas.

It all should be so perfect. So right. But as we drive through the searing Mojave Desert, the psychic's words ring in my ears, "I do not see an altar…"

Damn it. Miss Mary's gotten to me, too.

Chapter 46

THE FIVE-HOUR DRIVE from Orange County to Las Vegas is simple but taxing since Miss Mary's words are never far from my mind. *Did she curse me? Why did she say I would never make it to the altar? Did she mean something awful would happen on the way there?*

I try to block out these thoughts as I accelerate out of Westminster. We take a zigzag route along some of Orange County's most crowded freeways: San Diego (I- 405) south, Costa Mesa (State Route 55) north, and the Artesia Freeway (State Route 91) east until, now in western Riverside County, we finally connect with Interstate 15 north, which will take us straight to Vegas.

This heavily traveled six-lane superhighway, the only route between Las Vegas and metro Los Angeles—takes us up through the San Bernardino Mountains, rich and green at this time of year, and into what locals call the high desert, a flat, endless plain broken up by short, jagged mountains devoid of any signs of life. After passing through the desert city of Victorville, distinguished by little but its large freeway-side shopping mall, there is nothing but brown, rocky desert for mile after mile after mile.

It unnerves me.

"You okay?" Marlene asks.

"Sure. Why?"

"You haven't taken a breath in minutes."

"I'm fine," I assure her with a smile.

"Okay."

We catch a brief glimpse of civilization as we pass through Barstow with its massive railroad-themed McDonald's restaurant, after which we drive through two long straightaways that I swear extend for twenty miles each. Even though the speedometer says we are moving at eighty miles per hour—ten miles per hour above the posted limit—any visible ground features are so distant it seems as if we are barely moving at all.

"You don't have to drive so fast."

Yes, I do. I've got to get to that altar.

Around 1:00, we pull off to rest in the first human settlement we've encountered for hours, a tiny collection of restaurants, shops, and service stations called Baker. Outside of the local restaurants, signs boast the "world's tallest thermometer." Marlene wants to see it, but I couldn't care less. We're wasting time. Which is exactly what I tell her.

"Oh, c'mon, Tony. It'll be fun."

It turns out to be a 134-foot-tall tower with electric signs spaced out every fifteen feet or so displaying numbers from 30 to 130. According to this monument, the current temperature is 87 degrees. I assume that is downright chilly for this bone-dry desert enclave. I shudder to think what it must feel like here when the uppermost number is lit.

I would prefer to go the whole way without stopping, but Marlene begs me to pull over at a restaurant called The Mad Greek. She's eager to see what Greek food looks like out here in the wild, wild West. As it turns out, not much.

With walls papered in blue and white, and decorated with cheap imitation Greek statuary, the eatery is little more than a glorified coffee shop that, in addition to burgers, burritos, and corned beef hash, also happens to offer gyros, falafel sandwiches, and Greek salads, as well as hummus, baba ghanoush, *saganaki* (fried cheese) and spanakopita. I order a gyro on pita while

Marlene orders a barbecue chicken sandwich. The whole time I sit at the booth, my knee won't stop bouncing.

"What's wrong?"

"Nothing."

"You haven't touched your gyro. Is it good?"

"We should get back on the road soon."

But Marlene wants the full experience and makes us order dessert. Luckily, the pistachio baklava turns out to be the best part of the meal.

After lunch, we return to our car and follow the signs back to the freeway. Looking about, I see that Baker has perhaps two main streets, both of which are lined with businesses designed specifically to serve passing travelers. I see little in the way of housing or other industry. Where, I wonder, do the people who work here live? The nearest major towns are a good hour away. What kind of commute must these waitresses and gas station attendants have every day? What would compel them to work here?

"No wonder the Greek went mad," I tell Marlene.

"Someone's grumpy."

I decide not to tell her why, as if not voicing Miss Mary's premonition will lessen its power. After another interminable hour on the road, we finally leave the high desert and crest the hill that takes us into the Las Vegas Valley. We can clearly see the hotels of the Las Vegas Strip ahead of us, but as with everything else on this interminable trip, looks are deceiving. It still takes a good twenty minutes before we reach the exit for downtown.

"Jesus," I mutter between gritted teeth.

Marlene puts her hand on mine. "We'll be there soon, honey. Patience."

It's now 4:00 p.m., so I floor it straight to City Hall, determined to get a marriage license before the office closes. At the reception desk, Marlene and I are redirected to the Clark County Marriage License Bureau office. There, the process to obtain the license goes on and on. Sweat pours down my back as the minutes roll on by the big clock on the wall. At last, I can't take it anymore.

"It's supposed to be easy to get married in Vegas!"

"Tony."

Ignoring her, I anxiously lean into the clerk, a heavyset woman in her late fifties. "Look. Where is the closest wedding chapel?"

"The Lucky Little Wedding Chapel is right down the block." she points over my shoulder. "Here. I can give you a map to all the chapels in the area."

She hands me a glossy pamphlet titled, *Guide to the Chapels of Las Vegas: The Wedding Capital of the World!*

"Look how cute that is." Marlene points at the pictures.

I don't have time for cute. I stuff both the pamphlet and the marriage license into my breast pocket. Taking Marlene's hand, I whisk her back to our car.

"What's the rush? What are you doing?"

Five minutes later, we're at the Lucky Little Wedding Chapel, which looks like the kind of tiny frontier church you'd see in an old Hollywood Western. I usher Marlene into the lobby where we are greeted by a middle-aged woman wearing a long pioneer dress right out of *Little House on the Prairie.*

"We'd like to get married," I announce a little too loudly. "Here's our license."

"Do you have an appointment?"

"No." *You need an appointment?*

"We just got into town," Marlene explains, holding tightly to my arm.

"I'm sorry, but we're booked solid for the day," she says, even as a party of twenty college-age kids dressed in formalwear pushes past us into the main chapel. "Our first opening is at 10:30 the day after tomorrow."

Miss Mary's face looms in my mind's eye. I have visions of our casino burning down in the night—us never reaching the altar. Us never being together.

"No. That's too late. We have to do it today."

"*Have to?*" Marlene asks.

"Well, good luck," says the frontier woman. "This is our busy season."

Kicking up dirt clods, we return to my car in a hurry. As soon as we get to the door, Marlene whirls around on me. "Okay, just hold it right here. What in the world has gotten into you? You're not acting like yourself. You haven't all day. What's with you?"

I decide to tell her the truth. The real truth that goes even deeper than Miss Mary's prediction. Something that's built up inside of me for a long time. I pull Marlene into my arms. "All my life I've felt I was missing something. I thought it was material stuff: money, business, success. What I know now is that it was *you* I was missing. You're what I've been searching for all these years. Now that you're here—within my grasp—I can't let you go. I can't."

She pulls in me for a deep kiss. "Then, let's get this done already. Today."

In this together, we follow the map to another chapel a few blocks down. We hurry inside and are greeted by a woman who looks no more than twenty.

"We want to get married as soon as possible," Marlene says. "Do you have a time available?"

"I'm sure we can fit you in. You have any special type of service in mind?"

"Catholic," I say. "We'd like a priest."

"Oh." Her smile falls away. "I'm afraid we don't have one available just now. But we have an Elvis."

I check my watch. It's 6:00 p.m.

"We're not leaving," I tell her. "Find us a priest and bring him here. I don't care what it costs. I will pay."

"Well, I do know a priest," the young woman says thoughtfully. "But he's retired now. And blind."

"*Blind?*"

"He's kinda old. Got that macular degeneration."

Marlene turns to me. "What should we do?"

"It's okay if he's blind," I say. "As long as he can do the ceremony."

A half-hour later, the woman returns, guiding a short, bent-over man wearing a dark jacket and a priestly collar.

"This is Father Boyle," she says by way of introduction. "He's agreed to perform your ceremony."

"A pleasure to meet you, Father." I offer him my hand. "I know this is an inconvenience…"

"No inconvenience at all," he says in a surprisingly strong voice. "It is refreshing to find a couple still committed to the Holy Church."

"As we are to each other," Marlene says.

"Would you like me to get ya a Bible?" our hostess asks the priest.

"It would do me no good. My eyes…" he shakes his head wearily. "Fortunately, I've performed a few of these ceremonies during my good years. And while my eyes may have gone, my memory is still sharp. Shall we begin?"

And right there, Father Boyle begins to recite the ceremony by heart. As he does, he keeps shuffling around, trying to locate us. Marlene and I try our hardest not to laugh. Looking into her eyes, sharing this insane experience with her is so much fun I don't ever want it to stop. Miss Mary's words disappear from my mind. I'm completely lost in the moment with only one person, the love of my life.

It turns out Father Boyle's memory is, indeed, sharp. Without visual cues or need to consult the Bible, five minutes later he pronounces us man and wife.

"I love you," I whisper to Marlene.

"I love you, Tony."

I pull her in close for a kiss.

"You know," I say. "Miss Mary's prediction was wrong."

"Not entirely." She points. "This isn't a Catholic church. So, there was no altar."

Shrugging, I kiss her again.

The next day, we return to Orange County as a married couple.

"So, what are you going to do now?" Marlene asks me.

I've been thinking about this. Having sold my business, I have plenty of money and lots of free time. "I'm going to take a year off and just chill," I say, using an expression I picked up from Scott. "We can do all the tourist things I've never had time to do before. Disneyland. Knott's Berry Farm. Universal Studios…"

"Sounds like fun."

And it is. For about three months, after which I get bored and restless. I wasn't born to chill. I need to do something. It's time to start hunting white tigers again. With Marlene.

Chapter 47

IF I AM going to go back to work, I have two choices: Either I can start my own business, or I can work for someone else. Starting another business has distinct advantages. I can again be boss so no one can tell me what to do. If the business succeeds, I'll reap the lion's share of benefits (or the white tiger's).

But, as I know all too well from experience, being a business owner has its downsides. Hours can be long and hard. I will need to hire and manage employees. Starting a business also requires capital. Yes, thanks to my sale of Coco's Mediterranean Foods, I now have plenty of cash. Yet investing this money back into a new enterprise will put my capital at risk. Potentially, I could lose everything it's taken me my entire life to accumulate.

Frankly, I'm getting too old to take big chances. I decide that, just like I did when I first came to America, I will work for someone else.

If I am going to work for someone else, I again have two choices: Either I can look for a salaried position—a 9-to-5 job—or I can look for a sales position based on commission. A salaried position offers security, predictability and, in many cases, benefits, like health insurance and 401(k) retirement contributions. On the other hand, a salaried job might lock me into a daily schedule, limiting the amount of income I can generate. If I work on commission, my income will be determined by my own efforts. I will be the master of my own fate. Then again, the elements necessary for success might not always be under my control. Plus, I would be responsible for paying for my own health insurance and retirement contributions, which can be expensive.

Still, achieving such success in virtually everything I have tried since coming to America, I feel confident I can prosper at anything I commit myself to. And I don't want to be limited to a monthly salary. To tell the honest truth, I want the challenge—the thrill—*the adventure*.

So, I decide to look for a commission sales job.

To find such a position, I start where all job hunters begin in the 1990s: the newspaper want ads. Scanning entries in *The Orange County Register*, I see one ad headlined, "Unlimited $$$ Opportunity. Set Your Own Hours!" I am intrigued. Reading further, I notice the job involves selling meat products door-to-door from a truck. Hmmm… That doesn't sound glamorous. Yet the ad says I can earn a "very healthy commission." Having punched my share of time clocks back in Boston, I am attracted to the idea of setting my own hours. And the product is food, which is something I know how to sell.

All day long the words from the ad gnaw at my brain, tempting me. I do some research into the company behind the promotion. It's called Country Fed and has an A rating from the Better Business Bureau. The few articles and reviews I can find at the library make the outfit sound legitimate and financially solid. The hell with it. I make an appointment for an interview.

The next day, I travel to the company's headquarters, located in a modern office park in Anaheim Hills. There I meet with the sales manager, George Teller, a pudgy man in his early fifties.

"I just sold my company," I explain. "It was a lucrative sale, but I'm bored. I want to go back to work. I like selling."

George doesn't have much in the way of a neck, but he manages to give me a sideways glance. I gather it's not often that applicants who've just sold their company call upon him.

"Here's how it works," he tells me after a long pause. "We sell high-quality frozen steaks, chicken, and seafood by the case. Each case contains fifty meals. Sell ten cases and you earn $1,000 on top of your regular 20 percent commission. We expect you to sell ten cases per week. If you fail twice to make your quota, you're out."

"I can do that."

George doesn't believe me. "I'm going to be honest with you. This job ain't for everybody. Most people can't hack it. They quit after two weeks."

"I like a challenge."

George snorts. "Challenge. I got guys who sleep in their cars."

"I want this job."

"It's hard work. Not much fun."

I lean in close. "Look. I can't go back to Disneyland again." It takes every ounce of strength not to grab George by his throat and scream in his face. "I. Need. This."

He places both of his flabby hands on his belly. "Well, then. Welcome to Country Fed."

It takes less than five minutes to complete the paperwork that makes me an official salesman. The company provides me with a small Toyota refrigerated truck that they fill with cases of frozen foods. I'm allowed to choose any territory I want. I decide on just one city: Fountain Valley. Not only do I live here, which will significantly minimize my commuting time, but it's also highly residential, meaning there are many prospects crammed into just a few square miles.

With my handy *Thomas Guide* in the passenger's seat my first day, I begin to make my way through various neighborhoods. As I understand it, this entire area was built from farm and ranch land during a fifteen-year period from around 1965 to 1980. As a result, all of the houses have a similar look: lots of earth-toned wood siding and stucco.

I turn onto a tree-lined street and park so the Country Fed sign on the truck's side is clearly visible from the first house. I then step from the cab, go around to the back, and pull out a box of T-bone steaks. I sprint with the box to the front door, ring the bell, then step back so as not to appear intimidating.

A moment later, a woman appears in the doorway. She quickly looks me up and down. I'm wearing pressed tan slacks, a navy-blue sports coat, a red-striped shirt, and matching red tie.

"Good morning. I'm Tony, one of your neighbors, and I have here some delicious and healthy frozen meats I think your family is going to love—"

"Sorry, not interested." She steps back, reaching for the door.

"How would you like to save $50 a week on groceries?"

The woman hesitates for a nanosecond.

"And make fewer trips to the grocery store?"

She has yet to tell me to get lost. We're in a delicate holding pattern: One wrong move and this house of cards comes fluttering down. I press on.

"Instead of you driving to the supermarket every week, I can bring your family's meat straight to you." I open the box, revealing the large, inch-thick T-bone steaks within. "In each case you'll get ten T-bones, ten New York steaks, ten filet mignons, ten rib eyes, and ten hamburgers. That's fifty meals for just $220 per case. But buy *two cases*, and you'll get the second for half off. That's one hundred meals for just $330, or $3.30 per meal. Now what supermarket gives you a deal like that?"

Her brain tries to put up a wall of resistance, but what I'm saying sounds good—really good. It makes logical sense. And while she's mentally computing all kinds of factors: trips to the store, average meal price, thickness of the cuts, I'm beaming down at her a thousand-megawatt smile of pure, unadulterated warmth—and bullet-proof confidence.

Also, quick side note: The fact is, each case lists for $165, not $220. But I know from five minutes of listening to George's sob stories of sales guys that crashed upon the rocks of prospects' houses that offering 50 percent off an additional purchase gives the customer a powerful incentive to buy. In the end, the person pays the same $3.30 per steak, the company makes the same profit, and I can make more sales in half the time. It's a dynamite sales strategy, and it seems to be working. Instead of slamming the door in my face, the woman tentatively steps forward to examine my samples.

She points a shy pinky at the steaks. "They all look like this?"

"The T-bones, yes. All our steaks are grass-fed beef. No hormones. No antibiotics. They cook up so fresh and juicy, your family will love them."

Then something goes wrong. Some errant thought stops her cold. "But I can't buy a hundred steaks at once. I don't have that kind of room in my freezer."

I love objections. "Actually, I bet you do have some room in your freezer."

She puts her hand on her hip. "I'm telling you I don't."

She's getting testy now, but my smile doesn't waver. "How's this: I'll put the steaks in your freezer—

"*You'll* put the steaks in my freezer?"

"Sure. And whatever meat doesn't fit, you can have for free. How's that for a deal?"

No smile yet from her, but I swear the corners of her eyes are crinkling. "You're kidding, right?"

"I'm not kidding. Just tell me what you'd like: steak, chicken, or seafood."

"What seafood?" she asks, and she's already backtracking as I tango into her house. It's a dance between us. I lead, she follows. Part of her—the rational side— wants me to stay away—but the irrational side is curious—she wants to know where this will end.

I keep talking a mile a second, using my words like machine gun cover as I stealthily, confidently lead her back, back toward the freezer. I explain each case contains ten frozen trout, ten mahi-

mahi steaks, ten salmon steaks, ten cod fillets, and five pounds of jumbo shrimp. It's like a song I am singing, and at the end of each verse, I drop the same refrain. "It's just $3.30 per meal when you order two cases."

She stops me at the edge of the kitchen. "Let's try one case of steaks and one case of seafood," she says, careful to add, "*If* it all fits."

"Oh, it will fit… or it's free. Now, is that your freezer?"

Like Vanna White, she holds her arms out wide, displaying her totem of domesticity, the hub and birthplace of so many meals for her beloved family. I give it a good squint to signal I'm making careful measurements in my mind's eye. Then, I throw up a finger as if to say, 'One moment, madam!'

Before she can exhale, I zip back to truck, scooping up a case of steak and seafood from the freezer. Together, they weigh about thirty pounds, but they're light as glancing sunlight as I fling them onto a two-wheeled dolly for the trip from street to door.

She gives me a funny look as she takes in the cargo load—after all, minutes ago, she was sitting on the couch, watching a show, minding her own business—now here I am bringing in a cavalcade of meats—still she directs me to the kitchen and opens the refrigerator's freezer with a triumphant smirk.

As might be expected, it's stuffed with no shortage of grocery items: half-eaten bags of peas, tired leftovers, foiled covered patties, and a whole host of indeterminate odds and ends, all of which look freezer burned. There's not a whole lot of room here.

"Here's what I'm going to do," I say. "I'm going to remove everything you have and replace it with the new, fresh food. What I can't put back, I'll buy from you. Deal?"

"You'll *buy* it from me?"

I lift up the frozen peas for emphasis. "I'll buy it from you."

"Okay."

Ten minutes later, I have filled the freezer with my product, plus returned nearly all of the original contents, including several cartons of Neapolitan ice cream I'm certain she wants to keep. The few leftovers I can't fit, I hold in my hand. "So how much do you want for these?"

At last, her face breaks into a smile. "Forget it. It's garbage we were never going to eat anyway. How much do I owe you?"

"Three hundred thirty. And I take cash or checks."

She looks at me, then at the packed freezer. Then at me again. "Let me get my checkbook."

This is my new life. I do this four or five times every morning. Same thing all the time. At first, I meet resistance. But it slides right off as soon as I hit them with the fifty-percent-off-the-second-case deal, offering to pay for any food I can't fit in their freezer. Sale after sale, I close this way. Almost never do I fail to get two cases of product into a customer's freezer. And not a single customer asks me to buy their leftovers. Ever.

In my first quarter, I average between $12,000 and $14,000 in monthly commissions. George can't believe it. In fact, he looks like he's losing sleep over it. And weight. He just walks around, muttering, staring at me out of the corner of his eye, like I can't be real. Like I'm some magical unicorn someone's just found. He even puts a copy of one of my checks on the office wall to show other salespeople what can be done.

"We've never had a salesman like you," he says one day.

In late October, I come home from work for lunch with Marlene. She greets me with a big hug. Already I can tell she has news for me.

"I found a job," she announces.

"A job? What kind of a job?"

"As a customer service manager with a local furniture company. It pays $75,000 per year, plus benefits. We can both get health insurance."

I think about this for a minute. "That's a lot of money."

"Plus, health insurance."

"You know what? I have an even better offer for you."

Her face darkens. "Oh no. What?"

Chapter 48

I'VE DATED A lot of women over the years. I've *married* a lot of women over the years. But if I had met Marlene when I was a young man, I never would have looked twice at another female. I'd also have ten children by now and perhaps two dozen grandchildren. Marlene is the love of my life, and I want to spend as much time with her as possible. She's the other half of me—my heart.

"I want us to work together," I tell her.

"What do you mean?" she replies, shocked.

"We can be a team."

"But I went to three separate interviews."

"We'll sell together. Husband and wife."

"*Tony*. They're counting on me."

"I'll pay you the same $1,500 a week you would have made at the furniture company."

"I'm supposed to start tomorrow."

"Not only can we spend more time together, but your hours we'll be better. You'll only have to work from 8:00 a.m. to 1:00 p.m. After that, you can have your freedom. And spend time with your kids."

Marlene drops onto the couch. I can't make up my mind if she looks like a weight has been lifted or if the whole world is on her shoulders.

"But I bought a whole new wardrobe for this job."

"You can wear your new clothes with me. I'd love to see you in them."

She throws a pillow at me. "I'm serious. I was really looking forward to it. You know, they created a whole new department just for me. If I walk out now, they'll think I'm some kind of flake."

"Who cares what they think? You'll never see them again." The more I think about having Marlene with me every morning, the more I want it. "This is going to be good for you. For us. For our marriage. You'll love it. Trust me."

"All right. You win," she says with a sigh. "Let me call them up and tell them the bad news."

I wait in the living room while Marlene goes to the kitchen to call the furniture company. I catch only snippets of the conversation, but I can tell the person at the other end of the line is not happy. Marlene keeps apologizing and saying phrases like, "I know, I know."

Then she says, "It's not about the money. My husband really wants to do this, and I think I should give it a chance. It'll be good for our marriage."

About a minute later, Marlene returns to the living room. She looks like she's been beaten up emotionally, but she also looks happy.

"All right. It's done. I'm all yours, you crazy, crazy man."

"I'm crazy? You're the one who just quit her job."

"TONY!"

I calm her, pulling her into my embrace. "We're going to have a great time. And we're going to sell a lot of meat."

Marlene laughs. It's a laugh I look forward to hearing a lot of in the days and months ahead.

The next Monday, Marlene and I head out on our first husband-and-wife sales call. Marlene drives. I sit beside her, *Thomas Guide*

in my lap, navigating her through suburban Fountain Valley. It's just after 8:00 a.m. when we reach a modest two- story house, our first stop.

"Pull up just a bit. I want them to be able to see you from the front door."

As discussed, Marlene stays in the truck while I walk up to the entrance. This time, I am not carrying any samples. It's just me, my shorts and T-shirt, and my smile. Taking a deep breath, I ring the doorbell. I hear a dog bark within the house. There's the sound of movement, then the door opens to reveal a middle-aged Asian woman.

"Yes?" she asks cautiously.

"Good morning. My name is Tony. I'm one of your neighbors. I'm working with my wife, Marlene."

I motion to the truck parked at the curb. Seeing this, Marlene waves to me. Already I can see the woman tense. No matter. I keep on.

"We work for Country Fed Foods, offering delicious, top-quality frozen steaks at a fraction of what you'd pay for them at the grocery store. Not only are these restaurant-quality steaks, but we deliver them right to your door. Your family enjoys hot, juicy stakes, don't they?"

She looks like she just ate an entire sour lemon in one bite. "I would never buy meats from some random guy—"

"That's not a problem." I say with a smile. "I have a case in my truck. Wait right here and I'll show it to you."

I turn and floor it back to the truck. I don't even give the woman a chance to stop me. I return breathless with a case of frozen steaks. Before she can even begin to object, I'm talking a mile a minute. "See how thick these are?" I take one still sealed in its thick clear plastic package. "Thaw them out, slap them on the barbeque, and you'll have yourself a feast! And we also have chicken."

"I'm not—"

"Wait right here. I'll show you."

Setting down the case of steaks, I hoof it back to the truck. Again, I don't give the woman a chance to stop me. Seconds later I return to the door with a case of frozen chicken pieces.

"You get twenty breasts, twenty thighs, twenty legs, twenty wings, and twenty chicken patties. Great for sandwiches," I explain, taking out a sample for her to see. "These are all free-range chickens. No hormones. No antibiotics. Low-fat and very, very healthy. Imagine these on the grill, slathered with barbecue sauce. You can choose from the chicken, the steaks, or the seafood."

"I—"

"Wait right here. I'll show you."

For a third time, I run back to the truck. When I return to the house, I can still draw enough air to offer her a lengthy explanation on the seafood.

Does she tell me to go to hell? Nope.

"Look, why don't you come into the house?" she says. "Would your wife like to come in, too?"

"Oh, no. She has to stay with the truck. These meats are very valuable."

Again, I wave to Marlene, and she waves back. Then, as the woman holds the front door open for me, I carry the case of seafood into the foyer.

"This is a lot of food," she notes as I pass. "I don't see how I could ever fit it into my freezer."

"I bet I can make it fit. And anything I can't make fit, I'll give you for free. How's that for a deal?"

Using this approach, it takes Marlene and me just half a day to sell ten cases. We have already hit our weekly quota, and it's only 1:00 p.m. on Monday afternoon.

"I can't believe you," Marlene says as we share tacos at a local Mexican restaurant. "You're—you're like a machine."

I wave the compliment off. "I can do better. Just wait to see what I have in mind next."

Chapter 49

SELLING COUNTRY FED meats door-to-door, the most common objection I get from customers is not the price, and certainly not the quality of the product. It's the customer's lack of freezer space.

"It's too much! I don't have that much room!" I hear, stop after stop. *"Where am I going to put all this meat?"*

And, to be honest, they have a point. One case of sixty steaks takes up a lot of real estate. And I always try to sell two at once. That's more cubic footage than most family fridges can handle. Yes, I can usually find a way to make the meat fit—often at the expense of half-filled frozen food boxes and old, sad-looking leftovers—but doing so takes time, reducing the number of sales I can make in a given day. And time is money. I'm convinced that if I can just find a way to deal with this objection, I can double my daily sales. Easily.

Percolating in the back of my mind, this problem vexes me as Marlene and I stroll through the Fountain Valley Costco warehouse store (where I'm pleased to see they still carry my Coco's brand spanakopita in their refrigerated section). We're passing the appliance aisle when I suddenly stop. They're offering a 6.9-cubic-foot freezer chest for just $199.99. Wheels turn in my head.

"Excuse me a sec, honey," I tell Marlene.

She stares at me as I study the unit on display. It's a big white box, 2½ feet high, 3 feet wide, and 2 feet deep, with a hinged top set atop four small rubber feet. It's as basic as it gets, yet to me, it brims with untold possibilities.

"Buy two cases and your family can eat well for months," I tell my first customer the next day. Once again, I'm standing at a walkway to a single-family home as a middle-aged housewife hovers in her doorway. "But if you buy *ten cases*, you'll have enough dinners for a year. You'll eat like kings."

"But I don't have room for ten cases of meat," she objects. "My freezer is packed as it is."

"Not a problem," I assure her, ready for the push-back. "Because if you buy ten cases today, I'll give you a new freezer to put them in. For free."

Her eyes widen. "A new freezer? No way."

"I have one in the truck. It's brand new. Still in its factory box. Buy ten cases of food in any combination you want today and it's yours."

And like that, I make the sale. Yes, this freezer cost me $200—plus California state sales tax—but with this one deal, I nail my quota for the whole week. And as we all know, time is money.

I've now been selling Country Fed meat for six months. Along the way I've built a reputation. Throughout Fountain Valley, they call me Tony the Meat Man. Experts will tell you it's ten times easier to sell to established customers than it is to make new ones, and that's certainly my experience. Now, when I stop at a home where I've sold before, I don't have to go through my whole spiel again.

Customers greet me with checkbooks ready in hand. This is especially true of the happy recipients of free freezers. They can't wait to do business with me again. Referral business piles up too. And that's the best kind of business there is. Happy customers tell their friends and neighbors, and when they see my truck rolling down the street, they literally run outside to flag me down like I'm the ice cream man.

If my goal was to make a comfortable living, I could easily just work my existing customer list and still produce a good income. But *good enough* just isn't in my DNA. If it was, I'd still be at Knott's Berry Farm snacking on funnel cakes. Something in me is hungry for sales. I love it. It's my drug of choice.

Take today for example. I've just made my last sale. Or, so it would seem. My truck is empty. I'm just pulling away from a customer's house when, half a block down the street, I see a woman loading her two young daughters into a black SUV parked in their driveway.

"Pull up," I tell Marlene. "Block the driveway."

"What?" she asks, confused.

"I'm going to make another sale."

"But we don't have anything left to sell."

"Please do it. I can make this work."

At my direction, Marlene pulls us to a stop in front of the woman's driveway, preventing her from leaving. Grabbing a brochure from a cardboard box on the floor between us, I leap out, hurrying toward the idling car.

The woman looks alarmed by my unexpected appearance but I don't let that stop me. "I'm Tony the Meat Man," I announce, maintaining a safe distance from the vehicle. (I'm driven, not crazy.) "My wife and I were just over at the Valedezes' down the street when we saw you leaving. Your daughters are beautiful, and we all know how important it is that they eat healthy foods."

"You're trying to sell me something?" Her voice betrays not-so-subtle irritation. "I have to go. Could you move, please? The girls have soccer practice—"

"Just take a brochure." I say, offering. The woman hesitates, then takes the literature like it's infected with some disease.

"All our products are free of hormones and antibiotics," I continue, not ready to let her go. "The meat is flash-frozen at the source for maximum freshness. You'll get twice the quality at half the price you'll get at the supermarket."

"Let me see," one of the girls snatches the brochure from her mother.

"Hey. Give that back."

I don't let the family squabble throw me. In fact, I use the distraction. "Growing kids can really complicate your food budget. That's why the Valedezes order by the case. Buy two and you get the second one for half price. Buy three and you get a fourth case free. Buy ten and I'll throw in a free freezer."

This gets the mom's attention. "Wait. A free freezer?"

"Yep. Buy ten cases and it's yours. You and your beautiful daughters will eat like queens for a year."

The woman pauses, then turns back to me. "If I wanted these, how would I order? By phone?"

She put words like "if" and "would" in the last few sentences. She's trying to be noncommittal—but I know better. She wouldn't bother asking if she weren't already imagining that new freezer in her garage, piled high with meat she won't have to shop for.

"Just let me know what you want and I'll bring it straight to your door. My truck is empty right now—I'm completely sold out; can you believe it? But I can be back in half an hour. I promise."

"So, if I drop the girls off at soccer practice…?"

"I can meet you here in thirty minutes."

I hate to let a customer go before money has changed hands but I have no choice. I hurry back to the truck, and Marlene and I drive back to Country Fed HQ to pick up another ten cases of steaks, chicken, and seafood. Driving back to Fountain Valley, Marlene begins doubting me.

"Tony, she was trying to be nice. You didn't even bring the meat with you. She just wanted to get out of there."

Most people would think this way. Give the customer too much time to think about a deal—no matter how good it is—and they're likely to talk themselves out of it. However…

"Oh my God," says Marlene. "I can't believe it."

We're not even halfway up the driveway, and the mom is already out the door, checkbook in hand.

As it turns out, this is my best day yet. I've sold twenty cases of product—all before noon. Just because I turned a chance sighting into a selling opportunity. Or as Stephen Baldwin's character famously says in *Glengarry Glen Ross*, "A.B.C. Always be closing."

"You're doing great," I tell Marlene. For the past two weeks, she's been not only driving but also helping me sell. I work one side of a street; she works the other. If she's able to engage a customer in conversation, she calls me over, and I make the sale. This strategy allows us to cover the same territory in half the time. Plus, Marlene gets a kick out of it. We're really a team now.

At the end of another successful morning, we pull up to our neighborhood Wells Fargo bank to deposit all the checks we've collected. We have just one case of steaks left in the back, and we're both ready to call it a day. But when I step out of the cab, I get an idea.

"Open the back," I tell Marlene.

"Why?"

"I'm going to sell that last case of steaks."

She looks around dubiously. "Where? On the street?"

"In the bank."

"O-kay."

Amused, she pushes the button, releasing the rear door lock. I grab the case from the refrigerator, tuck it under my arm, and head inside. I pause by the entrance to look around. It's still lunch hour, so the bank buzzes with nearly a dozen men and women standing in line for tellers. All female, they sit along a long marble counter protected by thick bulletproof glass. About a year ago, a series of bank robberies plagued Southern California, prompting all the banks to adopt stricter safety procedures. In an area crisscrossed with high-speed freeways, robbers find banks like this to be tempting targets.

Wait until they get a load of me.

"Can I help you, sir?"

I turn to see a young banker approach in a charcoal pin-striped suit. He reminds me of Michael Douglas in Wall Street with his striped suspenders and slicked backed hair. I set my box on the floor and open it up. Suddenly the room goes very quiet. Before anyone can scream, "Robbery!" I carefully lay out plastic sealed steaks. The banker's face turns from fear to puzzlement.

"I have restaurant-quality meat for sale," I announce. "Special discount! 15 percent off. Today only."

I notice the uniformed security guard glance at the banker. Both men look confused. Is this a distraction for a heist? I see his right hand moving slowly for his sidearm still strapped to its holster.

Yet, I keep going.

"Those for sale?" says a curious customer in the back of the line.

"They all are: T-bones. Ribeyes. Pork chops. Hamburgers. All grass-fed, hormone-free, and no antibiotics."

"How much?" calls a young female employee from behind the glass.

Mollified, the guard drops his arm, and I start to sell. Within seconds, the line disintegrates as customers and employees alike drift over. In the coming decades, they will call this FOMO: Fear of Missing Out, but today's it's just simple crowd psychology. Demand breeds demand. Within fifteen minutes, I've sold every steak in my case. The slick-haired banker just stands there, blown away.

I show him the money I've just collected. "Sir, I think I'd like to make a deposit."

It's midwinter. In SoCal, that means cold and wet. It's 4:00 p.m. Usually, we're able to quit by 1:00, but this afternoon has been unusually slow. Still, I refuse to quit until I've reached my quota. I stop at a single-story house midway down a block of mid-1970s tract homes and knock on the door. I hear movement inside, then a woman in her late fifties opens it.

"Hi. I'm one of your neighbors. This is my wife. I'm here to tell you I can save you 50 percent on every one of your dinners. And you'll eat better than ever."

I hold up my sample case of Country Fed steaks. The rain is falling hard now, and both of us are getting soaked.

"Don't just stand there," the woman says. "Come in."

She leads us into a house filled with the kind of disposable knickknacks and tchotchkes they sell at the airport. Several chairs and sofas are squeezed into the small living room, leaving little space for walking. A man sits in one of the wing-back chairs, his eyes glued to cable news.

"This is my husband, Ben," she says, indicating for us to sit down. "Ben, they're selling frozen steaks."

Ben, in his early sixties and built like a truck driver, stares at me over the top of his bifocal glasses. I stare back. We say nothing for literally two whole minutes. It's perfectly silent. *And awkward.* Our two wives look increasingly uncomfortable as their alpha-male husbands sniff each other out.

Finally, Ben speaks. "Look, we both know this game," he says, his voice low and gruff. "Whoever talks first owns the product."

"Go get your credit card," I say. "You just bought ten cases of meat."

Marlene gasps. Ben stands, revealing himself to be at least six foot four.

Marlene tenses.

Is this huge man going to physically throw us out?

Instead, he extends his hand. "Thank you for the excellent salesmanship," he says with a smile.

I can't lose.

"We have a problem," George Teller says one day back at the office. George has never looked exactly healthy, but in the last year or so, he's gone downhill. Dark circles ring his eyes, and he's put the weight back on. "Corporate isn't used to writing $15,000 checks every week to one salesperson. Makes them nervous."

"So, what are you saying? You want me to stop selling?"

"We want you to become a manager. You'll get $600 a week, plus an override on every sale."

I have to think about this. The money sounds good, but I like being on my own. Also, managing other people is always a pain in the neck. If this is going to be worth my while, I'm going to have to do things *my* way.

"Okay," I say. "I will become a manager. But on one condition…"

Chapter 50

STANDING OUTSIDE COUNTRY Fed headquarters in Anaheim Hills, I beam with pride as ten brand new Toyota refrigerator trucks arrive at our company parking lot. This brings the total number in our fleet to twenty, doubling our sales capacity. Growing our sales staff was the "one condition" I made when accepting George's offer to become local sales manager.

Why did I make this demand? Simple. To keep my income at my current level, I need more salespeople generating commissions. I know what our staff is producing, and to be honest, the status quo isn't sufficient. It's not that we have bad salespeople. We don't. For the most part, our staff is just… average. I outsell the best of them two-to-one. If I'm going to take myself off the streets, the only way to compensate is through sheer numbers. Volume.

To get salespeople in our new trucks, I place a want ad in both *The Orange County Register* and the Orange County edition of *Los Angeles Times*. More than forty people respond. Marlene, now serving as administrative assistant, makes the appointments, spacing them thirty minutes apart. She sits with me during every interview, after which we compare notes. We're in agreement that the most important quality we seek is personality. Skills can be taught. Experience comes with time. But personality is something one is born with. Either you got it or you don't.

And I'm not just talking about charm or charisma, although those are both great qualities. No, I'm also talking about drive, optimism, and the ability to improvise. We're looking for people who won't take "no" for an answer, who can think on their feet, who instinctively know how to identify a prospect's needs, then present a product in a way that satisfies those needs.

These are all qualities I believe I possess that have allowed me to succeed in every field I have entered. Frankly, I don't believe a salesperson can survive, let alone thrive, without these attributes. If I'm going to make Country Fed the sales powerhouse I imagine, I need hustlers who think and behave as I do.

It takes Marlene and me a full week to get through all forty candidates. Out of this group, we pick ten—eight men and two women—to train and send into the field. I remember what George told me when I answered his original ad, that most of his sales force quit after just a few weeks. I imagine half the people I've just selected likewise will bail by month's end. Another two or three will likely leave after eight to ten weeks. Then I will be left with just two or three survivors. But these people will be golden. Again I will run the ad and again pick a new team of recruits to fill the vacant slots. Some will quit, but others will excel. I expect to repeat this natural selection process for at least six months until I have a staff of twenty A-level players: salesmen and women who are as good as, and maybe better, than I am. At that point, we will be unstoppable.

Certainly, good professional training and direction are essential to success. But so is personal support from management—from me. Three weeks into my tenure as sales manager, one of my best producers, Larry, comes to me, clearly upset. He joined Country Fed about a month before I did, and while his numbers never matched mine, he's always exceeded his weekly quota and never missed a day of work. I respect that kind of perseverance.

"What's wrong?" I ask.

"My wife is in the hospital," he says, his voice shaking. "She had to have her gallbladder removed."

I put my hand on his shoulder. "My God. Is she all right?"

"She's doing better. It took her three weeks to recover from the surgery, but she's back on her feet now."

"That's great," I say, relieved. "I had no idea. You never said anything."

"I didn't want special treatment. Her sister was there to take care of her so I could keep working."

"That's what family is for."

"The thing is, we just got our hospital bill," Larry continues, obviously uncomfortable. "Even with insurance, we still owe $5,000. What can I do to make the extra money?"

"You're already working six days a week. I don't see how you could work more."

"I could work Sundays, too. Just until I make enough."

"You know that's against company policy. We tried selling on Sundays once and got complaints. People don't like salespeople knocking on their doors when they're sleeping in or getting ready for church."

Larry looks miserable. "But if I don't pay the bill, it'll go to collections…"

I think about this for a moment. Larry is a good man. A good producer. The last thing I need is for him to be distracted by this kind of problem. Such people become desperate. And customers can smell desperation.

I reach into my desk and pull out my personal checkbook.

"Here," I say, writing out a check for $5,000. "Use this to pay your bill."

"What? I can't take this." He backs away, waving his hands.

I tear the check from the book. "It's a loan. Pay me back $250 a week for the next twenty weeks. I know your sales record. Shouldn't be a problem for you."

He takes the check and studies it. As if by magic, his whole body relaxes. "This is a lifesaver. I really appreciate it. You don't even know."

"I need you sharp. I need you focused. I need you happy."

"I won't let you down."

"I know that. Say hi to your wife for me. Tell her I'm glad she's feeling better."

"I will, Tony. I definitely will."

I have no doubt I have made the right decision. I can afford to lose $5,000. But I can't afford to lose a good salesman.

"We're going to have a national sales contest," says the voice over the loudspeaker. George, Marlene, and I sit in George's office listening to his speakerphone. The man on the other end is Dwayne Eckhart, co-owner and national sales manager of Country Fed Foods. We're part of a conference call involving dozens of district and local sales managers all over the United States. "Any sales manager whose office sells one hundred cases in the next two weeks wins tickets to the Super Bowl. Dallas Cowboys versus the Buffalo Bills. And, by the way, my money's on Buffalo."

Distant laughs echo through the speaker. Country Fed is headquartered in Atlanta, where this year's Super Bowl is to be played.

"Sounds great," George says, leaning into the speakerphone. "You might as well send the envelope to Tony now. No way he's gonna lose this."

"I have a better idea," I chime in. "Make the goal two hundred cases. Only it's not just two tickets. If we hit two hundred, it's me, my top four sales people, and our spouses."

"That's ten tickets," Dwayne says at the other end. I can practically hear him crunching the numbers to make this profitable. A few seconds later, he says, "Sure. If you can sell two hundred cases, you get ten tickets."

"Does that go for everybody?" another disembodied sales manager asks.

"It goes for everybody," Dwayne assures us, laughing.

I know why he's laughing. He doesn't think we can make those kinds of numbers. He thinks he's just made a sucker's bet.

And maybe he's right.

"How the hell are we supposed to make two hundred sales in two weeks?" grumbles Ben Ngyuen, one of my mid-level sales performers when I announce the contest to everyone after concluding our call. "We're already working two shifts. What's the most we've ever sold in a week? Eighty cases?"

Ben is right. For the past two months, I've had half my staff work from 7:30 a.m. to 4:00 p.m., while the other works from 4:00 p.m. until midnight.

"Eighty-two," I correct him. "But here's the thing. The night shift is underperforming. Badly. And I can't blame them. Who opens their doors to salesmen after nine o'clock?"

"I've been saying that for weeks," someone else chimes in. "We're wasting time."

"Only because we're selling to the wrong customers." I've been mulling over this problem for weeks, and the contest has finally prompted me to consider an innovative solution. "Why limit ourselves to *homes*? Where do people go at night? They go to clubs. Bars. Restaurants. Movie theaters. Grocery stores. ATMs. Those are the places we should be hitting."

"We can do that?" Larry asks.

"I once sold a case of steaks at a bank. You can sell anywhere people have money. Now, who wants to go to the Super Bowl?"

Cheers all around. Pumped, they high-five each other and get back to work. Is my sales strategy crazy? Hell, yes. But it begins working. Energized, my staff breaks all the normal rules of sales decorum. They camp out in front of dance clubs, hocking slabs of beef to sweaty couples. They park in front of liquor stores to nab 2:00 a.m. stragglers with the munchies. They intercept crowds coming out of movie theaters to sell them plastic-wrapped seafood and chicken.

They sell. Boy, do they sell. By the end of week two, we have moved 215 cases. A national record.

"Goddammit all, George, how the hell did you let this happen!" I hear Dwayne shouting over the phone the day after the contest ends.

"But you agreed..."

"Look. I know what I agreed to," Dwayne snarls. "But I figured you'd top out at maybe 105. 110. Hell, the most Chicago did was 117."

"You can blame Tony," George says, grinning at me.

"Thanks to him, now I have to shell out for ten Super Bowl tickets. And hotel rooms. And airfare. This is nuts. I could actually *lose* money on this!"

"Better to lose a little money now than to lose Tony forever," George says. "He held up his end of the bargain. Now we have to hold up ours."

Dwayne finally comes through, albeit kicking and screaming. Together, my four top salespeople and their spouses join Marlene and me on a non-stop American Airlines flight from LAX to Atlanta, Georgia. On the morning before the game, Dwayne invites us over to his mansion in suburban Dunwoody.

"Tomorrow, we're going to have another contest!" Dwayne announces as we gather in his living room. "Each couple is getting a fully stocked truck and a map of Atlanta metro. You all get to keep any commissions you make. And the first couple to sell out their entire truck gets an extra $1,000 bonus!"

I know what's going on here. He's trying to make back some of the money he had to shell out for this trip. The day after the game—which Dallas won 30-13— Marlene and I climb aboard one of Dwayne's trucks to take to the streets of this unfamiliar metropolis. Six hours later, we return, our truck empty. I'm happy to receive the commission, plus the $1,000 bonus, but this *contest* raises red flags in the back of my mind. The owners of Country Fed are not *incentivizing* us. They are taking advantage of us. These are not completely honest people I am dealing with.

Because of my success, Country Fed makes me district manager, which basically means I am responsible for all of California. My dream of only working until 1:00 p.m. every day has been forgotten. I am back to working long, long hours, six days a week. And it is no longer as easy for me as it used to be. I'm not myself. I'm tired. I'm thirsty all the time. I'm drinking water and soda at all hours, constantly running to the bathroom. My body is telling me something. But I'm not listening. I don't want to hear it. I don't want to stop.

Chapter 51

"WE'RE HAVING ANOTHER sales contest," Dwayne announces during our weekly national telephone conference call. "Any sales manager whose office sells three hundred cases in one month gets to come down to Atlanta and drive home in a brand news 1994 Mercedes-Benz C-Class!"

This gets my heart pumping. I want to win this contest. Bad. Not just for the car—which would look *wonderful* in my driveway—but to prove I can do it. I feel increasingly tired lately and fear I am growing too old to perform up to my own standards. Ever since I was a teenager back in Beirut, I believed I had the skills and ability to achieve anything I put my mind to. I remember working days on end with little sleep, managing two full-time jobs, and still having the energy to party all night while suffering no ill effects. Now, just putting in a normal eight-hour day leaves me exhausted. I mean *drained*. I have to win this contest—just to prove to myself I'm not slipping.

I call my sales staff together to pump them up for this contest. It's not an easy task. "A few months ago," I start, "we sold two hundred cases in two weeks. Now we have twice that amount of time to sell just 50 percent more product."

"Fifty percent more?" someone asks.

"But that's not possible!"

Even though my head hurts and I want to lie down, I keep it together. I can't appear weak to these people. They need a leader.

"It is possible. We're going to double our shifts."

I see heads looking around. They can't believe what I'm asking. It's nuts. But I know I've got to really incentivize them. If I don't, we're done. After all, if I can't *sell them* to make more sales, how can they go out there and close?

I cough into my handkerchief and dab my eyes. I keep my voice steady though I can barely stand on my feet. "Listen." I cough again. "We can do this!" My voice grows stronger as I pause to look each person in the eye. "And to sweeten the deal, I'm gonna throw in something extra. On top of what Eckhart's paying, I'm offering a $1,000 bonus to everyone who delivers 100 percent over quota. You're the best sales team in the country. You've proved it before, and you're going to prove it again."

A pause. Then they break into applause, cheering each other on. I try to keep my smile upbeat as they clap, but I can barely breathe.

Within weeks, my sales team delivers just as promised. A month later, on the weekly conference call, each local sales manager reports their final numbers.

"Two hundred seventeen cases," reports New York.

"Good, but not good enough," says Dwayne.

"A hundred and ninety-four cases," Miami reports.

"Not good," Dwayne says. "I'm disappointed."

"Three hundred and seventeen," I announce proudly.

Silence at the end of the line.

"I said, Los Angeles sold 317 cases."

"Tony, that's great. And congratulations," Dwayne says.

"When can I pick up my Mercedes?"

"We'll call you back with details."

I wait two days to hear from Dwayne. Frustrated, I ring him at the Atlanta office.

"I'm sorry, but Mr. Eckhart is in a meeting," his secretary tells me.

"Then get him out of the meeting," I say through clenched teeth. "He promised me a new car."

"Hold for a minute, please." The line goes silent. I wait. And I wait. And I wait. Finally, someone picks up on the other end.

"Tony? It's Dwayne. I'm here with Ken." Paul is Dwayne's younger brother. Together, they own and run Country Fed Foods.

I struggle to hold my temper. "You said you would call me about the Mercedes. I haven't heard anything."

"Yeah. Okay. Well, here's the thing," Ken says. "I'm going to be honest with you, Tony. We never expected anyone to actually *win* the contest."

"What are you talking about?"

"I mean, we created the contest to boost sales, but we never figured any team would actually sell three hundred cases in one month. Not even close."

"But what about the Mercedes?"

"That was just bait."

"So, you're saying there is no Mercedes."

"There is no Mercedes."

"You lied to us?"

"Like I said, we never expected anyone to actually…"

I don't hear any more of what Ken or Dwayne say. I can't. The blood is pounding so hard in my ears it has rendered me deaf to everything but my own rage. After what happened in Atlanta during the Super Bowl, I suspected these people couldn't be trusted. Now I know for certain they are crooks.

"Fine," I say, my voice shaking. "I'll leave the office keys on my desk."

This isn't a bluff. I call the sales team together and tell them the whole story. With that, Marlene and I leave. When we arrive home, I am exhausted. I just want to sleep. But an hour later, there is a knock at the door. Marlene answers. To my amazement, the entire sales staff has followed us home.

"We quit, too," Larry says. "The whole office shut down."

"We work for *you*, not them," Ben says.

I am touched, but worried, too. "No, you can't do this. You have families to support. Mortgages to pay. Go back to Country Fed."

"We won't," says someone else."

"We're only loyal to you. After all, you kept your promise. You paid us our bonuses."

Marlene grabs beers from the refrigerator, someone orders pizzas, and we end up having a big party. It doesn't break up until 1:00 a.m. I'm still tired. But damn if I don't feel great.

After the Country Fed fiasco, Marlene and I take a full month to recover. We still have plenty of money, so paying the bills is no problem. We just want to take it easy. While we do, Dwayne and Ken fly in from Atlanta to rebuild the California operation, but after three months, they finally shut the office down for good. They thought they were being so clever. Instead, they shot themselves in the foot.

Meanwhile, Scott has been discharged from the Army. He is married now, and his wife is pregnant. Since becoming a civilian he doesn't know what to do with his life. He comes over to our house one day to talk. I'm still not feeling great—I'm not exhausted like before, but I'm always thirsty and feel run down like I have a cold. Instead of worrying about myself, I focus on Scott.

The Army has done him a world of good. He's much slimmer now than when he left at eighteen. More muscular. His hair is neatly cropped, and when he stands, he stands erect, not slouched. It makes him look confident. I know now giving him that ultimatum was the right thing to do.

"You have a great personality. You always, have," I tell him. "You would do well in sales."

"I don't know anything about sales."

"I can teach you. You can ride along with Marlene and me and we'll show you how it's done."

He looks hesitant.

"Once you learn how to sell one thing, you can sell anything."

"You really think I can do it?"

"Yes, but this is serious," I stress. "You have to show up on time every day and be prepared to work."

"Just one problem."

"What?"

"You're not working anymore."

This stops me short. He has a point.

"I can fix that."

In no time, Marlene finds us another company. It's called Colorado Prime. It's basically the same operation as Country Fed, but it's not cold-calling. Telemarketers set appointments. Then, we go out and sell. Right away, this sounds much easier than going door-to-door.

Together, Marlene, Scott, and I go to the office to apply for jobs. I sit down first for an interview with Roy, the local sales manager. Seconds into the conversation, I manage to offend the guy after he tells me how much he earns.

"Wait," I say. "You're only making $37,000 per year?"

His face turns red. He tries to say something else but can't find the words. Moments later, he ends the interview and tells me to go wait outside. After interviewing Marlene and Scott, he makes them an offer.

"I'd like to hire you and Scott as a team," He says, looking right at Marlene. "Your record speaks for itself."

The three of us sit there, waiting.

"Thank you," Marlene says. "But what about Tony?"

Roy won't even look in my direction. "I don't see him as a good fit."

"Tony's very good with people," says Marlene. "A natural leader."

He finally turns to face me. "Frankly, you strike me as a troublemaker."

"He's the best salesman you'll ever have," Marlene says, in my defense. "And if you're not smart enough to hire him, you're not someone I want to work for."

"That's your position?"

"We're a team," Scott chimes in. "It's all of us or none of us."

That afternoon, we get a call at home from Roy. We're hired. All of us.

It turns out, Colorado Prime is a sophisticated operation. As part of our sales kit, we receive an impressive 3-foot-by-3-foot menu, printed on laminated cardstock, with colorful photos of the products in various combinations. We also receive instructions about how to use the menu in a sales environment. In addition to frozen steaks, chicken, and seafood, we will be pitching food-related products, such as barbeques, glassware, pots, pans, freezers, refrigerators, and even televisions. Since we can't be hauling all of these around in our car, the menu is the only way to market our full range of items.

Scott is true to his word and throws himself into working with Marlene and me. It's so nice to have my son back. Like old times. Each evening, he and I work from a flip chart the company provided to learn our sales pitch. Marlene plays along too, pretending to be the customer. She tries to jam us up with objection after objection, throwing us every conceivable curve ball a prospect might say.

At first, Scott stumbles on his answers—and even I have trouble refuting Marlene's airtight logic. Over the years, she must have memorized everything housewives said to our sales team to shut down sales—still, as I predicted, Scott is a natural at sales. Within weeks, he and I can outmaneuver every single objection. We've become veritable sales ninjas, capable of closing in any environment, no matter how unreceptive or hostile.

We begin working for Colorado Prime in August 1994. Unlike Country Fed, the company's telemarketers set up our appointments, so when we arrive at a house, the customers are, well... *primed* for us. We receive appointments all over Los Angeles, Orange, and Riverside counties, so we have to plan each week well in advance.

Compared to my last sales position, each encounter is more complicated and therefore harder to close. We are told to block out three hours for every sale. This means that, factoring in transportation, we can only do two visits per day. The goal is to sell each customer enough food to last eight months, as well as an upright freezer in which to store it all. To further incentivize the buyer, we discount the cost of food 20 percent to cover the freezer's monthly payments over three years. It's really a good deal, though. Even after the freezer is paid off, the 20 percent food discount remains for as long as they are customers of Colorado Prime. This strategy helps ensure customers keep reordering for three years at minimum and hopefully beyond.

We sell our barbeques and pot-and-pan sets the same way: Buy one and get a 30 percent discount off the food purchase. This covers the cost of the appliances and/or cookware, and, combined with the freezer purchase, the customer ends up getting a 50 percent food discount for life.

Same as before, I do most of the sales presentations myself while Marlene waits in the car. This means she's often alone for up to three hours at a time. She uses the downtime to complete the paperwork from previous sales and catch up on her reading. I know she's bored a lot, but she never complains.

Things hum along until early September, when I overhear two salespeople talking about a new contest. The big prize is a trip to Cancun. This is the first I've heard about this. Upset, I go talk to Roy.

"Why didn't you tell me about the Cancun contest?" I ask.

Roy never has gotten over my remark in the interview. I can tell he doesn't like me. Instead of offering an explanation, he smirks at me like I'm an idiot for even asking this. "Because it started in January."

"And?"

"And it ends at the end of this month. There's no way you can outdo people with a seven-month lead."

He turns to walk away but I call after him. "Really? How did I do last month?" I already know the answer to this question.

Though he stops, he keeps his back to me. "You did great."

I follow him to the end of the hallway where the sales tallies are kept. I notice he doesn't make eye contact when he says, "Thanks to you, we were the number one office in the country."

"Is that right?" I knew this already too.

Roy finally turns to me and yells. "So what? You'd have to do *three times* your numbers over the next three weeks—to even get close."

I give him my most innocent smile. "Just three times?"

Roy's face is beet-red. "I don't see how that's possible."

"You know, you have me doing two pitches a day."

"Yeah. That's right."

"Give me six."

He starts to walk away. "That's crazy."

I keep up with him. For a second, I forgot how tired I am. This is too much fun. "So, I'm crazy, Roy. Give me six."

"You can't do six. That's eighteen hours a day. Plus transportation. That's impossible."

"Only because each visit is supposed to be three hours long."

Stopping, he turns on his heel to point a finger at me. "That's the policy."

"And what if I can close a sale in just one hour?"

"The policy is *three* hours, goddamn it. Three! Believe me, we've tested it. Three hours is optimum. You need it. Everyone needs it to close."

"Not for me it isn't. Book me six visits a day until the end of the month. If I can't close the sales, you can fire me."

He's literally speechless for ten seconds. "Fine. It's your funeral." Roy walks off, adding, "I always knew you were a troublemaker."

Three weeks later, the contest concludes. The numbers are tallied. In just two months, I made more sales than any other salesman in the company, including those who started in January.

Marlene and I really enjoyed Cancun.

Despite my Mexican vacation, I'm still exhausted all the time. I'm also losing weight. A lot of weight. It's scary. My pants don't fit me anymore. I'm going through belts every few weeks. I look like I'm swimming in my shirts. Worried, Marlene tries to fatten me up with starchy foods, like rice and potatoes, but they just make me feel worse. At last, I see a doctor.

"You should be happy," he tells me after a quick examination. "Most people would die to be so thin."

Neither Marlene nor I are satisfied with this diagnosis, so Marlene visits our local pharmacy and describes my symptoms to the pharmacist.

"Sounds like diabetes to me. You need to buy a test kit. Right away."

We take it home. Inside, there's a strip I'm supposed to pee on. Before I do, Marlene shows me the color match card that goes from light brown (healthy) to dark brown (unhealthy).

After peeing, I compare my color to the chart and gasp. The color my strip has turned isn't even listed. Because it's pure black.

Chapter 52

"I HAVE A question about your diabetes test strips," Marlene says to the representative on the other line. "My husband followed the instructions on the package and the strip came out black. Can you tell me what that means?"

There is an awkward silence, the kind that never means anything good. My mouth has turned uncomfortably dry, so I go into the kitchen to pour myself a glass of water. I am always thirsty lately, but this is something different. This is the taste of fear.

"Can you see the expiration date on the box?" the rep asks. For a moment, I feel a glimmer of hope. Maybe the test spoiled and the results mean nothing.

"October 15, 1997," Marlene reports.

"That's two years from now."

Marlene and I share a look. The problem is not the test. *It's me.* I gulp down the entire glass. It doesn't make any difference.

"Look. I think you should call 911," the rep suggests. "Like now. Your husband may be close to falling into a diabetic coma."

We don't call 911. Beyond my persistent thirst and a general sense of fatigue, I feel fine enough. Certainly not on death's door. Instead, we make an appointment to see another doctor and run more tests. He specifically checks me for diabetes. The results are not encouraging.

"Well, the normal range for fasting blood sugar is between 80 and 100," he says. I'm sitting on a cushioned table in a white-walled examination room while Marlene stands behind me, hands on my shoulders. Both of us have been expecting the worst. "And your number is 400. A lot of your body's cells are dying because this condition has been untreated for so long."

Marlene's grip tightens on my shoulders.

"I don't understand. How did I get this? What did I do wrong?"

"First of all, Tony, diabetes—especially Type II diabetes, which is what we're talking about—is usually not caused by any one single thing. Part of it is based on genetics. Some people are just more predisposed to it than others. The other part is lifestyle. Being overweight can contribute to it. So can lack of exercise and eating a high-fat, low-fiber diet. And stress. What do you do for a living, again?"

"Sales."

Marlene grips my shoulders even tighter.

"Uh-huh. You see, what happens is your body becomes insulin resistant," the doctor continues. "That means that while your pancreas is producing sufficient insulin to transport glucose to your cells, the cells aren't accepting the insulin. Glucose, or sugar, begins to build up in your bloodstream, and that's what causes the symptoms you've been experiencing."

"So, what do we do now?"

"Yeah, is this going to kill me?"

The doctor nods. "If you keep living and eating the way you have been, then yes, it will kill you. Fast."

I let out a small scream as Marlene's nails break skin on my back. "Sorry, Tony."

"But," the doctor looks me in the eyes, "I believe we're still at the stage where we can manage this with proper medication and lifestyle changes."

"You said *manage*, not *cure*."

"That's right. This is now a *permanent* condition. But, like I said, if you manage it correctly, you can go on to live a long, healthy life. You're the one in control."

I turn to Marlene. I know he's right. All these years, I've been running, going, nonstop. Pushing it to the limit. It's finally caught up with me.

"Tony?" Marlene asks me with tears in her eyes. She doesn't finish the question. She doesn't have to.

"I will," I tell her.

The doctor prescribes a medication to manage my insulin levels and refers us to a dietician who can create a meal plan to lower my blood sugar. After the appointment, Marlene drives us home. I'm still too shaken to consider taking the wheel. Instead, I stare out the window, wondering if I will actually be able to change my ways, and if doing so will make any difference. I'm only in my forties, yet I feel Death closing in on me.

"I've never felt so old."

"You're not going to die," Marlene says cheerfully. Gone are the tears. She's returned to being my sunny optimist. "You heard what the doctor said. We can control this. It just takes a little planning and effort. Since when have you ever failed at anything you put your mind to?"

I turn to her and force a smile. Again, I remember why I fell in love with her. She knows me better than I know myself. No way I'm going to leave this woman a widow.

Later that week, Marlene meets with the dietician the doctor recommended. She teaches her how to prepare meals low in simple carbohydrates, which are, basically, sugars that can aggravate my condition. She also advises me to take chromium and vanadium supplements. I go to my local Mother's Market to buy these minerals. I'm happy to see chromium available over-the-counter. But I'm disappointed to discover vanadium is nowhere to be found.

"Vanadium? I've never heard of it," says the manager after I tell him about my situation.

"My doctor says this is good for diabetes," I explain, showing him my note. "I'm sure you have a lot of customers who could use this, too. You really should stock it."

"I'll look into it," he promises. And he does. A month later, vanadium is on the shelves of every Mother's Market in Orange County.

The doctor's management plan takes a while to work, but after a few weeks, I'm already feeling stronger and less thirsty. We check my blood sugar levels daily before breakfast. I'm thrilled to watch it drop from 400 to 300 to 200 and finally down to 110. Marlene was right. I can succeed at whatever I put my mind to.

The first thing I want to do now is go back to my first doctor, the one who said I should be thrilled I'm losing so much weight—and shake him. But I have better things to do with my time.

"I have good news and bad news," Scott says. We're sitting at a corner table in our favorite local Italian restaurant. Scott and Marlene have just ordered a sausage pizza. I'm contenting myself with an antipasto salad. "I'm leaving Colorado Prime."

"What?" Marlene asks.

"It's just not working for me. I just can't sell like you do, Dad."

For the moment, I'm speechless. Scott has managed to turn an excuse into a compliment, and I'm unsure how to respond.

"So, what are you going to do?" Marlene asks, again taking the lead. "Have you at least looked for another job?"

"As a matter of fact, I have one." Marlene and I share a joint sigh of relief. "I'm going into the mortgage business with Jimmy."

He's talking about his half-brother, the son I had with Sara, whom I've barely spoken to in years. I've heard rumors of Jimmy, who's now in his late twenties, going into real-estate financing, but I had no idea he was an entrepreneur.

"Well, I have to admit, I'm a bit disappointed," I confess. "But if you can make this work, I'm all for it. You know all we want is for you to be happy."

"Jimmy really knows what he's doing. We're going to make this work."

I have my doubts, but I remain silent. Not that anything I say will make a difference at this point. Scott is as stubborn as I am.

In May of 1995, Marlene and I take a trip to Lebanon. This is the first time I've been home in more than fifteen years. Marlene's mother has property here, specifically an undeveloped parcel on a spectacular bluff overlooking the Mediterranean Sea.

"I've been thinking about it," Marlene says. We sit high up on a large boulder perched above a 30-foot-high cliff, feeling the cool sea breeze caress our skin. In the distance, we can see the majestic peak of Mount Lebanon cresting into paper-thin clouds. The air rumbles with the sound of waves crashing on the rocks below. "With everything that's been so crazy this past year—the fact I almost lost you— maybe it's time we retire," Marlene says. "Think about it. With the money we have, we could move here and live comfortably."

It's an attractive proposal. The civil war has been over for years, and the country is recovering nicely thanks to millions in foreign investments. Down deep, I still miss my homeland—our shared homeland. I take Marlene's hand and kiss it. "If that's what you want, I want it too."

Returning to California, we begin making plans to move. Marlene contacts one of her cousins, a homebuilder, to design a dream house for the site in Lebanon. Eventually, they come up with a plan Marlene says is perfect. "I can't wait to show it to you."

A few days later, we stop at a diner for breakfast. Marlene and I have just been served bacon and eggs—no toast with jam for me anymore—when we hear a scream.

Across the dining room we see a large man who looks to be in his fifties on the floor, clutching at his chest. Immediately, cell phones emerge from pockets and purses. Within five minutes, an ambulance arrives. EMTs check the man's vital signs. Seconds later, they have an oxygen mask over his face and are carrying him out on a stretcher. The reality of what's happened hits me. *I could be this man.*

"What if this happens in Lebanon?" Marlene asks, once again reading my mind.

I imagine the scenario: I keel over at the table. Marlene calls the operator for an ambulance. Being three miles from the nearest town and fifteen miles from the nearest hospital, it could take thirty minutes or more before help arrives. And by then, I could be as dead as the bacon now congealing on our plates.

"Maybe we should stay in Orange County," I say.

"Maybe we should," she agrees.

We give up talking about land on the Lebanese seacoast… and plans for Marlene's dream house.

It's now autumn of 1996 when the Colorado Prime's district manager asks me to join him in the office's small conference room.

"I'd like to make you sales manager for the Cerritos office," he says. "You've been our top producer for three years running. Get six people to do what you're doing, and we'll be the top district in the country."

We've been down this road before. This time I'm ready. "I can do that," I reply confidently. "But I don't want you or anyone from corporate calling me and telling me how to do my job."

He chuckles. "You don't like to be micromanaged."

"Never have."

"If this office does six sales a week, you won't hear a peep from us."

I almost have to laugh, too. I'm already selling more than six packages a week. This should be a walk in the park.

"I'll take it," I say without hesitation.

Six sales a week may be corporate's goal, but my dreams are bigger. The average Colorado Prime office has three sales reps. The first thing I do is hire ten, then double the number of telemarketers. My aspirations may be high, but the way Marlene looked at me in that doctor's office is never far from my mind. It's not me that's going out there, killing myself for sales. Instead, I train the staff myself, helping each rep to establish empathy with their prospects while focusing on the benefits buying in bulk can deliver.

Within a month, we're generating thirty-five sales a week. Then forty-five. Then I get a phone call from the district manager.

"You're killing us, Tony," he groans. "Corporate's computer program is only set up to handle forty sales a week per office. And no one's ever come close. Now what are we supposed to do?"

"Buy a new computer program?"

It's a good thing they do, because a few months later, we're generating ninety sales a week. Our best week: nine-nine sales. I'm mad we couldn't make it an even one hundred.

In 1998, after four years, Jimmy's mortgage company goes under, and Scott is again out of a job.

"I want to open my own mortgage company," he tells me one day. "We can own it together. Fifty-fifty. You fund it, I'll run it."

"What kind of funding are we talking about?" I ask skeptically.

He gives me a figure. It's substantial but not unreasonable. In fact, considering his line of business, I'd be more skeptical if he had asked for less. His wife is pregnant again, and this is no time for him to be out on the streets. So, I call my lawyer and we create a corporation.

Scott finds a 5,000-square-foot office in Costa Mesa, the city just south of Fountain Valley. He hires twelve telemarketers. First National Lending is in business. I pray to God he can make this work. More than anything, I want my boy to be a success.

Chapter 53

"I WANT US to look for a house," Marlene says one day.

"We already have a house," I remind her.

"This is different. Maria told me her grandfather needs to sell his place in Lake Isabella."

Maria came as a secretary with my job. A total pro, she's been working for Colorado Prime for almost fifteen years, during which she's been able to raise two boys and send them off to college.

"It would be a great place to retire," Marlene adds. "It's out in Kern County— away from it all."

Although I have now been living in Southern California for more than a decade, my knowledge of local geography remains confined to Orange, Los Angeles, and Riverside counties. I have a vague notion that Kern County is some place north of Los Angeles. Otherwise, to me, it might as well be on the far side of the moon. More importantly, I have other misgivings about Marlene's plan.

"First of all, I don't want to retire. Not any time soon. "Secondly, if I *did* retire, it sure wouldn't be to Kern County. I don't know a thing about it."

Marlene pats my hand, giving me her sweetest smile. "That's why we're going to drive up and look. I told her we'd go this weekend."

"This weekend! Why did you tell her that?"

"Because she asked."

"Driving halfway to San Francisco is not how I want to spend my Saturday."

"But I promised."

Marlene looks at me the way she always does when she's determined to get her way. But I'm not a happy man. It seems stupid to wake up bright and early—ruining a perfectly good day—to brave the horrors of L.A. traffic just to see a home I don't even want.

And I don't keep these feelings to myself, either. In fact, I complain throughout the entire four hours it takes us to get to Lake Isabella, which turns out to be in the southern Sierra Nevada mountains, two hundred miles north of Los Angeles. The lake is surrounded by high, jagged hills covered with scrub-like vegetation. What shade there is to be found is in the form of small groves of mesquite trees composing the shoreline.

Maria's grandfather's house is at the end of a long dirt road. I have put Marlene through so much whining and grumbling that by the time we finally park, she is livid with me.

"It's not worth it. I wish we'd never come." Slamming the door behind her, Marlene storms off.

"Look, I'm sorry," I yell after her.

She won't even look at me. Or the house we drove out here to see. This couldn't get any worse. Not only did we waste the day driving here, but also, I managed to infuriate my wife. Eager to leave as soon as possible, I amble over to the rustic, ranch-style house. Perhaps if I do my diligence, give it a once-over, that will be that and we can go. I'll work on making it up to Marlene later.

Drawing closer, I notice more about the home. A lack of wear and weathering, coupled with the pristine condition of the roof, suggests a recent construction. Maria's grandfather, a thin, sinewy man who looks to be in his early seventies, rises from his wicker chair on the porch.

"Tony Assali." I offer my hand. "I work with your granddaughter."

"Right. Maria told me you were coming up."

"It was a long drive. Mind if I use your bathroom?"

"It's inside. Second door on the right."

I immediately find the bathroom. I'm in and out in under two minutes. I don't even bother to look at the rest of the home.

But as I exit back onto the porch, I get a familiar odd, disorienting sensation, like the universe is talking to me. I don't know what it's saying, but I feel a compulsion that I can neither explain nor resist. I take a seat in the empty chair next to the old man, who seems at peace in this remote setting.

"So, how much for the house?" Even I'm surprised by the words coming out of my mouth.

"A hundred seventy-five thousand," he replies without hesitation. He's obviously given this thought.

"I don't think so. Not in this market." I have no idea what I'm talking about. Nor do I know what Kern County real estate goes for these days. Possessing not the slightest interest in moving here, I've done zero research into local home values or market trends.

He counters. "$165,000." Suddenly, this has become a negotiation. Maybe there's a bargain to be had here. If so, I might be able to make a tidy profit even if I never set foot here again.

I look around. The view is beautiful. The way the sun flashes off the lake is almost ethereal and the smell of the mesquite, intoxicating. For a brief moment, I almost imagine myself living here.

"One hundred twenty-five thousand, cash," I say with a tone of finality. "No escrow."

"Sold!"

Again, we shake hands. And just like that, I've bought a house. For reasons I cannot begin to explain.

Reeling from the adrenaline coursing through my body, I stumble back to the mesquite grove where Marlene remains seated, fuming. Nearby is a large rock with a sign attached that reads, "2½ Acres Available for Development."

I take out a pen and write down the contact phone number.

"You want to look at the house now?"

"No, let's just go home," she pulls herself to her feet.

"You sure?"

"What's the point? Let's just go."

"Fine. You drive. I'm beat."

"Fine," she says, grabbing the keys from my hands.

As we drive down twisty Highway 178, I pull my new Ericsson cell phone from my pocket and check the signal. Surprisingly, I get two bars, even in this rural location. Yes, even now, the universe is working to accommodate me.

I call the contact number from the sign offering land for sale. "You have a lot for sale on Lake Isabella?" I say to the man who answers.

"That's right. Two and a half acres."

"How much?"

"Twenty-five thousand dollars."

"I don't have that. But I can give you twenty thousand, cash. No escrow. Can you do that?"

"I can do that," he says.

I glance over to see Marlene staring at me like I'm a madman. "What are you doing?" she whispers.

"Great. I'll have the cash for you this time next week. The name is Assali. Tony Assali."

"What the hell did you just do?" Marlene demands as I snap the phone shut.

"I just bought the land next to Maria's grandfather's house."

"Why?"

"You liked what you saw up there, didn't you?"

"Yes. Kind of. I don't know. But there's no way I'm going through the hassle of building a house on an empty lot."

"I don't want to build there, either," I agree. "In fact, I don't want *anybody* building there. They might have horses. Horses attract horse flies. And I don't want horseflies in my house."

"What are you babbling about?" Marlene says, increasingly agitated. "Wait a minute. Are you actually thinking about buying that house?"

"No, I'm not thinking about it. I already bought it."

At this point, Marlene nearly loses control of the car. I reach over to steady the wheel until she recovers.

"But we never even looked at it! And you complained the whole way down here. Why would you do such a crazy thing?"

"I had to. I just knew it was the right thing to do."

Marlene doesn't say anything more. After several minutes, though, I see her shoulders relax. She loosens her white-knuckle grip on the wheel.

"Another white tiger?" she finally asks.

"You know it."

The next weekend, we drive back to Lake Isabella with two cashier's checks, one for $125,000, the other for $20,000. Maria's grandfather has the paperwork ready, and we sign the necessary documents. The house is ours.

Now, for the first time, Marlene gets to see the home's interior. This is only my second visit, if you count my brief visit to the restroom. As soon as Marlene steps inside, she stops cold. I watch in fascination as she glides from room to room as if in a dream. I knew she would like the house, but this much?

"What's going on?" I ask.

"Go back to the car."

"Why?"

"Just go back to the car. Look in the trunk."

I do as she says. I open the trunk and peer inside. I see nothing but some old grocery bags, an unused first aid box, some loose receipts, and a Frisbee I bought years ago for a trip to the beach.

Then I notice something toward the rear of the compartment: a large heavy cardboard tube, the kind you might use to mail posters or other large printed documents. I lean down to grab it. Removing the round plastic cap from one end and sliding out the rolled papers inside, I recognize what this is immediately: the floor plan Marlene drew for us back when we were thinking of building in Lebanon years ago.

I bring the blueprints back to the house. Shaking, Marlene unrolls the blueprint on the kitchen table, anchoring its curled edges with salt and pepper shakers, an ashtray, and a napkin holder. I gaze at the plan in rising disbelief.

It looks exactly like the house we're standing in.

"When was this built?" I ask Maria's grandfather.

"1995."

Goosebumps rise along my arms as I check the notation on the blueprint. Yes, it's dated 1995. Maria's father was building this house at the same time, two hundred miles away, while Marlene was drawing these plans. It's as if they were psychically linked. *Is this why I had to buy the house the moment I saw it?*

Picking up the plan, we walk through the house. Every room matches the blueprints. Even little details, like the position of the fireplace, are identical. The only difference is that instead of the living room picture window overlooking the Mediterranean, it opens onto Lake Isabella.

"This is my dream house," Marlene grips my hand. "How is this possible?"

So much for life's ups and downs. Even though we are flourishing, it pains me to know my son is not. Scott's mortgage business is foundering. He's making deals but not showing profits. So far, I have sunk more than $250,000 into this venture. Finally, I tell him I'm pulling out.

"What about the money you've invested?" he asks.

"I don't know."

And truthfully, I don't. All night long I agonize about this situation. As Scott's father, I want the best for him, yet part of me knows he has to fend for himself to be a man—to build resilience and confidence. On top of that, there's the fact that I must protect my future with my wife. I can't drag her into a mess she didn't create.

The next day, I call my lawyer and draw up the papers to give Scott 100 percent ownership of the company. This isn't what he wanted, nor I for that matter, but I don't know what else to do. He will have to do what I was once told: sink or swim.

Chapter 54

MY OUTPUT AS Colorado Prime's local sales manager for Cerritos continues to set records. As a result, I'm earning $40,000 to $50,000 a month, more than I have ever made in my life. And just as it did with Country Fed, my success raises red flags with upper management.

"Bonuses are designed to be incentives," explains our company's new vice president, who is visiting Southern California from the main New York City office. "They're rewards for exceptional work."

"You don't think I'm doing exceptional work?" I say, confused.

"If you're getting rewards *every* month, then your work is no longer exceptional. The bonuses defeat the purpose."

"Huh?"

"Look. You're making too much money," the regional sales manager explains. He, too, is visiting from San Diego. "To be honest, it's pissing off the other sales managers."

"Pissing them off? But I'm bringing in sales for *our* company."

This logic bounces right off these guys based on what the regional sales manager says next. "The bottom line is, we have to even things out, or we're going to have a rebellion on our hands."

My head spins as I listen to this. Capitalism is supposed to reward hard work and success. So why am I being punished for being successful?

"We're going to raise your sales goals by 50 percent," the VP states flatly. "That should put your take-home pay back in line where it should be."

I stare at these two supposedly sane and experienced business executives, trying to determine what could be going through their minds. Do they honestly think I am eager to work harder for less money? Even crazier, do they really want me to generate *fewer* sales? Maybe they just want me to walk out—the way I left Country Fed after the bosses stiffed me—so they can replace me with someone desperate enough to work fourteen hours a day for peanuts.

Fortunately, I'm not desperate. Despite all of the money I lost investing with Scott, I still have enough socked away to retire anytime. But then I realize something. This confrontation isn't about money. It's not even about *me*. It's about *them*. These guys are scared, scared that if this office continues to perform head-and-shoulders above all the others, someone above them in the company will start asking questions. Someone is going to pressure them to repeat our performance—companywide. And they can't do that. My success is putting their jobs at risk. And this puts me in a very interesting position.

"Okay, I agree to your terms," I tell the two suits. "Under one condition."

"And that is?" the San Diego regional manager says cautiously.

"I get to run this whole office."

I see their eyes go wide but I continue anyway.

"My condition is that I get to be autonomous. No questions asked. No more interference from New York or San Diego."

Yep, it's the same condition I've demanded virtually everywhere I've worked. And the bosses always relent because they have everything to gain and nothing to lose. I expect this time will be no different.

"And you can still hit your numbers?" says New York.

"Of course."

"And how do you plan to do that?" asks San Diego.

"What did I just say?" I smile. "No questions."

The two executives share a look.

The next day, I am notified the Cerritos office is mine—and mine alone. Immediately, I go to work. I double our sales staff and telemarketing team, making sure to hire the absolute best people I can find. Then I increase our sales training sessions from two to four times per week. I know these people are already working their asses off, but I can't help recall what I did with Marlene and Scott to improve my own sales game. Not content to rest on my laurels, I had my wife grill us over and over until we were highly honed sales machines. In order to scale, I need to take the same training regimen to my personnel.

And just as I did with Country Fed, I make sure my salespeople needn't worry about making ends meet, even if it means I have to front them money out of my own pocket. Over the next six months, the loans I arrange total more than $200,000. Why do I do this? Because I know if you don't feel confident, you can't sell. Therefore, I consider these loans a good investment. And the investment pays off. We hit our new, higher sales quotas… *and then some.*

Management is happy. Our sales team is happy, too. Everyone is making money. To celebrate, I take the whole office—all the sales reps and their spouses—on a weekend trip to Las Vegas. I take care of all the airline tickets so we can all travel together. I also take care of the hotel and dining bills. On our last night, Marlene and I go to the hotel's five-star restaurant, a steakhouse catering to visiting businessmen on expense accounts. You can't touch anything for under forty dollars. When we arrive, I see a few empty tables near the windows.

"I have to use the men's room," I tell Marlene. "Would you please get us one of those tables?"

When I return, I find her waiting for me by the restaurant entrance.

"What's going on?"

"The hostess said we need a reservation," Marlene explains, clearly frustrated. "We'll have to go someplace else."

This makes no sense. I can still see at least four empty tables. "I'm going to talk to the hostess."

I cross to the front desk where I find an extremely tall, extremely attractive looking woman of about thirty typing data into a screen.

"My wife and I would like a table. I see you have some empty ones near the window."

"I'm sorry, sir, but this restaurant is reservations-only," the hostess explains with practiced charm. "If you want, I can see if there's an opening at the Italian restaurant."

"I'd like to speak to your manager, please."

"Of course, sir. Just a moment."

A few moments later, a stocky middle-aged man with slicked-back hair arrives. "Can I help you, sir?"

"My name is Tony Assali and my wife and I would like a table by your window."

The manager's eyes bug wide and his mouth drops. A split-second later, he composes himself and grabs a set of leather-bound menus.

"Of course, Mr. Assali. Right this way."

I motion Marlene to join us, and we're led to a large semi-circular booth at the far end of the restaurant.

"Is this acceptable, sir?"

"Absolutely," I say, confused by the sudden deference.

Over the next ninety minutes, Marlene and I are treated like royalty. The staff is quick and attentive, eager to make sure every part of our meal is to our satisfaction. The steaks we order are hot and juicy and melt like butter in our mouths. Our wine glasses are kept full to the brim. We are each given a premium dessert "on the house." I've never experienced such first-class service in all my life. When the check finally arrives, I include a generous tip.

Several minutes later, I tell one of my salesmen about our experience and he cracks up laughing.

"What's so funny?" I ask, thrown by his reaction.

"Don't you know?" he asks between giggles. "One of the biggest mob families in town is named Assali. The manager figured you were related."

"You're kidding. There are Lebanese gangsters in this town?"

Marlene is exhausted after dinner. But I'm feeling lucky and want to play more slots.

"Why don't you go back to the room," I suggest. "I'll be up in half an hour."

"You sure?"

"Promise."

Marlene heads for the elevators as I begin to stroll through the casino. The floor is still busy at this hour, the air humming with electronic tones, beeps, and tunes. Five minutes later I locate a Double Diamond dollar machine in an uncrowded corner. I sit down, slide five $20 bills into the cash slot, bet the $3 maximum, and push the button. The wheels spin and bring up nothing. So, I bet another $3 and try again, which is when a miracle happens.

Chapter 55

I PAUSE TO check my watch. It's just after 3:00 a.m. The casino has quieted down, but a dozen or more die-hards are still plugging away at their slot machines, desperate for Lady Luck to bestow favors on them. I'm exhausted and dehydrated, and my bladder feels like it's going to burst, yet I press on. I bring the heel of my right hand, which has been sore for the past hour, to the Bet Max button for the umpteenth time. I don't even watch the wheels spin. I know what the outcome will be.

I'm about to play again when a shadow appears on the machine's glass face. I turn to see Marlene standing over me. She's in her pajamas, bathrobe and slippers. Seeing her dressed this way in a public area is shocking, and for a moment I suspect I'm hallucinating.

"Goddamn it, Tony, it's three o'clock in the morning. Are you out of your mind? You promised you would come to bed. *Hours ago*."

I wait until Marlene has completed her thought, then silently present the plastic bucket in front of me. Make that *three* buckets. Each filled to the brim with silver dollars.

"That's a lot of money."

"Yes, it is."

"You won that all tonight?"

"Watch this."

Taking nine silver dollars from the first bucket I plug them into the machine. Then I hit Bet Max. The wheels spin and lock into place, and the air rings with melodious chimes as the numbers on the display panel rapidly zoom past 50... 100... 150... 200... 250... 300... 350... 360. At the same time, the chute at the base of the machine clangs wildly as silver dollars pour like water gushing from a hose. I grab another plastic bucket to capture this latest silver cascade.

"The machine must be broken," I explain. "It pays out 40-to-2 with every $9 bet."

"No!" She covers her mouth with her hand.

"It's been doing this all night. That's why I haven't left."

I nod over my right shoulder. Marlene turns to see two large uniformed security men hovering by a pillar not ten feet away. One of them holds a large roll of yellow tape.

"Why don't they stop you? Why don't they just shut you down?"

"They can't. It's the law. They can't turn off the machine until I leave. That's why I'm still here."

"You mean you've been sitting here since nine o'clock?" she gasps.

"Yep."

"Have you had anything to drink?"

"They stopped serving me free cocktails four hours ago."

"Have you gone to the bathroom?"

"I told you, the moment I stand up, they'll shut the machine down."

"You must be dying."

"Tell me about it."

"What can I do?"

"Play with me."

"I can do that?"

"Why not? Couples do it all the time."

I give Marlene nine silver dollars. One by one, she carefully plugs them into the machine.

"Now hit Bet Max," I instruct.

She does. The wheels spin, then lock, and again the machine sings in triumph. Another $360 payout.

"Now slide in here," I say, giving her my seat. "I've warmed it up for you."

I look back at the two security guards. They take a tentative step forward, but I continue to stand over Marlene's shoulder as she again feeds the one-armed bandit. Realizing they still have no legal recourse, they retreat to their former positions.

"Keep playing," I tell Marlene. "I'm going to the men's room. Don't pause for a second. And don't let them intimidate you. I'll be back in five minutes."

The nearest men's room is located at the far wall a hundred yards away. I hurry through the mazelike casino at a near sprint, balancing my urgency against my fear that any sharp jolt will release my tenuous control over my bladder. My luck holds some more, and I make it in time.

A few minutes later, I return to the Double Diamond machine to find Marlene continuing to play unmolested.

"Having fun?"

"You bet!"

We continue to play as a team. Every hour, one of us takes over while the other visits the restroom. Around 7:00 a.m., fatigue finally wins out, and we decide to call it quits. I grab three buckets of coins and Marlene picks up two more. Slowly, with joints aching, we carry our load to the nearest cashier's window. We're barely ten feet from the machine when the two security guards, equally exhausted, swoop in to wrap their yellow tape around the machine.

"Too late, suckers," I mutter to myself.

Arriving at the window, we set our buckets on the counter top.

"We'd like to cash out, please," I announce to the cashier. One by one, we empty our contents through the small slot in the thick glass window. The cashier takes the silver dollars to a big clunky machine that makes a rhythmic clanking sound as it counts automatically.

"Would you like this in cash or a cashier's check?" she asks.

"Check," says Marlene without even consulting me. I don't protest. No one should risk walking around with this much cash, even in a heavily guarded facility like this hotel.

Five minutes later, the cashier returns with a check for $42,870. In my sleep-deprived state, I can't help but chuckle. I've just paid off the weekend's entire $37,000 cost and made a few grand for myself in the process.

Why am I so lucky? Why do good things like this keep happening to me? Is it just coincidence—or maybe a *karma* thing? All my adult life, I have tried to do good… and then some. Back in Boston, I arranged to give money to the church. I have kept families together with personal loans. I worked to make sure my own family was safe and secure. I have always kept my promises. I like to think my *luck* is a reward for the efforts I have made to help others.

Any remaining doubts about the good karma plays in my life vanish a few months later. I'm back in the Cerritos office when the San Diego district manager enters, accompanied by a professional photographer.

"What's going on?" I ask cautiously.

"Tony, I have something special for you," San Diego says. "It's a certificate honoring you for achieving $10 million in annual sales."

I'm stunned as he joins me behind my desk and presents me with a framed certificate signed by all the top corporate brass. Holding up the framed document, he takes my hand, and we pose for pictures.

"Plus," San Diego continues. "We'll be presenting you with a $100,000 bonus check at our annual gala next month. Again, congratulations."

After San Diego and his photographer leave, several of my sales reps crowd into my office to marvel at the certificate.

"You earned this," one of them says.

"You need to hang this up," another insists.

Two of the reps exit only to return a few minutes later with a hammer and some picture hooks.

"This will look perfect right here," one of them says, positioning the massive glass frame on the wall directly behind my desk.

"Go ahead," I say.

Together, the two reps nail the hangers into the wall, then carefully hang the framed certificate.

"Looks great," one says admiringly.

I have to agree. It *does* look great. And it feels great, too, being recognized for my hard work and accomplishments.

Basking in my sudden celebrity, I lean forward, only to hear a sharp crack behind me.

Someone screams. "Tony, look out!"

Chapter 56

"TONY, I JUST heard about—"

"Marlene, don't move!" One of the reps behind me shoots his arm forward, commanding Marlene, who has just entered the office, to freeze.

"You too. Don't move, Tony," the other says. "Not a muscle."

All four of us now stand like silent statues, as if the world has become frozen in time. After about ten seconds, I can no longer stand the suspense. Carefully, I begin to turn my swivel chair around.

"Tony, don't!" one of the reps shouts.

But I keep turning. I have to. I have to see what's happening behind me. Finally, I've turned a full 180 degrees so I'm facing the back wall. The first thing I see is the framed certificate, its glass shattered. And then, as my eyes refocus, I see what caused the two reps such anxiety.

Several large glass shards, including a blade-shaped triangle about three inches long, hang suspended in midair. I try to wrap my mind around what I'm seeing, but it makes no sense. This is like some kind of freeze-frame you might see in a movie, but this isn't a movie. This is real life. And the laws of physics, including gravity, are supposed to be in effect. But they clearly are not.

As I watch in awe, one of the sales reps slowly reaches forward and oh-so-carefully plucks the largest shard out of the air.

He then gently sets it down on the desk behind me. Emboldened, he then plucks a second, smaller shard from where it hangs suspended, careful not to cut his finger on its knifelike edge, and sets it down on the desk beside the first piece. Finally, he captures the third shard between his thumb and forefinger and sets it on the desk with the others. The danger gone, we all let out a collective breath. I turn back to look at Marlene, who continues to stand stone-still, eyes wide, mouth agape.

What just happened? From the position and angle of those glass shards, it's clear they could have cut my neck badly had they continued to fall. They could have even killed me. But something stopped them. Something I can only guess is not of this world. But what? And why?

A few weeks later, I return to Las Vegas. This time, on the company's dime. Colorado Prime has brought the entire company here for a big awards celebration, just as the suit from San Diego promised. Management has booked what must be half the rooms in a four-star hotel on the Las Vegas Strip—plus a ballroom enormous enough to host a national political convention.

They've erected a large stage at one end of the ballroom, complete with a theater-like proscenium. It is from here, backed by a huge projection screen, that the company's head honchos will make their congratulatory speeches and narrate professionally shot video clips documenting the success the company has enjoyed over the past twelve months.

Seated at a large, circular table, the remains of my steak dinner in front of me, I take in the sheer vastness of this spectacle. There must be fifteen thousand people here: salespeople, managers, and executives from throughout the country, plus their spouses. Every fifteen seconds or so, the cavernous hall echoes with thunderous applause as a speaker announces the breaking of some sales record or congratulates a manager for a job well done.

I turn to Marlene, seated at my right. She wears a gold-laced gown whose iridescent fabric sparkles like tiny diamonds. Her hair has been professionally styled. A thick, gold marine chain adorns her neck, matching the earrings I bought her just for this occasion. I've never seen her look more beautiful.

We're minutes away from the moment I'm scheduled to be called up to receive my $100,000 bonus check when one of the company vice presidents appears behind me. "Tony, can I talk to you for a minute?"

"Sure. What's up?"

"Just come with me."

Marlene throws me a look of concern as I rise and follow the VP to a far corner.

"Something wrong?"

"Nothing's wrong," he assures me with a thin smile. "Richard Smith is going to call your name in just a minute. When you go on stage, he's going to give you an envelope."

"Yes." I knew that already.

"The envelope's going to be empty," the VP says. "Just pretend like there's a check in there."

This can't be happening again. "Wait a minute. What about the $100,000 I was promised?" Already I can feel my stomach tightening.

His thin smile returns. "You'll get it in about a month. It's a cashflow thing. You know…"

He pats me on the shoulder, and I return to our table. From my expression, Marlene senses something amiss. "What's wrong? What did he say?"

Before I can respond, the company president is introduced to a round of applause. He takes his place before the center podium.

"We've had a great night tonight, haven't we? And an outstanding year," he says.

More applause from the crowd. I can see Marlene is not clapping. She's staring at me, so I offer her my own thin smile.

"But the evening would not be complete without recognizing the truly stellar work of our top local sales manager," Richard continues. "He's only been with us for two years, but in that short period he's helped his office set record after record for monthly sales. This year, his group posted numbers in excess of $10 million, an all-time company record. For his outstanding production, we are pleased to present this bonus check for $100,000."

A collective gasp rises from the crowd as Richard holds up an envelope emblazoned with our company logo.

"Ladies and gentleman, let's give it up for our Sales Manager of Year, Tony Assali of Cerritos, California!"

And the crowd goes wild. The room explodes with applause as fifteen thousand people rise to their feet. The floor shakes like an earthquake. Whooping and hollering, my sales staff forms a human chain as I rush toward the stage. I bound up the steps, waving to the crowd like a guy who's just won a presidential nomination.

Richard presents me with the envelope. The roar from the crowd is deafening. I look inside. As promised, it's empty. Feigning a smile for the second time tonight, I move down the line of suited executives, shaking their hands in succession. Finally, I return to Richard and look him in the eye.

"Aren't you going to shake my hand?" he asks.

"No," I reply, still offering my phony smile. "I don't trust you."

It turns out I have good reason to be skeptical. A month passes and no check. Six weeks. No check. Seven weeks. No check. Finally, our regional manager demands Richard pay me or he'll quit. Reluctantly, he sends me the money I have been promised. But the bitterness remains.

Chapter 57

PRIOR TO THE turn of the first millennium A.D., widespread fear whipped throughout Europe. People thought the world was about to end. Superstition suggests unusual meaning can be found in round numbers, and many believed that in the year 1,000, end-time would come. This, of course, did not happen. Armageddon was not fought, and history marched on unabated. One thousand years later, a new type of millennial panic sets in. This one is not rooted in Christianity but in the more modern religion of science. Rather than the Second Coming, we fear the Y2K bug. For those who didn't live through Y2K hysteria or don't know what all the fuss was about, it so happened that many first- and second-generation computers were not powerful enough to handle years expressed in four digits. Accordingly, their designers calibrated them in only two digits, as in 60 for 1960 and 99 for 1999.

But what would happen when the year 2000 arrived? How would these computers read "00"? As the year zero? 1900? No year at all? These early programmers did not believe this would be a problem. The year 2000 was decades away, and they figured that by the time it arrived, all of these early computers would have long been retired, replaced by more powerful, more capable machines.

How naïve they were. They did not foresee that many of these "ancient" computers would become the backbone of municipal utility and national military agencies throughout the Western world, organizations lacking the funding and initiative to regularly update their hardware. As a result, thousands of such machines were still in use. This required hundreds of millions of dollars to be spent on programming patches people hoped would prevent cyber-doom, the complete collapse of our modern infrastructure.

Here in California, we watch in tense anticipation as the year 2000 first arrives on the far side of the world. In Japan, then China, then India, and then Europe and Africa, the new millennium dawns without incident. No computers crash. No nations go dark. We begin to breathe easier as midnight continues to sweep west, first into Canada, then to the U.S. East Coast, the Midwest, and finally to us here along the Pacific, again without incident. The lights stay on. Water continues to flow. Airplanes do not come crashing to Earth. Whether the original fears were overblown or the Y2K patches worked doesn't matter. The Apocalypse has been averted.

However, at Colorado Prime, we find ourselves dealing with a potential meltdown of our own. In the year 2000, the Federal Trade Commission (FTC) begins hearings on whether or not to establish a Do Not Call Registry. This is an opt-out list individuals and businesses can join to prevent telemarketers from phoning them. The financial penalties for violating the list are severe. Only charities and political organizations exercising their First Amendment right of free speech are exempt. Much to our horror, the FTC leadership approves the creation of this no-call list, and tens of millions of people sign up. Since telemarketing has been the foundation of our company's sales strategy from the beginning, this is devastating.

By the time 2003 rolls around, the Do Not Call Registry has taken effect and, as predicted, choked our ability to find new customers at the source. Civilization does not perish as a result of the new law, but our long-struggling company sure does. In early spring, management decides to shutter all the local offices, including Cerritos. Opting to remain in business no matter what, the top brass decides it will only take reorders through the main New York office.

Fresh out of a job, I start a meat-retailing company of my own. With a partner, I form L.T.T. Foods. In a pattern similar to what happened when I left Country Fed a decade ago, I bring twenty-one sales reps from Colorado Prime to my new enterprise. These people want to work for me, and I want to do good by them. At L.T.T., we struggle to use what telemarketing we still can under the new rules. Severely limited, we next turn our sales approach to door-to-door soliciting, a skill with which I have much experience. The company is not a raging success, but it pays the bills. And it keeps me mentally occupied. Many years after Marlene suggested I retire, I still cannot bring myself to cash out, nor even kick back. Inactivity is just not in my DNA.

One day, I come home from work to find Lorraine, my stepdaughter, waiting for me in the kitchen.

"I have something for you," she says. Reaching into her purse, she pulls out a personal check. Surprised, I look at the amount: $3,000. Even more baffling, it's signed by Scott.

"What's this for?"

"Scott said he's going to give you $3,000 every month until he's paid back all the money you gave him to start First National Lending," Lorraine explains. This throws me for a loop. Calling it quits with Scott caused a rift between us that has only grown wider over time. In fact, we haven't spoken for the past five years

"Scott asked you to do this for him?"

"Yes."

"Where is he now?"

"Outside. In his car."

My breath catches in my throat. I arrived just a few minutes ago without noticing Scott—my son to whom I haven't spoken in half a decade—parked outside.

"Would you tell him to come inside? I want to talk to him."

Lorraine knows the difficult history between Scott and me. "You're sure?"

Suddenly I am transported back in time, back to when Scott was just a baby. I remembered the joy I felt when he arrived at the hospital, how happy I felt raising him on my own, tucking him in at night, reading him bedtime stories. I recall how proud I felt watching him play baseball and how sad I was when his life spiraled out of control.

For years, I haven't talked to this man. I've hardly spoken his name because of the private pain it causes me. So many wonderful and positive things have happened in my life in the five years we haven't talked—but clouding all of the good is a shadow reminding me all is not right in the world, for I don't have my son. My boy.

"You're sure?" she asks again.

"Please," I say, choking on the word. "Ask him to come in."

Lorraine heads outside. While she's gone, I drop into a chair. I suddenly feel so much older. A few minutes later, Scott walks through the front door. His head hangs forward. His shoulders sag. He's unable to lift his eyes to meet mine. Without a word, I leap out of the chair, wrapping my arms around him. He's taller than I am, and the embrace is awkward, but it doesn't matter. We both cry. It takes us many minutes to recover the ability to speak.

"Let's go to dinner," I suggest, wiping tears from my eyes.

"Sure, Dad."

We choose to go to the same restaurant where Lorraine works as a waitress. After ordering, Scott begins to talk.

"I don't know how you do it," he confesses. "Everything you touch turns to gold. Everything I do fails."

"First National is going under?"

"Not yet. But we have problems. I think people are stealing my files. The numbers just aren't where they're supposed to be."

"Is there anything I can do?"

"I'd like you to manage the business. Marlene can handle the books. Between the two of you, I bet you can straighten everything up within a month."

I ponder this for a moment. The last time I agreed to come onboard with Scott, it led to problems. What if the same thing happens again? When I mention this to Scott, he shrugs my concerns off.

"I've learned a lot. It's not like before. You'll see."

From the corner of my eye, I notice Lorraine across the restaurant. She stands at attention before a group of four people, pencil in hand, taking their orders. She happens to glance over my way, and I smile at her. Once again, nostalgia overtakes me tonight, and I am transported back to my days at the Wayfarer Hotel, my little wine glass jingling on a chain as I hurried on to the next customer. How bold I was back then. How fearless. I could hardly speak English, yet there I was selling overpriced bottles to America's upper crust.

I turn to Scott. "How can I turn my back on you? You have my support."

He smiles. "I knew I could count on you."

I tell him I will agree to his request with some modifications. "I'll handle your sales and marketing. But I want you to handle administration. You have ten years of experience in mortgage lending. You know this industry. I don't."

"I'll teach you."

"I'm counting on that."

Over the next few weeks, Marlene also throws herself into her new role. Just like before, we act as a trio, a team. While she is busy learning to process mortgage applications, I train my L.T.T. sales reps how to sell home loans. I even buy mailing lists of people on the Do Not Call Registry, hire a small team of telemarketers, and write a sales script. Like everything I do, I go all in.

After three weeks of training and preparation, we're ready to roll in the mortgage business. I tell my partner I am quitting L.T.T. and taking my reps with me. He is angry with me and orders his attorney to hit me with a lawsuit, but his counsel can't find solid ground on which to base such a suit. The fact is, I have done nothing wrong.

Several days into our new venture, I am reviewing our mortgages when I notice we are paying $900 on each application for something called "escrow." I do not understand what this is, nor why it is so expensive, so I consult Scott.

"Escrow is a third-party service that's part of every real estate deal," he explains. "The escrow company holds money from both sides, like the earnest money a buyer pays in advance. It verifies both sides have met the conditions necessary for the sale to be finalized. Then it releases the funds."

"And this costs $900?" I ask, still not quite believing what I'm hearing.

"That's the going rate."

"And why can't we just do it ourselves and save the fee?"

"Well, that would require us to set up a separate company."

"Great. Then let's set up a separate company."

And we do. As I soon learn, there are two types of escrow: in-house, which is regulated by the California Department of Real Estate, and another regulated by the State Department of Corporations. Following the law, we hire an escrow officer with many years of experience in the field.

Remembering back to the night when I saw Lorraine working so hard at the restaurant, how it reminded me of myself when I was coming up, I ask her to join us in this new venture. To me, it's the perfect choice. After all, Lorraine has been working with her mother processing our loan applications for years part-time.

"But I like working with Mom," she says.

"And you're doing a great job," I say. "But right now, we need you."

"But I don't know anything about escrow."

"Neither did I. Until recently. But you're smart. You'll learn. You've also got a great personality."

She offers me the beginning of that sweet smile I cherish, so I press my case further. "And the money's better."

Still somewhat reluctant, Lorraine signs on. It doesn't take long for her to see she made the right choice, as the new business becomes profitable. Very profitable, very fast. But there is tension between Scott and Marlene. The two most important people in my life have big personalities. Big personalities come with big opinions. After months of sharing those opinions in confrontational ways, the situation climaxes with a blowout in the middle of the office. After several minutes of shouting, Marlene storms out. Once I calm her down, I return to Scott. He's breathing heavily, also clearly upset. After healing our longtime rift, the last thing I want is to lose my son again.

"If we stay together, we're going to keep having problems," I tell him. "So, here's what's going to happen. The lending company is yours. But I'm taking the escrow company. We can still do business together, but we'll be in separate offices. Separate buildings."

"Do I have any say in this?" he asks.

"Sure. Do you have a better idea?"

He hesitates. "Not really."

So, we pack up and find new offices. The first thing I do is change our status from in-house to an independent entity. This will allow us to sell our services to any mortgage broker, not just to Scott and First National.

It's only been a year, but I've gone from selling meat to selling mortgage loans to selling escrow services. What's next?

Chapter 58

STARTING AN ESCROW company is not easy. It takes time. And effort. At the moment, it's just Lorraine and me processing the intakes. To keep cash flowing, Marlene becomes a licensed mortgage broker. To lower our overhead, the three of us work out of our house. Everywhere we turn are file cabinets, computers, and boxes overflowing with documents. Marlene and I now eat, sleep, and breathe business 24/7. It's exhilarating—and overwhelming.

About a month after we leave First National Mortgage, our doorbell rings. Curious, I open the front door to find ten of its sales reps standing on our sidewalk.

"We're here to work for you," one of them says.

"I'm flattered, but I don't have a company. It's just me and Lorraine." I point to the papers scattered on the coffee table. "We don't even have an office."

"Well, we're leaving First National anyway," another rep says and sighs. "So, if you don't hire us, we'll have to find someone who will."

"Don't do that. Not yet. Give me twenty-four hours to work this out."

As soon as the reps depart, Marlene and I discuss options.

"Those guys do know the mortgage business. I could bring them on with me. There wouldn't be much of a learning curve," Marlene says.

"True. But where would we put them? We're already bursting at the seams."

"We'd need an office. A *real* office. Then we can go back to having a home. A real home."

She's right, so we rent space in a small building a few blocks away. We also hire those ten reps from First National. This does not represent a major financial burden to us since the whole sales staff makes its money on commission. We only have to provide them with desks, telephones, and computers, all of which we buy used.

Excited by this venture in ways I haven't been in years, I concentrate on the escrow company, which I name EscrowQuick. It's also such a relief to know I can depend on Lorraine to process all the applications we generate. A wonderful protégé, she's intelligent and steady.

To build our client base, I begin canvassing for customers, enticing Orange County's many real estate agents with a $100 discount on all escrows. How do I find these agents? I go to open houses every weekend and introduce myself. I also make a point to invite agents to see my offices in Fountain Valley to show off our team. The strategy works. Within a year, EscrowQuick is one of the most profitable escrow services in Orange County.

But then comes 2007. For the past few years, the real estate market has been booming—so much so it feels like being on a magical carnival ride that will never end. Both my escrow service and Marlene's mortgage company have been flourishing, closing deal after deal after deal. But good times can't last forever.

After hearing rumors about growing cracks in the system for a long time, on April 7, calamity strikes. New Century Financial, headquartered in nearby Irvine, California, declares Chapter 11 bankruptcy. One of the largest holders of subprime mortgages in the country, it sold high-interest mortgages to customers with less-than-stellar incomes and credit ratings.

In retrospect, it makes sense that so many of these customers defaulted. Still when it happens, it unnerves Marlene and me. Just a few weeks earlier, we put $15,000 down on a new 4,000-square-foot house in Corona, a city in western Riverside County. Ever since writing the check, Marlene has been uneasy, and the collapse of New Century Financial forces her anxieties to the surface.

"I think we should pull out altogether," she tells me. "The real estate market's in trouble. This is no time to buy a house."

"But if we pull out, we'll lose our deposit. Fifteen thousand dollars is a lot of money."

"But not as much as $800,000," she reminds me, referring to the sale price of the house we've contracted to purchase. "If the market collapses, we could be seriously underwater. We could lose our shirts."

I consider Marlene's scenario. Since we're both dependent on the real estate business, any market downturn will affect our incomes directly. If that income stream dries up, we'll have to dig into our life savings to cover mortgage payments. And for what? A four-bedroom house we really don't need?

"Fine," I agree. "I'll cancel the contract."

And I do. As a result, we lose the $15,000. And as the coming months will reveal, this was the smartest move we could've made.

Just a few weeks after the New Century bankruptcy, I get a call from Scott's bookkeeper. "We're being killed by our subprime mortgages. We need $11,000 by the end of the week to keep our doors open. Can you help?"

"I'm sorry, I can't. Things are going to get worse before they improve. I think the best thing Scott can do is cut his losses."

I wish I could help my son, but I know this would be throwing good money after bad. It's not the time to be investing in the mortgage business. At the end of the week, First National Mortgage goes under. This is not the first mortgage company to go out of business, and it won't be the last. As we move into 2008, the Great Recession takes hold. The Gross Domestic Product (GDP) falls steeply. The Federal Reserve Bank repeatedly lowers its interest rates, trying to stop free fall. In February, President George W. Bush signs the Economic Stimulus Act of 2008, including income-tax rebates and tax breaks for companies seeking to buy new equipment.

Nothing helps. The toxic subprime mortgages driving the boom market have become poison spreading to every part of the economy. In March, Bear Stearns, the eighty-five-year-old brokerage house, collapses and is bought by JPMorgan Chase. In July, the parent company of Countrywide Financial, a major mortgage lender specializing in subprime loans, shutters. And in September, just two months before the election pitting Republican John McCain of Arizona against Democratic Senator Barack Obama of Illinois, the economy is hit with a triple whammy: First, the U.S. Treasury takes over the federal mortgage program known as Freddie Mac and the Federal National Mortgage Association known as Fannie Mae. Then the Lehman Brothers investment house goes under in the biggest bankruptcy in U.S. history, involving more than $600 billion in debt. Finally, AIG, a company insuring other insurance companies, is relieved of its crippling $85 billion debt by the government after assuming an 80 percent ownership due to the fact that it views AIG as "too big to fail."

Even as the U.S. economy goes into a tailspin, taking much of the industrial world with it, we somehow press forward. As Marlene predicted, home sales are way, way down, but some property is still selling, and someone has to do the escrows. Lorraine and I work hard to keep EscrowQuick afloat while Marlene opens a center to process FHA loans for local brokers, a service few other local specialists are providing. Thankfully, demand is so high she has to hire three more processors to keep up, requiring us to look for even larger accommodations.

We find a building in Fountain Valley with two open offices: suites 101 and 104. Self-contained, they're situated not only at opposite ends of a corridor but also on opposite sides. I take both. Suite 101 is for EscrowQuick. Suite 104 is for Marlene's FHA loan-processing company. To economize, I have one set of stationery bearing the Suite 101 address printed for each company.

A year later, the tenant in Suite 102 moves out. It's a big space, about 4,000 square feet, large enough to fit both of our businesses. I meet with the landlord to discuss moving into the vacant unit.

"I'd like to consolidate both of my companies into Suite 102," I tell him.

"That shouldn't be a problem," the landlord says.

"Good. I just have one request."

"What's that?"

"I want to change the suite number from 102 to 101."

"Why?"

"So, I don't have to print new stationery."

The landlord considers this for a few seconds. "Makes sense to me."

So, we get our new suite. We also get a great deal: Just $1 per square foot for five years. Recessions can be profitable if you know how to manage them.

Getting great deals on office space comes with a price. Real estate throughout SoCal is suffering, and as a result, our income takes a nosedive. I don't want to let any of my employees go. They all have families to support. Family has made all the difference in my life, and I can't imagine letting down even one employee. So, I keep paying them, even as business dries up. This just isn't sustainable, though. Within months, I tap out our corporate cash reserves.

"What will we do?" Marlene asks me one night.

"I don't know," I say.

Though insolvency hounds me day and night, threatening to destroy everything I put together all these decades, I cannot erase the faces of my employees from my thoughts. Every time I consider laying someone off or failing to make payroll, I think of my own mother and father, my brothers and sisters, who came to this country with so little. What would have happened if people had turned their backs on us?

After careful deliberation, I dig into my personal finances to make sure I do not miss even one month of payroll. It works. For a time. Finally, in December 2009, my back against the wall, I have no other choice. I file for Chapter 7 personal bankruptcy. This allows me to keep my creditors at bay. It also allows me to keep my company open and my employees paid.

I have to wonder, *what if I had retired back when Marlene advised me to? What if I hadn't started selling meat, brought Scott into the business, financed his mortgage company, then broke off to start this escrow business?* I could be sitting on $1 million, *plus*, instead of standing in bankruptcy court along with a hundred other hard-luck cases. But these misgivings instantly disappear when I look at the men and women whose livelihoods I fought to preserve. Every day, I have the honor and privilege to see them smiling at me, knowing we built this together. If they wouldn't give up on me, then how could I give up on them? People say it's easy to do good when times are good but the real test of character comes when times are bad. And these are definitely the worst times I can remember.

Chapter 59

BANKRUPTCY CARRIES A stigma. The very word connotes failure. Destitution. *Defeat.* But while I understand the moral blemish bankruptcy carries, I also recognize it as a legitimate and useful legal instrument that can keep productive, hard-working businesses afloat during difficult times. Operating under Chapter 7 protection, Marlene and I take no paychecks for a full year. In spite of mounting pressures, I continue marketing our services, building our loyal customer base, while Lorraine keeps her end of the bargain. I was right to put my faith in her. Giving no quarter to the travails of the Great Recession, she excellently performs her job, processing applications.

Money trickles in, and I somehow manage to pay my staff's salaries out of my own pocket. We stay in business. And because our doors remain open while other escrow companies close theirs, more and more files come our way. It becomes a war of attrition that I am determined to win. And I do. Just six months after filing for Chapter 7 protection, I pay off all of our creditors. The bankruptcy is formally discharged. Not only have we survived while most of our peers have gone the way of Pan Am, Texaco, and Circuit City, we've done even better—we didn't lay off a single employee. This is truly one of the proudest achievements of my life.

In the midst of this growing silver lining comes the darkest patch of gray. About four years ago, my mother began showing symptoms of dementia. At first, the signs were subtle. She would ask something, then ask the same question five or ten minutes later. Then she stopped recognizing people. She even got lost driving to stores she had visited hundreds of times.

"Your mother needs help," Marlene tells me one day after receiving yet another frantic call. "This can't go on. She can't be left alone anymore."

"I know," I say sadly.

It's too hard to say what I'm thinking, so I don't, but in my heart, I know what's coming. Mom needs to move into a facility that can care for her. This recognition is not easy to accept. On the outside, my mother looks the same. But now I see confusion in her eyes. Fear. I have read enough about Alzheimer's to know that, every day, a little piece of her mind is breaking off, never to return.

I scout the area for assisted living centers. When I visit them, I'm horrified by the sight of elderly men and women, many frail and in wheelchairs, staring off into space or talking to figures who aren't there. I can't help but feel that committing my mother, the woman who brought me into this world all those years ago, will only accelerate her decline. I also know keeping her at home is not an option. Not for her. And certainly not for us. With great reluctance, I find a memory care facility near our home and move her in. She resists, assuring Marlene and me she's fine even though it's obvious to everyone she isn't.

"This is normal," the facility administrator tells us. "Moving is one of the great traumas anyone can go through, and it's doubly difficult for dementia patients."

"So, what can we do?"

"Give her time. Let her get used to the routine. In fact, it's best you not visit her for the next two weeks."

"You mean, we shouldn't come see her?" Marlene asks.

The administrator nods. "Yes, even though it sounds wrong, like the last thing you'd want to do, the truth is, she needs to get used to her new home."

"Her new home," I say, letting the words sink in.

"Any distraction is just going to slow her acclimation," she adds.

Reluctantly, I do as I'm told. For two weeks I stay away, letting the facility staff tend to my mother's needs. Afterward, Marlene and I arrive for our first visit. I'm surprised to find Mom in good spirits. She says she is comfortable in her new room. She has even managed to make friends.

"Good," I tell her. "I'm so proud of you."

Unfortunately, her mental decline not only continues. It accelerates. In early September 2009, I get a call from the same facility administrator.

"I understand your mother is Catholic," he says. "You may want to contact a priest."

"Oh no. What is it?"

"She's having severe difficulty breathing. She won't last the night."

My worst fear—the reality I've avoided facing for years—is coming true. Still, I keep it together as I call a nearby church to arrange for a priest to administer last rites. Marlene and I remain in the room after the priest departs. I am determined to be with my mom until the end.

The next morning, September 4, my mother passes. Although my heart is heavy with grief, my sorrow is mixed with a strange combination of relief and elation. My mother lived a full and happy life. She got to see her children grow up and to become successful and free in America. She had the joy of being a grandmother. This is not a time to mourn a death but a time to celebrate a life.

"Have you ever heard of BNI?"

I'm having lunch with Jeff Sheldon, a local entrepreneur who occupies a suite in our building directly down the hall from EscrowQuick. About forty years old, fit, and never without a coat and tie, something unusual for Southern California, Jeff continually impresses me with his sharp mind.

"No, what's that?"

"BNI means Business Network International. It's a referral group."

"You mean like a leads club? A bunch of business owners get together and try to sell themselves?" I've tried this type of organization before and see little value in it.

"Not quite. At BNI we can refer anyone *but* ourselves."

"I don't get it."

"Let's say a member is looking for a new dentist. You like your dentist so you refer him. Or maybe you need a printer. In that case, another member might refer you to his printer."

I like Jeff, but I'm still unconvinced. "How many people belong to this BNI?"

"There are more than two hundred thousand members in seventy-five countries."

If this were a cartoon, my jaw would have dropped to the table.

"That's a lot of referrals," I whistle.

"The referrals build trust. And over time, that trust leads to more business. As we say, 'Givers Gain.'"

"Sounds interesting," I admit. "How do I sign up?"

A week later, I attend my first BNI chapter meeting. There are about thirty members present although I'm told the local group actually has more than five times this number. There's a healthy mixture of men and women, young and old, natives and immigrants, like myself. In the weeks to come I make plenty of connections but do not get many referrals. Not at first. In fact, it takes me a year to get a referral that closes. Still, I'm persistent. During this time, I do what I can to help other members. I recommend dentists. Car dealers. Restaurants. Anything they need, they come to Tony.

Soon, I am the number one referral-giver in the whole Orange County, California, region. And one by one, bit by bit, referrals start to come my way. By the end of year two, 75 percent of my escrow business is a result of BNI referrals.

In 2016, a massive fire tears through the Lake Isabella area. Marlene and I watch the news in horror as we see the fire line get closer to our dream house on the lake. We watch anxiously as the TV shows huge bomber-sized aircraft dropping water and fire retardant on the blaze, which still shows no sign of weakening.

Marlene sobs. "We're going to lose the house."

She's right. There's nothing we can do about it, so I put my arm around her shoulders and say the only thing I can think of: "We can always rebuild."

The next day, we get a call from Sylvia Steinmetz, one of our neighbors. She was forced to flee her home and spent the night in a local motel. Now she plans to return to assess the damage.

"Let us know how bad it is," Marlene says. "Or even if there's anything left."

Using her phone's camera, Sylvia sends us a live video feed as she walks down the dirt road toward the nearby properties. Once-mighty mesquite trees have been reduced to blackened skeletons. The ground around them looks like dusty charcoal with a landscape resembling a war zone.

At last, our cluster of vacation houses appears on screen. All we can make out are collapsed walls, smashed glass, and brick chimneys standing naked against the sky.

"It's horrible," Sylvia cries off camera. "All gone. Everything's gone."

But then Sylvia turns a corner, and our house comes into view. "Oh, my God, Tony," Marlene gasps.

Chapter 60

IT'S A WEEKDAY and I stand before my BNI group, giving a keynote address, telling my fellow networkers the story of my life. Over the years I have heard many keynote addresses. Most of the time, attendees lose attention after the first few minutes. Pretending to listen, the audience goes back to looking at their phones. Not today. Nearing the end of my story about our home in Lake Isabella, I command the room. No one is looking at their phones. No one can even sip their coffee. Everyone stares at me. I have their full attention.

"It was another miracle," I tell them. "There were twenty houses on our block, and only one was spared. *Ours*. I don't know why this happened, but it did. I have been very blessed in my life and feel very fortunate. Thank you for listening. And thank you for supporting me over the years."

Everyone claps. They rise to their feet, cheering. This, too, has never happened in any BNI meeting. They don't give standing ovations.

Suddenly, a hand goes up from the audience. "What did all of these amazing things teach you?" a man asks.

The timer with the watch frowns. It's his job to make sure I don't go past my allotted time to speak, and already, I'm over by fifteen seconds. Still, he can see that no one wants me to stop talking, so I answer. "What I learned from being in this great country is that you can do what you like here. There's freedom in America. Freedom to reach the unreachable. Coming from where I did—seeing what I have—I know that isn't the case anywhere else."

"Okay," says the timer. "I think that'll do it. Thank you, Tony—"

Another hand shoots up. Someone else has a question. "All these things that happened to you—they're so amazing. I mean, they don't seem real. How can you explain it?"

Ignoring the timer, I turn to the young lady asking the question. "I don't have all the answers, but if you do things right, there is no limit. If you act honestly, if you stay positive, things will open up to you. I promise."

I can see by the look on this young woman's face that something I've said affects her deeply. Her expression changes. She looks like she's fighting back tears. "But life isn't like that. It's not just some walk in the park. It's hard."

People are growing uncomfortable. They squirm in their seats.

I ignore them, focusing on the young lady. "Yes, there are ups and down, but you have to keep it together even when you lose the people you love the most. Even in the face of great loss, life doesn't stop."

Tears roll down the young lady's face. Something tells me she is dealing with something very difficult right now.

"Every day brings fresh challenges," I tell her softly. "We all know that. There are no perfectly charmed lives. As humans, we were born to struggle—to face obstacles. What makes a life beautiful is how you live it. You can give in to the pain and the problems, you can give up—or you can try. *You can lead by example.* You can show people the way to treat others." I look around the room at the many men and women who've helped me over the years, whom I've helped back. Isn't this reciprocity what it's all about? Not just this group, but *every* group—every association, every family, every union of souls. "Most importantly," I tell them. "When life is the toughest, you can choose to give. And the more you give, the more you get back."

The room fades away, and I am no longer talking to a group of professionals. Instead, I face my children and grandchildren. We are in Lebanon atop Mount Hermon, the land of our ancestors. My family stands before me, listening to my words.

"I have regrets in life," I say, trying not to let my voice break. "Did I focus on business too much? Yes. It doesn't excuse what I did, but I am a finisher. When I start something, I give it everything. If I had to do things differently, I would make better decisions with my personal relationships. I married my first wife too quickly. As a result, I had to raise Scott on my own. He didn't get the benefit of the female touch. He got lost for a time as a result."

I can see Scott in the crowd. We lock eyes. "Scott, you didn't get enough of me over the years and for that, I am sorry."

I turn to look at the others. "My second marriage was also made hastily. The third time I shouldn't have gotten married at all. I've made mistakes."

My throat is dry. I need water. I need to sit down. I feel exposed, embarrassed. When I blink again, I can't believe my eyes. All of my family members are with me. Even those who are no longer with us on this Earth: my mom, my dad, my brother. All of my friends, too. Somehow, they are all with me here. Smiling at me.

Out of the crowd, Marlene steps forward and takes me by the hand. This simple act is enough. It gives me strength to finish what I have to say to all of them. "If I met Marlene when I first came to America, I would probably have many more kids by now…"

They laugh, allowing me to relax.

"Marlene came along just when I needed her most," I continue. "I think this is how the universe works. Life gives you what you need when you need it. Miraculous things have happened in my life, but I would bet miraculous things have also occurred in yours if you really think about it. All of this wonder surrounding us—it cannot all just be happenstance. Life is beautiful. And every waking second is proof we are very fortunate to be alive, to share this world for such a short time."

Marlene comes closer, and I kiss her. Holding her hand, I turn to all of them, my family, my loved ones, everyone who ever meant something to me, and say, "Thank you for this experience. I love you all."

Photos

My sister Coco's late husband Nadim, my sister Nunu, Scotty, and I hang out together, circa 1973.

Taken in Beirut, circa 1965. From left: my sister Coco, my sister Josephine, my mother Victoria, my brother Joe, and my sister Nunu.

Scotty and me in front of our condo in Salem, New Hampshire, circa 1972.

My parents: Toufic and Victoria, at a historical castle in Lebanon, circa 1960.

My family poses for a photo together after I was sent to America, circa 1973.

Tony Assali with Michael Ashley

Prior to my leaving for the U.S., my family and I enjoy a fun winter's day together. From left: sister Josephine, sister Nunu, mother Victoria, brother Joe, sister Coco, and me, circa 1968.

Picture of me in Canada, circa 1975.

Posing for the camera during my tenure at Sallinger's clothing store, circa 1978.

With Nunu's husband (also named Tony) at our home in Stoneham, Massachusetts. Check out my cool GTO in the background. (It was my first car in America.) Circa 1976.

Tony Assali with Michael Ashley

Cover of national brochure for the Sheraton Hotels, featuring me serving Irish Coffee to patrons, circa 1970.

Close-up of me in my element.

Marlene, the white tiger I sought my whole life (and finally caught), circa 2018.

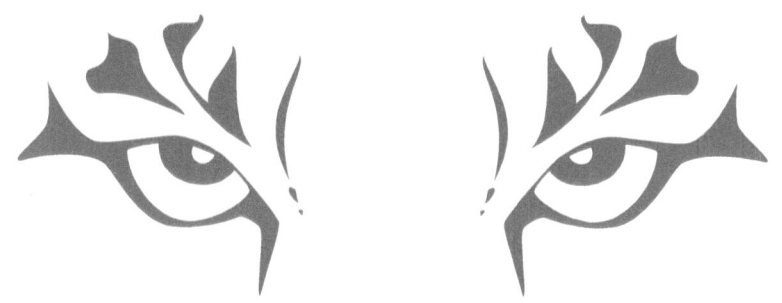

About the Authors

Tony Assali

WHEN CIVIL WAR broke out in Lebanon, Tony's home country, his parents sent him to America with just $28 in his pocket. They hoped he would secure a foothold in the U.S. so they could soon join him. But Tony did much more than that—he achieved the American dream.

Do you enjoy hummus? You might wish to thank Tony for bringing the tasty Mediterranean dish to American supermarkets in the 1980s—just one of the many feats of this serial entrepreneur. Along the way, Tony also built million-dollar companies in multiple sectors: apparel, food, retail, and real estate.

It's no wonder BNI founder Ivan Misner, Ph.D., wrote the foreword to this memoir. Tony exemplifies BNI's motto: Givers Gain. Never a taker, he has always put others' interests first. Fulfilling his parents' wishes, Tony brought his whole family to the U.S. and found them all jobs. Later, when he assumed a managerial position and his sales force needed confidence to close deals, Tony lent them his own money. Soon after opening his own escrow company, the housing market collapsed in 2008. Did Tony ever miss payroll? Not once—he also kept his entire staff without laying off a single worker.

Time and again, Tony has been rewarded for his kindness and something else—his ability to see business opportunities others can't, or won't, due to their limited thinking. In this memoir, *Catch the White Tiger*, Tony reveals the secrets to his success: kindness and unflinching confidence in his vision.

The former president of Coco's Mediterranean Foods, Inc., Tony has owned/operated EscrowQuick, Inc. since 2007. A distinguished public speaker with a transformational message, Tony is available for your next event. Contact him at: www.tonyassali.org.

Michael Ashley

MICHAEL ASHLEY IS a four-time best-selling author who has ghostwritten books for CEOs and business executives in many sectors, including finance, marketing, technology, health, law, and real estate. Thought leaders, including Michael Gerber, David Oreck, and Montel Williams, have endorsed Michael's work. His clients have appeared on *Inside Edition* and in prestigious publications, including *Entertainment Weekly*, *The Orange County Business Journal*, and *Pelican Hill Magazine*.

Prior to founding his own content company, Ink Wordsmiths, Michael, a regular contributor to *Forbes*, worked as a screenwriting consultant to Disney, a contributor to the *Huffington Post*, a copywriter, blogger, and newspaper reporter. He holds a Master of Fine Arts degree from Chapman University and teaches writing courses. Using the power of words, he enables his clients to share their stories to grow their personal brands. You can contact him via email at michael@inkwordsmiths.com.

www.ingramcontent.com/pod-product-compliance
Lightning Source LLC
Chambersburg PA
CBHW020307010526
44107CB00001B/6